Hong Kong Inland Revenue Ordinance

International Law & Taxation Publishers

London

Hong Kong Inland Revenue Ordinance

ISBN 1-893713-31-8

International Law & Taxation Publishers
London

http://www.internationallawandtaxationpublishers.com

Contents

CHAPTER 112

INLAND REVENUE ORDINANCE

ARRANGEMENT OF SECTIONS

Part I - Introductory

Part II - Property Tax

Part III - Salaries Tax

Part IV - Profits Tax

Part XIII - Repayment

Part XIV - Penalties And Offences

Part XV - General

CHAPTER 112

INLAND REVENUE

To impose a tax on property, earnings and profits.

PART I - Introductory

Short title

1.   This Ordinance may be cited as the Inland Revenue Ordinance.

Interpretation

2.(1)   In this Ordinance, unless the context otherwise requires-

"active partner", in relation to a partnership, means a partner who takes an active part in the control, management, or conduct of the trade or business of such partnership;

"agent", in relation to a non-resident person or to a partnership in which any partner is a non-resident person, includes-

> *(a)*   the agent, attorney, factor, receiver, or manager in Hong Kong of such person or partnership; and

> *(b)*   any person in Hong Kong through whom such person or partnership is in receipt of any profits or income arising in or derived from Hong Kong;

"approved charitable donation" means a donation of money to any charitable institution or trust of a public character which is exempt from tax under section 88 or to the Government, the Urban Council or Regional Council, for charitable purposes;

"assessable income" means the assessable income of a person in any year of assessment as ascertained in accordance with sections 11B, 11C and 11D; and "net assessable income" means assessable income as adjusted in accordance with section 12;

"assessable profits" means the profits in respect of which a person is chargeable to tax for the basis period for any year of assessment, calculated in accordance with the provisions of Part IV;

"assessor" means an assessor appointed under this Ordinance;

"assistant commissioner" means an assistant commissioner of Inland Revenue appointed under this Ordinance;

"authorized representative" means a person authorized in writing by any other person to act on his behalf for the purposes of this Ordinance;

"basis period" for any year of assessment is the period on the income or the profits of which tax for that year ultimately falls to be computed;

"bill of sale" means a bill of sale registrable under the Bills of Sale Ordinance (Cap. 20);

"body of persons" means any body politic, corporate or collegiate and any company, fraternity, fellowship and society of persons whether corporate or not corporate;

"business" includes agricultural undertaking, poultry and pig rearing and the letting or sub-letting by any corporation to any person of any premises or portion thereof, and the sub-letting by any other person of any premises or portion of any premises held by him under a lease or tenancy other than from the Crown;

"certificate of deposit" means a document relating to money, in any currency, which has been deposited with the issuer or some other person, being a document which recognizes an obligation to pay a stated amount to bearer or to order, with or without interest, and being a document by the delivery of which, with or without endorsement, the right to receive that stated amount, with or without interest, is transferable, and, in the case of any such document which is a prescribed instrument by virtue of paragraph (a) of the definition of "prescribed instrument" in section 137B of the Banking Ordinance (Cap. 155), includes any right or interest referred to in paragraph (b) of that definition in respect of such document;

"Commissioner" means the Commissioner of Inland Revenue appointed under this Ordinance;

"corporation" means any company which is either incorporated or registered under any enactment or charter in force in Hong Kong or elsewhere but does not include a co-operative society or a trade union;

"debenture" means a debenture as defined in section 2(1) of the Companies Ordinance (Cap. 32);

"deposit" means a deposit as defined in section 2(1) of the Banking Ordinance (Cap. 155);

"deputy commissioner" means the deputy commissioner of Inland Revenue appointed under this Ordinance;

"executor" means any executor, administrator, or other person administering the estate of a deceased person, and includes a trustee acting under a trust created by the last will of the author of the trust;

"financial institution" means-

>   *(a)*   an authorized institution licensed or registered under the Banking Ordinance (Cap. 155);

>   *(b)*   any associated corporation of such an authorized institution which, being

exempt by virtue of section 3(2)(a) or (b) or (c) of the Banking Ordinance (Cap. 155), would have been liable to be licensed or registered as a deposit-taking company or restricted licence bank under that Ordinance had it not been so exempt;

"Governor" means the Governor of Hong Kong and includes the officer for the time being administering the Government;

"Hong Kong currency" means money which is legal tender in Hong Kong;

"husband" means a married man whose marriage is a marriage within the meaning of this section;

"incapacitated person" means any minor, lunatic, idiot, or person of unsound mind;

"inspector" means an inspector appointed under this Ordinance;

"limited partnership" has the same meaning as in section 3 of the Limited Partnerships Ordinance (Cap.37);

"marriage" means-

> *(a)* any marriage recognized by the law of Hong Kong; or

> *(b)* any marriage, whether or not so recognized, entered into outside Hong Kong according to the law of the place where it was entered into and between persons having the capacity to do so,

but shall not, in the case of a marriage which is both potentially and actually polygamous, include marriage between a man and any wife other than the principal wife, and "married" shall be construed accordingly;

"mortgage" means a security by way of mortgage or equitable mortgage for the payment of any definite and certain sum of money advanced or lent at the time, or previously due and owing, or forborne to be paid, being payable, or for the repayment of money thereafter to be lent, advanced or paid, or which may become due upon an account current, together with any sum already advanced or due, or without, as the case may be, and includes-

> *(a)* conditional surrender by way of mortgage, or further charge, of or affecting any property whatsoever; and

> *(b)* any conveyance of any property whatsoever in trust to be sold or otherwise converted into money, intended only as a security, and redeemable before the sale or other disposal thereof, either by express stipulation or otherwise; and

(c)   any instrument for defeating or making redeemable, or explaining or qualifying any conveyance, transfer or disposition of any property whatsoever, apparently absolute, but intended only as a security; and

(d)   any instrument relating to the deposit of any title deeds or instruments constituting or being evidence of the title to any property whatsoever or creating a charge on any property whatsoever; and

(e)   any mortgage by an equitable owner of his equitable rights; and

(f)   any warrant of attorney to enter up judgment;

"net chargeable income" means net chargeable income calculated in accordance with section 12B;

"occupational retirement scheme" has the meaning assigned to it by section 2(1) of the Occupational Retirement Schemes Ordinance (Cap. 426);

"owner" in respect of land or buildings or land and buildings, includes a person holding directly from the Government, a beneficial owner, a tenant for life, a mortgagor, a mortgagee in possession, a person with adverse title to land receiving rent from buildings or other structures erected on that land, a person who is making payments to a co-operative society registered under the Co-operative Societies Ordinance (Cap. 33) for the purpose of the purchase thereof, and a person who holds land or buildings or land and buildings subject to a ground rent or other annual charge; and includes an executor of the estate of an owner;

"person" includes a corporation, partnership, trustee, whether incorporated or unincorporated, or body of persons;

"precedent partner" means the partner who, of the active partners resident in Hong Kong

(a)   is first named in the agreement of partnership; or

(b)   if there is no agreement, is specified by name or initials singly or with precedence to the other partners in the usual name of the partnership; or

(c)   is first named in any statutory statement of the names of the partners;

"profits arising in or derived from Hong Kong" for the purposes of Part IV shall, without in any way limiting the meaning of the term, include all profits from business transacted in Hong Kong, whether directly or through an agent;

"receiver" includes any receiver or liquidator, and any assignee, trustee, or other person having the possession or control of the property of any person by reason of insolvency or bankruptcy;

"recognized occupational retirement scheme" means an occupational retirement scheme-

(a) which, prior to the commencement of section 2 of the Inland Revenue (Amendment) (No. 5) Ordinance 1993, was a retirement scheme approved by the Commissioner under section 87A where such approval has not subsequently been withdrawn;

(b) registered for the time being under section 18 of the Occupational Retirement Schemes Ordinance (Cap. 426);

(c) in respect of which an exemption certificate has been issued under section 7(1) of the Occupational Retirement Schemes Ordinance (Cap. 426) and has not been withdrawn;

(d) which is operated by an employer who is-

(i) the government of a country or territory outside Hong Kong; or

(ii) any agency or undertaking of or by such a government which is not operated for the purpose of gain; and

(e) contained in or otherwise established by any Ordinance;

"river trade limits" has the same meaning as in the Merchant Shipping Ordinance (Cap. 281);

"specified form" means a form specified under section 86;

"spouse" means a husband or wife;

"standard rate" means the rate specified in Schedule 1;

"tax" except for the purposes of Parts XII and XIII, means any tax imposed by this Ordinance (including provisional salaries tax charged under Part XA, provisional profits tax charged under Part XB and provisional property tax charged under Part XC) other than additional tax, but for the purposes of Parts XII and XIII "tax" includes additional tax;

"trade" includes every trade and manufacture, and every adventure and concern in the nature of trade;

"trustee" includes any trustee, guardian, curator, manager, or other person having the direction, control, or management of any property on behalf of any person, but does not include an executor;

"wife" means a married woman whose marriage is a marriage within the meaning of this section;

"year of assessment" means the period of 12 months commencing on 1 April in any year;

"year preceding a year of assessment" means the period of 12 months ending on 31 March immediately prior to such year of assessment.

(2)   For the purposes of the definition of "financial institution" in subsection (1)-
"associated corporation", in relation to a bank or deposit-taking company, means-

> *(a)*   a corporation over which the bank or deposit-taking company has control;

> *(b)*   a corporation which has control over the bank or deposit-taking company; or

> *(c)*   a corporation which is under the control of the same person as is the bank or deposit-taking company;

"control", in relation to a corporation, means the power of a person to secure-

> *(a)*   by means of the holding of shares or the possession of voting power in or in relation to that or any other corporation; or

> *(b)*   by virtue of any powers conferred by the articles of association or other document regulating that or any other corporation,

that the affairs of the first-mentioned corporation are conducted in accordance with the wishes of that person.

(2A)   For the purposes of the definition of "recognized occupational retirement scheme" in subsection (1) -

> *(a)*   a scheme which is registered for the time being under section 18 of the Occupational Retirement Schemes Ordinance (Cap. 426) shall upon registration be regarded as a recognized occupational retirement scheme as from-

> > **(i)**   the date on which the application for such registration was made; or

> > **(ii)**   the date on which the terms of the scheme came into effect,

> whichever is the earlier; and

> *(b)*   a scheme in respect of which an exemption certificate has been issued under section 7(1) of the Occupational Retirement Schemes Ordinance (Cap. 426) and has not been withdrawn shall upon the issue of the certificate be regarded as a recognized occupational retirement scheme as from-

> > **(i)**   the date on which the application for the certificate was made; or

> **(ii)**   the date on which the terms of the scheme came into effect, whichever is the earlier:

Provided that if such date is earlier than the first commencement date of the Occupational Retirement Schemes Ordinance (Cap. 426), the scheme shall be regarded as a recognized occupational retirement scheme as from such commencement date.

(3)   For the purposes of this Ordinance a husband and wife shall be deemed to be living apart when they are living apart-

> *(a)*   under a decree or order of a competent court in or outside Hong Kong;

> *(b)*   under a duly executed deed of separation or any instrument of similar effect; or

> *(c)*   in such circumstances that the Commissioner is of the opinion the separation is likely to be permanent.

Establishment of Board of Inland Revenue. Power of Governor to appoint a Commissioner and other officers

3.(1)   *(a)*   There shall be a Board of Inland Revenue composed of the Financial Secretary and 4 other members appointed by the Governor, of whom not more than one shall be an official in the employment of the Government. A member so appointed shall hold office until he shall resign or be removed from office by the Governor.

> *(aa)*   The Board of Inland Revenue shall have a secretary who shall be the deputy commissioner.

> *(b)*   members of the Board of Inland Revenue shall form a quorum for the transaction of business and when the Financial Secretary is present he shall be the chairman.

> *(c)*   All matters coming before the Board of Inland Revenue shall be decided by a majority of votes, and in the case of an equality of votes the chairman or presiding member shall have a second or a casting vote.

> *(d)*   The Board of Inland Revenue may transact any of its business by the circulation of papers without meeting; and a resolution signed by a majority of the members shall be as valid and effective as if it had been passed at a meeting by the votes of the members so signing.

(2)   For the purposes of this Ordinance, the Governor may appoint a Commissioner, a deputy commissioner, assistant commissioners, assessors and inspectors.

(3) An assistant commissioner exercising or performing any power, duty, or function of the Commissioner under this Ordinance shall be deemed for all purposes to be authorized to exercise or perform the same until the contrary is proved.

(4) All powers conferred upon an assessor by this Ordinance may be exercised by an assistant commissioner.

Exercise of powers and duties

3A.(1) Where under this Ordinance any power is conferred or any duty is imposed on the Commissioner and so long as it is not provided that the power or duty shall be exercised or performed by the Commissioner personally, such power may be exercised or such duty may be performed by the deputy commissioner or by an assistant commissioner.

(2) Except where a provision of this Ordinance provides that a power or duty shall be exercised or performed by the Commissioner personally, the Commissioner may, subject to such limitations as he may think fit, authorize in writing any public officer to exercise any power or perform any duty conferred or imposed upon him by this Ordinance.

Official secrecy

4.(1) Except in the performance of his duties under this Ordinance, every person who has been appointed under or who is or has been employed in carrying out or in assisting any persons to carry out the provisions of this Ordinance shall preserve and aid in preserving secrecy with regard to all matters relating to the affairs of any person that may come to his knowledge in the performance of his duties under this Ordinance, and shall not communicate any such matter to any person other than the person to whom such matter relates or his executor or the authorized representative of such person or such executor, nor suffer or permit any person to have access to any records in the possession, custody or control of the Commissioner.

(2) Every person appointed under or employed in carrying out the provisions of this Ordinance, shall before acting under this Ordinance take and subscribe before a justice of the peace an oath of secrecy in such form as the Board of Inland Revenue may specify.

(3) No person appointed under or employed in carrying out the provisions of this Ordinance shall be required to produce in any court any return, document, or assessment, or to divulge or communicate to any court, any matter or thing coming under his notice in the performance of his duties under this Ordinance, except as may be necessary for the purpose of carrying into effect the provisions of this Ordinance.

(4) Notwithstanding anything contained in this section, the Commissioner or any officer of the Inland Revenue Department authorized by the Commissioner in that behalf may communicate any matter which comes to his knowledge, including a copy of any return, accounts or other document submitted to him in connection with this Ordinance-

    (a)   to the Commissioner of Rating and Valuation, to the Collector of Stamp Revenue, or to the Estate Duty Commissioner, or

    (b)   to the income tax authority of any part of the Commonwealth to such an extent as the Commissioner may deem necessary to enable the correct relief to be given from income tax in that part in respect of the payment of tax under this Ordinance, or

    (c)   to the Attorney General, or any public officer authorized by him, for the purpose of reporting under section 68(5) an appeal to the Board of Review, or

    (d)   to any person appointed under or employed in carrying out the provisions of the Business Registration Ordinance (Cap. 310), as regards any matter required to be notified to the Commissioner pursuant to section 8(1) or (2) of that Ordinance by the person submitting such return, accounts or other document.

(5)   Notwithstanding anything contained in this section, the Commissioner may permit the Director of Audit or any officer of that department duly authorized by the Director of Audit in that behalf to have such access to any records or documents as may be necessary for the performance of his official duties. The Director of Audit or any officer so authorized shall be deemed to be a person employed in carrying out the provisions of this Ordinance for the purpose of subsection (2).

(6)   Notwithstanding anything contained in this section, where the Commissioner is of the opinion that any tax deemed to be in default under the provisions of section 71(1) has for the time being become irrecoverable, he may communicate to the Financial Secretary the names and descriptions of the persons charged with such tax together with particulars of the tax in default.

PART II - Property Tax

Charge of property tax

5.(1) Property tax shall, subject to the provisions of this Ordinance, be charged for each year of assessment on every person being the owner of any land or buildings or land and buildings wherever situate in Hong Kong and shall be computed at the standard rate on the net assessable value of such land or buildings or land and buildings for each such year.

Provided that-

  (a) *(Repealed)*

  (b) where the owner of the land is not the owner of the buildings thereon, separate assessments shall be made for the land and for the buildings;

  (c) *(Repealed)*

  (d) *(Repealed)*

  (e) *(Repealed)*

(1A) In subsection (1), "net assessable value" means the assessable value of land or buildings or land and buildings, ascertained in accordance with section 5B-

  (a) *(Repealed)*

  (b) less-

    (i) where the owner agrees to pay the rates in respect of the land or buildings or land and buildings, those rates paid by him; and

    (ii) an allowance for repairs and outgoings of 20% of that assessable value after deduction of any rates under subparagraph (i).

(1B) The percentage allowance specified in subsection (1A) may be amended by resolution of the Legislative Council.

(2)   *(a)* Notwithstanding subsection (1), any corporation carrying on a trade, profession or business in Hong Kong shall, on application made in writing to the Commissioner and on proof of the facts to the satisfaction of the Commissioner, be entitled to exemption from the property tax for any year of assessment in respect of any land or buildings or land and buildings owned by the corporation where the corporation would be entitled under section 25 to a set-off of the property tax which, if exemption were not granted under this subsection, would be paid by the corporation; and the property shall be and remain exempted from property tax for each year of assessment in which the circumstances are such as to qualify the property for such exemption for that year.

(b) *(Repealed)*

(c) Every corporation exempted from property tax under this subsection in respect of any land or buildings or land and buildings shall, within 30 days after the event, notify the Commissioner in writing of any change in the ownership or use thereof or in any other circumstances affecting such exemption.

(2A)-(5) *(Repealed)*

5A. *(Repealed)*

Ascertainment of assessable value on or after 1 April 1983

5B.(1) This section shall apply to any year of assessment commencing on or after 1 April 1983.

(2) The assessable value of land or buildings or land and buildings for each year of assessment shall be the consideration, in money or money's worth, payable in that year to, to the order of, or for the benefit of, the owner in respect of the right of use of that land or buildings or land and buildings.

(3) Any consideration payable before the year of assessment commencing on 1 April 1983 in respect of a period of the right of use which starts after, or extends beyond, 1 April 1983 shall, for the purposes of this section, be deemed to be payable in equal monthly instalments during the period of the right of use or during a period of 3 years ending on 31 March 1986, whichever is the shorter.

(4) Any consideration payable in respect of a period of the right of use which is not contained within any one year of assessment shall, for the purposes of this section, be deemed to be payable in equal monthly instalments during the period of the right of use or during a period of 3 years commencing at the start of the period of the right of use to which the consideration relates, whichever is the shorter.

(5) *(Repealed)*

(6) In this section, "consideration" includes any consideration payable in respect of the provision of any services or benefits connected with or related to the right of use.

6. *(Repealed)*

7. *(Repealed)*

Interpretation

7A.   In this Part-

"buildings", except for the purposes of section 5(2), includes any part of a building;

"land or buildings or land and buildings" includes piers, wharves and other structures;

"occupied", in relation to land or buildings or land and buildings, means land or buildings or land and buildings which are being put to beneficial use.

7B.   (*Repealed*)

Bad debts

7C.(1) In ascertaining the assessable value of any land or buildings or land and buildings under this Part for any year of assessment commencing on or after 1 April 1983, there shall be deducted any consideration in money or money's worth, payable or deemed to be payable on or after 1 April 1983 to, to the order of, or for the benefit of, the owner in respect of the right of use of that land or buildings or that land and buildings and proved to the satisfaction of the assessor to have become irrecoverable during that year of assessment.

(2)   Consideration previously deducted as irrecoverable and recovered during any year of assessment shall be treated as consideration mentioned in section 5B(2) payable in that year of assessment in respect of the right of use of the land or buildings or land and buildings in respect of which that consideration was payable.

(3)   Notwithstanding section 70, where a person is entitled to deduct any consideration under subsection (1) but the land or buildings or land and buildings has no or insufficient assessable value from which to deduct that consideration in the year of assessment in which, under that subsection, that consideration is deductible, that consideration, or that consideration to the extent to which it cannot be deducted in that year, shall be deducted from the assessable value of that land or buildings or that land and buildings in the latest year of assessment in which that assessable value is sufficient.

PART III - Salaries Tax

Charge of salaries tax

8.(1)   Salaries tax shall, subject to the provisions of this Ordinance, be charged for each year of assessment on every person in respect of his income arising in or derived from Hong Kong from the following sources-

        (a)   any office or employment of profit; and

        (b)   any pension.

(1A)   For the purposes of this Part, income arising in or derived from Hong Kong from any employment-

        (a)   includes, without in any way limiting the meaning of the expression and subject to paragraph (b), all income derived from services rendered in Hong Kong including leave pay attributable to such services;

        (b)   excludes income derived from services rendered by a person who-

                (i)   is not employed by the Government or as master or member of the crew of a ship or as commander or member of the crew of an aircraft; and

                (ii)   renders outside Hong Kong all the services in connection with his employment; and

        (c)   excludes income derived by a person from services rendered by him in any territory outside Hong Kong where-

                (i)   by the laws of the territory where the services are rendered, the income is chargeable to tax of substantially the same nature as salaries tax under this Ordinance; and

                (ii)   the Commissioner is satisfied that that person has, by deduction or otherwise, paid tax of that nature in that territory in respect of the income.

(1B)   In determining whether or not all services are rendered outside Hong Kong for the purposes of subsection (1A) no account shall be taken of services rendered in Hong Kong during visits not exceeding a total of 60 days in the basis period for the year of assessment.

(2)   In computing the income of any person for the purposes of subsection (1) there shall be excluded the following-

        (a)   the official emoluments received by the Governor;

(b)   the official emoluments of consuls, vice-consuls and persons employed on the staff of any consulate, who are subjects or citizens of the state which they represent;

(c)   subject to subsection (4) any sum received by way of commutation of pension under-

    (i)   a recognized occupational retirement scheme upon termination of service, death, incapacity or retirement;

    (ii)   the Pensions Ordinance (Cap. 89);

    (iii)   the Pension Benefits Ordinance (Cap. 99); or

    (iv)   the Pension Benefits (Judicial Officers) Ordinance (Cap. 401);

(ca)   in the case of a pension attributable to services rendered in any office or employment, other than employment by the Government, so much of the pension as is not attributable to services rendered in Hong Kong;

(cb)   subject to subsection (4) any sum, other than a pension, withdrawn from a recognized occupational retirement scheme upon termination of service, death, incapacity or retirement, but, if the scheme is set up by an employer not chargeable to tax under Part IV, the sum excluded by this paragraph shall not exceed, in the case of that part of the sum withdrawn which represents the employer's contributions, an amount equal to 15% of the employee's income from his office or employment for the year preceding the date of withdrawal multiplied by the number of completed years of his service with that employer;

(d)   the emoluments payable by the Governments of the members of the Commonwealth, other than the Government of Hong Kong, to members of Her Majesty's forces and to persons in the permanent service of those Governments in Hong Kong in respect of their offices under those Governments;

(e)   wound and disability pensions granted to members of Her Majesty's forces;

(f)   gratuities granted to members of Her Majesty's forces in respect of services rendered during war;

(fa)   the Hong Kong War Memorial Pensions and additional benefits paid under the Hong Kong War Memorial Pensions Ordinance (Cap.386);

(g)   any amount arising from a scholarship, exhibition, bursary, or other similar

educational endowment held by that person where he is receiving full time instruction at a university, college, school, or other similar educational establishment;

(h)   the emoluments payable by the Government of the United Kingdom to persons in the temporary service of that Government who are in the opinion of the Commissioner serving in Hong Kong on United Kingdom based terms whereby they are normally employed in the United Kingdom but are liable for overseas service or are recruited in the United Kingdom specially for service in Hong Kong;

(i)   any amount received by way of periodical payments in the nature of alimony or maintenance by a person from his or her spouse or former spouse;

(j)   income derived from services rendered as master or member of the crew of a ship or as commander or member of the crew of an aircraft by a person who was present in Hong Kong on not more than-

    (i)   a total of 60 days in the basis period for that year of assessment; and

    (ii)   a total of 120 days falling partly within each of the basis periods for 2 consecutive years of assessment, one of which is that year of assessment;

(k)   any salary or other remuneration paid by another person who is chargeable to profits tax under Part IV which, but for section 17(2), would be deductible in computing the profits or losses of such other person for the purposes of that Part.

(3)   For the purposes of subsection (2)(c) and (cb)-

"retirement" means-

(a)   a retirement from the service of the employer at some specified age of not less than 45 years; or

(b)   a retirement after some specified period of service with the employer of not less than 10 years; or

(c)   the attainment of the age of 60 years or some specified age of retirement, whichever is the later;

"termination of service" means a termination of employment with the employer other than upon retirement, death or incapacity.

(4)   *(a)* Any amount received on termination of service from a recognized occupational retirement scheme as represents the employer's contributions under the scheme may only be excluded under subsection (2)(c) and (cb), as the case may be, to the extent that the amount does not exceed the proportionate benefit calculated in accordance with paragraph (b).

     (b) The proportionate benefit is the sum not exceeding the amount bearing the same ratio to the accrued benefit of the relevant person as represents the employer's contributions under the scheme as the number of completed months of service with the employer bears to 120 months:

       Provided that in the case of a recognized occupational retirement scheme approved by the Commissioner under section 87A at any time prior to its repeal by the Inland Revenue (Amendment) (No. 5) Ordinance 1993 (76 of 1993), where any amount payable upon termination of service in accordance with the rules of the scheme, as approved by the Commissioner prior to the repeal of that section, exceeds the proportionate benefit calculated in accordance with this paragraph, that amount shall be taken to be the proportionate benefit.

     (c) For the purpose of paragraph (b)-
"accrued benefit" means the maximum benefit a person would have been entitled to receive under an occupational retirement scheme in respect of his service recognized for the purposes of the scheme if, at the date of termination of the person's employment, retirement (as defined in subsection (3)) has instead taken place.

Definition of income from employment

9.(1) Income from any office or employment includes-

     (a) any wages, salary, leave pay, fee, commission, bonus, gratuity, perquisite, or allowance, whether derived from the employer or others, except-

       (i) the value of any holiday warrant or passage granted by an employer to an employee in so far as it is used for travel;

       (ii) any allowance for the purchase of any such holiday warrant or passage in so far as it is expended for that purpose;

       (iii) any allowance paid by an employer to an employee for the transportation of the personal effects of the employee in connection with any journey on which a holiday warrant or passage referred to in subparagraph (i) or (ii) is used in so far as the allowance is expended for the transportation of the personal effects of the employee; and

        (iv)   subject to subsection (2A), any amount paid by the employer to or for the credit of a person other than the employee in discharge of a sole and primary liability of the employer to that other person, not being a liability for which any person was surety;

(aa)   so much of any amount (other than a pension falling under section 8(1)(b)) received by an employee before or after his employment ceases, whether by way of commutation or otherwise, from a pension or provident fund, scheme or society, other than a recognized occupational retirement scheme, as represents the employer's contributions to that fund, scheme or society;

(ab)   so much of any amount (other than a pension falling under section 8(1)(b)) received by an employee, whether by way of commutation or otherwise, under a recognized occupational retirement scheme-

        (i)   by reason other than termination of service, death, incapacity or retirement of the employee as represents the employer's contributions under the scheme in respect of the employee;

        (ii)   by reason of termination of service as represents such part of the employer's contributions under the scheme in respect of the employee that exceeds the proportionate benefit calculated in accordance with section 8(4)(b);

(ac)   any payment received by an employee pursuant to a judgment given under section 57(3)(b) of the Occupational Retirement Schemes Ordinance (Cap. 426) that is attributable to his employer's contributions to the occupational retirement scheme in respect of which the judgment was given;

(b)   the rental value of any place of residence provided rent-free by the employer or an associated corporation;

(c)   where a place of residence is provided by an employer or an associated corporation at a rent less than the rental value, the excess of the rental value over such rent;

(d)   any gain realized by the exercise of, or by the assignment or release of, a right to acquire shares or stock in a corporation obtained by a person as the holder of an office in or an employee of that or any other corporation.

(1A)   *(a)*   Notwithstanding subsection (1)(a), where an employer or an associated corporation-

        (i)   pays all or part of the rent payable by the employee; or

    (ii)   refunds all or part of the rent paid by the employee,

such payment or refund shall be deemed not to be income;

    (b)   a place of residence in respect of which an employer or associated corporation has paid or refunded all the rent therefor shall be deemed for the purposes of subsection (1) to be provided rent free by the employer or associated corporation;

    (c)   a place of residence in respect of which an employer or associated corporation has paid or refunded part of the rent therefor shall be deemed for the purposes of subsection (1) to be provided by the employer or associated corporation for a rent equal to the difference between the rent payable or paid by the employee and the part thereof paid or refunded by the employer or associated corporation.

(2)   The rental value of any place of residence provided by the employer or an associated corporation shall be deemed to be 10% of the income as described in subsection (1)(a) derived from the employer for the period during which a place of residence is provided after deducting the outgoings, expenses and allowances provided for in section 12(1)(a) and (b) to the extent to which they are incurred during the period for which the place of residence is provided and any lump sum payment or gratuity paid or granted upon the retirement or termination of employment of the employee:

    Provided that -

    (a)   if such place of residence be a hotel, hostel or boarding house the rental value shall be deemed to be 8% of the income aforesaid where the accommodation consists of not more than 2 rooms and 4% where the accommodation consists of not more than one room;

    (b)   if such place of residence be other than a hotel, hostel or boarding house any person may elect to have -

        (i)   in respect of the years of assessment up to and including the year of assessment commencing on 1 April 1982, the assessable value ascertained in accordance with section 5A; or

        (ii)   in respect of the years of assessment commencing on or after 1 April 1983, the rateable value included in the valuation list prepared under section 12 of the Rating Ordinance (Cap.116) or, if the place of residence is not so included, the rateable value ascertained in accordance with Part III of that Ordinance,

substituted for rental value at 10% as aforesaid.

(2A)   Subsection 1(a)(iv) shall not operate to exclude -

>   *(a)*   any benefit capable of being converted into money by the recipient; or
>
>   *(b)*   any amount paid by an employer in connection with the education of a child of an employee,

from income from any office or employment.

(3)   A pension shall include a pension which is voluntary or is capable of being discontinued.

(4)   For the purposes of subsection (1) -

>   *(a)*   the gain realized by the exercise at any time of such a right as is referred to in paragraph (d) of that subsection shall be taken to be the difference between the amount which a person might reasonably expect to obtain from a sale in the open market at that time of the shares or stock acquired and the amount or value of the consideration given whether for them or for the grant of the right or for both; and
>
>   *(b)*   the gain realized by the assignment or release of such a right as is referred to in paragraph (d) of that subsection shall be taken to be the difference between the amount or value of the consideration for the assignment or release and the amount or value of the consideration given for the grant of the right,

(a just apportionment being made of any entire consideration given for the grant of the right to acquire the said shares or stock and other shares or stock or otherwise for the grant of the right to acquire those shares or stock and for something beside):

Provided that neither the consideration given for the grant of the right nor any such entire consideration shall be taken to include the performance of any duties in or in connection with the office or employment by reason of which the right was granted, and no part of the amount or value of the consideration given for the grant shall be deducted more than once under this subsection.

(5) Where salaries tax may by virtue of subsection (1)(d) become chargeable in respect of any gain which may be realized by the exercise of a right, salaries tax shall not be chargeable under any other provision of this Ordinance in respect of the receipt of the right.

(6) For the purposes of this section

>   "associated corporation" means-
>
>   *(a)*   a corporation over which the employer has control;
>
>   *(b)*   if the employer is a corporation-

    (i)   a corporation which has control over the employer; or

    (ii)   a corporation which is under the control of the same person as is the employer;

"child of an employee" means any child of an employee or of his or her spouse or former spouse, whether or not born in wedlock, and includes the adopted or step child of either or both of them;

"control", in relation to a corporation, means the power of a person to secure-

    (a)   by means of the holding of shares or the possession of voting power in or in relation to that or any other corporation; or

    (b)   by virtue of any powers conferred by the articles of association or other document regulating that or any other corporation,

that the affairs of the first-mentioned corporation are conducted in accordance with the wishes of that person;

"employee" includes a holder of an office;

"place of residence" includes a residence provided by an employer or an associated corporation notwithstanding that the employee is required to occupy that place of residence by or under his terms of employment and whether or not by doing so he can better perform his duties;

"retirement" and "termination of service" have the same meaning as in section 8(3).

Salaries tax on spouses to be paid separately unless they elect to be jointly assessed

10.(1) In the case of a husband and wife, unless an election is made under subsection (2), salaries tax shall be payable on the net chargeable income of each spouse ascertained under this Part by the spouse to whom the income has accrued.

(2)   Where in any year of assessment a husband and wife, not being a wife living apart from her husband, both have assessable income and-

    (a)   either the husband or wife is entitled to allowances under Part V which are in excess of his or her net assessable income as reduced by approved charitable donations under section 12B(1)(a); or

    (b)   both also have a net chargeable income and the aggregate of the salaries tax which would be payable by them if subsection (1) applies exceeds the salaries tax which would be payable if an election is made under this subsection,

an election may be made by them, subject to section 11, to be assessed to salaries tax in the manner specified in subsection (3).

(3) Where an election is made by a husband and wife under subsection (2) salaries tax shall be payable on their aggregated net chargeable income as ascertained under section 12B(2) and in the case of an election-

> *(a)* under subsection (2)(a), the spouse who would have been chargeable to salaries tax in the absence of such an election;

> *(b)* under subsection (2)(b), the spouse who is nominated by them,

shall be chargeable to salaries tax in respect of such aggregated net chargeable income.

(4) Where a husband or wife is deceased an executor shall have the same right to make an election under subsection (2) as the deceased would have had if the deceased had not died.

(5) For the purposes of subsection (3), where an election is made under subsection (2) by a husband and wife who married one another in the year of assessment to which the election relates, they shall be deemed, for the purposes of ascertaining their aggregated net chargeable income for that year, to have married at the commencement of that year.

The time and manner in which an election or the withdrawal of an election for joint assessment is to be made

11.(1) An election shall be made in the specified form jointly by the husband and wife and, subject to subsection (3), may be withdrawn by them jointly by notice in writing given to the Commissioner.

(2) An election shall relate to the year of assessment specified in such form and it, and any withdrawal thereof under this section, may be made at any time-

> *(a)* within that year of assessment or the following year of assessment; or

> *(b)* before the expiration of a period of one month following the time when the assessment for the year of assessment becomes final and conclusive under section 70,

whichever is the later, or within such further time, if any, as the Commissioner may allow as being reasonable in the circumstances.

(3) Where an election is withdrawn under this section it shall, for the purpose of assessing the net chargeable income of the husband and wife, be deemed never to have been made and any assessment made prior to such withdrawal on the basis of the election may be adjusted by the Commissioner to take account of the withdrawal.

(4) A husband and wife who under this section have withdrawn an election may not again make an election in relation to the year of assessment to which the withdrawn election relates.

(5)   In this section "election" means an election made under section 10(2) and, where a nomination under section 10(3)(b) is required, includes such nomination.

11A.   (*Repealed*)

Ascertainment of assessable income

11B.   The assessable income of a person in any year of assessment shall be the aggregate amount of income accruing to him from all sources in that year of assessment.

Office or employment of profit

11C.   For the purpose of section 11B, a person shall be deemed to commence or cease, as the case may be, to derive income from a source whenever and as often as he commences or ceases-

> *(a)*   to hold any office or employment of profit; or

> *(b)*   to become entitled to a pension.

Receipt of income

11D.   For the purpose of section 11B-

> *(a)*   income which has accrued to a person during the basis period for a year of assessment but which has not been received by him in such basis period shall not be included in his assessable income for that year of assessment until such time as he shall have received such income, when notwithstanding anything contained in this Ordinance, an additional assessment shall be raised in respect of such income:
>
> Provided that for the purposes of this paragraph income which has either been made available to the person to whom it has accrued or has been dealt with on his behalf or according to his directions shall be deemed to have been received by such person;

> *(b)*   income accrues to a person when he becomes entitled to claim payment thereof.

> Provided that-

> **(i)**   any lump sum payment received on or after 1 April 1966, being a lump sum payment or gratuity paid or granted upon the retirement from or termination of any office or employment or any contract of employment of an employee or a lump sum payment of deferred pay

or arrears of pay arising from an award of salary or wages, whether such a payment is paid by an employer to a person during employment or after that person has left his employ, shall upon the application in writing of the person entitled to claim payment thereof within 2 years after the end of the year of assessment in which the payment is made be related back and shall then be deemed to be income which has accrued during the periods in which the services or employment, in respect of which the payment was made, were performed or exercised, or, if the relevant periods of service or employment exceed 3 years, the payment shall be deemed to be income accruing at a constant rate over the 3 years ending on the date on which the person became entitled to claim payment thereof or ending on the last day of employment, whichever is the earlier; and, notwithstanding section 70, an application made by any person under this proviso for the adjustment of an assessment shall, to that extent, be regarded as a valid objection to the assessment under section 64; and

(ii) subject to proviso (i), any payment made by an employer to a person after that person has ceased or been deemed to cease to derive income which, if it had been made on the last day of the period during which he derived income, would have been included in that person's assessable income for the year of assessment in which he ceased or is deemed to cease to derive income from that employment, shall be deemed to have accrued to that person on the last day of that employment.

Adjustments to assessable income

12.(1) In ascertaining the net assessable income of a person for any year of assessment, there shall be deducted from the assessable income of that person-

(a) all outgoings and expenses, other than expenses of a domestic or private nature and capital expenditure, wholly, exclusively and necessarily incurred in the production of the assessable income;

(b) allowances calculated in accordance with Part VI in respect of capital expenditure on machinery or plant the use of which is essential to the production of the assessable income;

(c) the amount of any excess carried forward to that year of assessment in accordance with section 12A(3);

(d) the amount of any excess required by subsection (3) to be deducted.

(2) Where any machinery or plant is not used wholly and exclusively in the production of assessable income, the amount of the allowances provided for in subsection (1)(b) shall be reduced in the proportion considered by the assessor to be fair and reasonable.

(3) If in the case of a husband and wife who have made an election under section 10(2), the aggregate of deductions claimed for any year of assessment by either spouse under subsection (1)(a), (b) and (c) exceeds the assessable income of that spouse in that year, the excess shall be deducted from the assessable income of the other spouse for the purpose of determining the net assessable income of that other spouse in that year.

(4)   (*Repealed*)

(5) The amount of assessable income for any year of assessment of a person shall, for the purposes of ascertaining his net assessable income, be increased by the amount of any balancing charge directed to be made under Part VI on that person in respect of the machinery or plant used in the production of the assessable income.

Treatment of losses

12A.(1) Where in any year of assessment the aggregate of the outgoings, expenses and allowances deductible under section 12(1)(a) and (b) from the assessable income of a person exceeds the amount of his assessable income, the amount of the excess shall, subject to subsection (4), be carried forward and set off against his assessable income in subsequent years of assessment.

(2) The aggregate amount set off against a person's assessable income in subsequent years of assessment shall not exceed the amount of any excess under subsection (1).

(3) Subject to subsection (4), a set off by a person under this section shall first be made against his assessable income for the year of assessment next succeeding the year of assessment in respect of which the excess occurred and, so far as it cannot be so made, against his assessable income for the next year of assessment and so on until the excess has been completely set off.

(4) Where in any year of assessment the net chargeable incomes of the husband and wife are aggregated by reason of an election made under section 10(2), any excess carried forward into that year under this section shall-

> *(a)*   be set off primarily against the assessable income of the spouse whose deductions resulted in the excess and then, so far as it cannot be so set off, against the assessable income of the other spouse; and

> *(b)*   then, and so far as it cannot be set off in accordance with paragraph (a)-

> > **(i)**   where no election is made under section 10(2) in respect of the following year of assessment, in accordance with subsection (3); or

> **(ii)** where an election is made under section 10(2) in respect of the following year of assessment, in accordance with paragraph (a),

and so on from year to year until the excess has been completely set off.

Ascertainment of net chargeable income

12B.(1) The net chargeable income of a person for any year of assessment shall, subject to subsection (2), be such amount as is arrived at after deducting from his net assessable income-

> *(a)* such approved charitable donations as are provided for under section 12BA; and
>
> *(b)* such allowances as are under Part V permitted for that person.

(2) In the case of a person chargeable to salaries tax under section 10(3), that person and his or her spouse shall have but one net chargeable income, and it shall be the amount arrived at after deducting from the aggregate of their net assessable incomes-

> *(a)* such approved charitable donations as are provided for under section 12BA; and
>
> *(b)* such allowances as are under Part V permitted in their case.

(3) *(Repealed)*

Charitable donation

12BA.(1) Subject to subsections (2) and (3), the amount of charitable donations that, in ascertaining net chargeable income, may be deducted-

> *(a)* in the case of a person whose assessable income is aggregated with that of his or her spouse by reason of an election made under section 10(2), from the aggregate of their net assessable incomes; and
>
> *(b)* in the case of any other person, from the net assessable income of that person,

shall be the aggregate of approved charitable donations which are made during that year by that person and by his or her spouse, if in any case such aggregate amount is not less than $100.

(2) Every deduction claimed by virtue of subsection (1) shall be claimed on the specified form and the deduction shall be permitted only if the claim contains such particulars and is supported by such proof as the Commissioner may require.

(3) No deduction shall be permitted under subsection (1) for any year of assessment in respect of-

(a)   any sum which is allowable as a deduction under section 16, 16B, 16C or 16D;

(b)   a sum in excess of 10% of-

    (i)   the assessable income as reduced by the deductions provided for under section 12(1)(a) and (b); or

    (ii)   in the case of a husband and wife who have made an election under section 10(2), the aggregate of the assessable incomes of both spouses as reduced in each case by the deductions provided for under section 12(1)(a) and (b).

(4)   Notwithstanding anything contained in this section, a charitable donation shall not be taken into account in ascertaining the net chargeable income of more than one person and, where a deduction of the same donation is claimed or allowed in respect of the net chargeable income of more than one person, section 33(2) to (4) shall apply with the necessary modifications to such a deduction as they do to a dependent parent allowance, a dependent grandparent allowance or a child allowance; and section 33 shall, where this subsection applies, be construed as if a reference to such an allowance included, in the case of a donation so claimed, a reference to an allowance to which section 33(2) applies and, in the case of a donation so allowed, an allowance to which section 33(3) applies.

Calculation of salaries tax

13.(1)   Subject to subsection (2), salaries tax shall be charged at the rates specified in Schedule 2 on the net chargeable income of a person for each year of assessment ascertained in accordance with this Part.

(2)   The amount of salaries tax so charged shall not exceed the amount which would have been chargeable had the standard rate been charged on the whole of-

(a)   the net assessable income as reduced by approved charitable donations provided for under section 12BA; or

(b)   in the case of a spouse chargeable to salaries tax under section 10(3), the aggregate amount of his or her net assessable income and that of his or her spouse as reduced by approved charitable donations provided for under section 12BA.

PART IV - Profits Tax

Charge of profits tax

14.(1) Subject to the provisions of this Ordinance, profits tax shall be charged for each year of assessment at the standard rate on every person carrying on a trade, profession or business in Hong Kong in respect of his assessable profits arising in or derived from Hong Kong for that year from such trade, profession or business (excluding profits arising from the sale of capital assets) as ascertained in accordance with this Part.

(2) In the case of-

   (a) a corporation; and

   (b) a corporation ("relevant corporation") to which a share of the assessable profits of a partnership is apportioned under section 22A and is charged in the partnership name under section 22,

profits tax shall be charged on the assessable profits of that corporation, or on that share of the assessable profits of that relevant corporation, as the case may be, at the rate specified in Schedule 8.

Certain amounts deemed trading receipts

15.(1) For the purposes of this Ordinance, the sums described in the following paragraphs shall be deemed to be receipts arising in or derived from Hong Kong from a trade, profession or business carried on in Hong Kong-

   (a) sums, not otherwise chargeable to tax under this Part, received by or accrued to a person from the exhibition or use in Hong Kong of cinematograph or television film or tape, any sound recording, or any advertising material connected with such film, tape or recording;

   (b) sums, not otherwise chargeable to tax under this Part, received by or accrued to a person for the use of or right to use in Hong Kong a patent, design, trademark, copyright material or secret process or formula or other property of a similar nature, or for imparting or undertaking to impart knowledge directly or indirectly connected with the use in Hong Kong of any such patent, design, trademark, copyright, secret process or formula or other property;

   (c) sums received by or accrued to a person by way of grant, subsidy or similar financial assistance in connection with the carrying on of a trade, profession or business in Hong Kong, other than sums in connection with capital expenditure made or to be made by the person;

   (d) sums received by or accrued to a person by way of hire, rental or similar

charges for the use of movable property in Hong Kong or the right to use movable property in Hong Kong;

(e)   *(Repealed)*

(f)   sums received by or accrued to a corporation carrying on a trade, profession or business in Hong Kong by way of interest derived from Hong Kong;

(g)   sums received by or accrued to a person, other than a corporation, carrying on a trade, profession or business in Hong Kong by way of interest derived from Hong Kong which interest is in respect of the funds of the trade, profession or business;

(h)   sums received by or accrued to a person by way of refund to that person of a contribution made by him as employer to a recognized occupational retirement scheme, but to the extent only that such sums were allowed as deductions in ascertaining the assessable profits of that person under this Part;

(i)   sums, not otherwise chargeable to tax under this Part, received by or accrued to a financial institution by way of interest which arises through or from the carrying on by the financial institution of its business in Hong Kong, notwithstanding that the moneys in respect of which the interest is received or accrues are made available outside Hong Kong;

(j)   sums received by or accrued to a corporation carrying on a trade, profession or business in Hong Kong by way of gains or profits arising in or derived from Hong Kong from the sale or other disposal or on the redemption on maturity or presentment of a certificate of deposit or bill of exchange;

(k)   sums received by or accrued to a person, other than a corporation, carrying on a trade, profession or business in Hong Kong by way of gains or profits arising in or derived from Hong Kong from the sale or other disposal or on the redemption on maturity or presentment of a certificate of deposit or bill of exchange where such gains or profits are in respect of the funds of the trade, profession or business;

(l)   sums, not otherwise chargeable to tax under this Part, received by or accrued to a financial institution by way of gains or profits arising through or from the carrying on by the financial institution of its business in Hong Kong from the sale or other disposal or on the redemption on maturity or presentment of a certificate of deposit or bill of exchange notwithstanding that-

    (i)   the moneys laid out for the acquisition of the certificate or bill were made available outside Hong Kong; or

      (ii)   the sale, disposal or redemption is effected outside Hong Kong; and

   (m)   sums received or receivable by a person as consideration in respect of the transfer of a right to receive income, as provided for in section 15A.

(1A) Subsection (1)(j) or (k) shall not apply to gains or profits arising in or derived from Hong Kong, other than gains or profits received by or accrued to a person whose trade, profession or business comprises or includes trading in certificates of deposit or bills of exchange, to the extent to which such gains or profits relate to a period prior to 1 April 1981; and gains or profits received by or accrued to any person from the sale or other disposal or on the redemption on maturity or presentment, on or after 1 April 1981, of a certificate of deposit or bill of exchange purchased or otherwise acquired by that person before that date, shall be determined by reference to such amount as the Commissioner may consider such certificate of deposit or bill of exchange would have realized if it had been sold in the open market at the close of business on 31 March 1981 and not by reference to the amount, if any, paid by that person in so purchasing or otherwise acquiring such certificate of deposit or bill of exchange.

(1B) *(Repealed)*

(2) Where, in ascertaining for the purposes of this Part the profits of a trade, profession or business carried on in Hong Kong, a deduction has been allowed for any debt incurred for the purposes of the trade, profession or business, then, if the whole or any part of that debt is thereafter released, the amount released shall be deemed to be a receipt of the trade, profession or business arising in or derived from Hong Kong at the time when the release was effected.

(3) Where in the basis period for any year of assessment a financial institution was not a financial institution for the whole of that period, in that, if the institution is a bank it was not licensed for the whole of that period or if the institution is a deposit-taking company it was not registered for the whole of that period, then subsection (1)(i) and (l) shall apply only in respect of such part of the basis period during which the bank or deposit-taking company was licensed or registered, as the case may be.

(4) The amendments to this section effected by the Inland Revenue (Amendment) Ordinance 1984 shall not have the effect of rendering chargeable to tax sums received or accrued to any person prior to 1 April 1984 which were not chargeable to tax immediately prior to the coming into force of that Ordinance.

(5) The amendments to this section effected by the Inland Revenue (Amendment) (No. 2) Ordinance 1986 shall apply to sums received or accrued by way of interest, gains or profits on or after 1 April 1986, and the provisions of this section in force immediately prior to the coming into force of that Ordinance shall continue to apply to such sums received or accrued prior to 1 April 1986 as if such amendments had not been enacted.

Transfer of right to receive income

15A.(1) Subject to subsection (3) where-

> *(a)* a right to receive income from property is transferred by a person to another person; and

> *(b)* consideration has been received or is receivable in respect of the transfer,

the amount of the consideration shall, notwithstanding the exclusion relating to the sale of capital assets contained in section 14, be treated as a trading receipt arising in or derived from Hong Kong by the transferor from a trade, profession or business carried on in Hong Kong.

(2) The reference in subsection (1) to the amount of consideration shall, in the case where consideration is paid or given otherwise than in cash, be construed as a reference to the money value of the consideration.

(3) Subsection (1) shall not apply in relation to a transfer of a right to receive income from property where the right arose from the ownership by the transferor of a legal or equitable estate or interest in the property and, before or at the time of that transfer, the transferor also transferred that estate or interest to the transferee.

(4) In this section-

"income" means any profits, rent, interest or royalty chargeable to tax under Part IV;

"property" means any property whatsoever;

"right to receive income from property" means a right to have income that will or may be derived from property paid to, or applied or accumulated for the benefit of, the person owning the right.

(5) This section shall apply to any agreement made for the transfer of a right to receive income from property within the meaning of subsection (4) entered into or effected after 25 February 1987 other than an agreement made in pursuance of a legally enforceable obligation incurred on or before that date.

15B. *(Repealed)*

Valuation of trading stock on cessation of business

15C. Where a person ceases to carry on a trade or business in Hong Kong the trading stock of the trade or business at the date of cessation shall be valued for the purpose of computing the profits in respect of which that person is chargeable to tax under this Part as follows-

(a)   in the case of any such trading stock-

    (i)   which is sold or transferred for valuable consideration to a person who carries on or intends to carry on a trade or business in Hong Kong; and

    (ii)   the cost whereof may be deducted by the purchaser as an expense in computing the profits from such trade or business in respect of which such purchaser is chargeable to tax under this Part,

the value thereof shall be taken to be the amount realized on the sale or the value of the consideration given for the transfer;

(b)   in the case of any other such trading stock, the value thereof shall be taken to be the amount which it would have realized if it had been sold in the open market at the date of cessation.

Post-cessation receipts and payments

15D.(1) Where a person who has ceased to carry on a trade, profession or business in Hong Kong, receives any sum which, if it had been received before such cessation, would have been included in the profits of the trade, profession or business in respect of which the person is chargeable to tax under this Part, then to the extent to which the sum has not already been included in such profits that sum shall be deemed to be profits of the trade, profession or business for the year of assessment in which the cessation occurred.

(2)   Where a person who has ceased to carry on a trade, profession or business in Hong Kong pays any sum which, if it had been paid before such cessation, would have been deductible in computing the profits of the trade, profession or business in respect of which the person is chargeable to tax under this Part, then to the extent to which the sum has not already been deducted in computing such profits, that sum shall be deducted in ascertaining his profits for the year of assessment in which the cessation occurred.

Stock borrowing and lending

15E.(1) This section applies where-

(a)   in relation to a stock borrowing under a stock borrowing and lending agreement, the borrower has used the borrowed stock obtained from a lender for one or more than one specified purpose and has effected a stock return;

(b)   if any distribution is made or a right or option is issued in respect of the borrowed stock during the borrowing period, regardless of whether that event occurs before or after the borrowed stock is disposed of by the borrower to a third party, the lender receives from the borrower the distribution or identical property, the right or option or an identical right or option, or a compensatory payment equal to the value of the distribution or the value of the right or option;

(c) the lender does not dispose of, whether by transfer, declaration of trust or otherwise, the right to receive any part of the total consideration payable or to be given by the borrower under the stock borrowing and lending agreement;

(d) both the borrower and the lender were dealing with each other at arm's length in relation to the stock borrowing and the stock return; and

(e) the lender does not enter into the stock borrowing with the purpose, or main purpose, of avoiding or deferring the inclusion of any amount in profits in respect of which the lender is chargeable to tax under this Part.

(2) For the purpose of determining whether an amount, other than any fee payable under a stock borrowing and lending agreement, should be taken into account in ascertaining the profits in respect of which a lender is chargeable to tax under this Part in respect of a stock borrowing or a stock return, the lender is to be treated as if-

(a) the stock borrowing, to the extent of the quantity and description of the borrowed stock in respect of which the stock return is subsequently made, had not been entered into;

(b) the stock return had not been made;

(c) the lender had, at all times during the relevant borrowing period, held the borrowed stock in respect of which the stock return is made; and

(d) the stock which is the subject of the stock return were the borrowed stock in respect of which the stock return is made.

(3) Where-

(a) a lender receives from a borrower in relation to the borrowed stock a distribution or identical property or a right or option or identical property; and

(b) had the borrowed stock continued to be held by the lender at all times during the borrowing period an amount would have been included or excluded, as the case may be, in ascertaining for a year of assessment the profits in respect of which the lender is chargeable to tax under this Part in respect of the distribution or the right or option,

then an equal amount shall be likewise treated in ascertaining the chargeable profits of the lender for that year of assessment.

(4)　　Where a lender receives from a borrower in relation to the borrowed stock a compensatory payment in respect of a distribution made or right or option issued during the borrowing period, then in determining whether an amount is to be included or excluded, as the case may be, in ascertaining for a year of assessment the profits in respect of which the lender is chargeable to tax under this Part in respect of the compensatory payment, the lender is to be treated as if-

> *(a)*　　the distribution had been made, or the right or option had been issued directly to him in respect of the borrowed stock; and

> *(b)*　　he had disposed of the distribution or right or option immediately after its making or issue, as the case may be, for a consideration equal to that compensatory payment.

(5)　　In determining the amount, if any, other than a fee payable under a stock borrowing and lending agreement, to be taken into account in ascertaining the profits in respect of which a borrower is chargeable to tax under this Part in respect of a stock borrowing or a stock return, the borrower is to be treated as if the stock borrowing and the stock return respectively had been carried out for a consideration equal to the market value of the borrowed stock at the time of the relevant stock borrowing.

(6)　　Where a person has entered into a stock borrowing and lending agreement under which a stock borrowing has been effected, and at the time of making an assessment of profits tax on that person for any year of assessment the assessor is of the opinion that the requirements specified in subsection (1) have been or will be satisfied, the assessor may make the assessment on the basis that this section is applicable.

(7)　　　Where-

> *(a)*　　an assessment has been made on the basis that this section is applicable; and

> *(b)*　　after the making of the assessment, the assessor becomes satisfied that this section is not applicable,

then the assessor may accordingly adjust the assessment.

(8)　　In this section-

"borrower", "borrowed stock", "lender", "specified purpose", "stock borrowing", "stock borrowing and lending agreement" and "stock return" have the same meanings as in the Stamp Duty Ordinance (Cap. 117);

"borrowing period", in relation to any borrowed stock, means the period commencing when that stock was borrowed under a stock borrowing and ending when a stock return is effected in relation to that stock;

"distribution" includes-

> *(a)*　　an interest payment;

> *(b)*　　a dividend;

> *(c)*　　a share issued by a company to a shareholder in the company where the share is issued as a bonus share;

> *(d)*　　an amount credited by the trustee of a unit trust to a unit holder other than by way of redemption, realization or liquidation;

> *(e)*　　a unit issued by the trustee of a unit trust;

"option" includes-

> *(a)*　　in relation to a company, an option to acquire shares in the company;

> *(b)*　　in relation to a unit trust, an option to acquire units in the unit trust;

"right" includes-

> *(a)*　　in relation to a company, a right to acquire shares in the company or to acquire an option;

> *(b)*　　in relation to a unit trust, a right to acquire units in the unit trust or to acquire an option.

Ascertainment of chargeable profits

16.(1) In ascertaining the profits in respect of which a person is chargeable to tax under this Part for any year of assessment there shall be deducted all outgoings and expenses to the extent to which they are incurred during the basis period for that year of assessment by such person in the production of profits in respect of which he is chargeable to tax under this Part for any period, including-

> *(a)*　　where the conditions set out in subsection (2) are satisfied, sums payable by such person by way of interest upon any money borrowed by him for the purpose of producing such profits, and sums payable by such person by way of legal fees, procuration fees, stamp duties and other expenses in connection with such borrowing;

> *(b)*　　rent paid by any tenant of land or buildings occupied by him for the purpose of producing such profits, but not exceeding, in the case of rent paid to the

tenant's spouse, or by a partnership to one or more of the partners thereof or to a spouse of any such partner, an amount equal to the assessable value of the land or buildings;

(c)   tax of substantially the same nature as tax imposed under this Ordinance, proved to the satisfaction of the Commissioner to have been paid elsewhere, whether by deduction or otherwise, by any corporation which is managed and controlled in Hong Kong or by a person other than a corporation who carries on a trade, profession or business in Hong Kong, during the basis period for the year of assessment in respect of profits chargeable to tax by virtue of section 15(1)(f), (g), (i), (j), (k) or (l):

Provided that no deduction shall be made under this paragraph if the corporation or person concerned is eligible for relief under Part VIII in respect of such profits;

(d)   bad debts incurred in any trade, business or profession, proved to the satisfaction of the assessor to have become bad during the basis period for the year of assessment, and doubtful debts to the extent that they are respectively estimated to the satisfaction of the assessor to have become bad during the said basis period notwithstanding that such bad or doubtful debts were due and payable prior to the commencement of the said basis period:

Provided that-

(i)   deductions under this paragraph shall be limited to debts which were included as a trading receipt in ascertaining the profits, in respect of which the person claiming the deduction is chargeable to tax under this Part, of the period within which they arose, and debts in respect of money lent, in the ordinary course of the business of the lending of money within Hong Kong, by a person who carries on that business;

(ii)   all sums recovered during the said basis period on account of amounts previously allowed in respect of bad or doubtful debts shall for the purposes of this Ordinance be treated as part of the profits of the trade, business or profession for that basis period;

(e)   expenditure incurred in the repair of any premises, plant, machinery, implement, utensil or article employed in the production of such profits;

(f)   expenditure incurred in the replacement of any implement, utensil or article employed in the production of such profits:

Provided that no allowances have been or shall be made under the provisions of Part VI in respect of such implement, utensil or article;

(g)   notwithstanding section 17, a sum expended for the registration of a trade mark, design or patent used in the trade, profession or business which produces such profits;

(ga)   the payments and expenditure specified in sections 16B, 16C and 16E, as provided therein;

(h)   such other deductions as may be prescribed by any rule made under this Ordinance.

(2)   The conditions referred to in subsection (1)(a) are that-

(a)   the money has been borrowed by a financial institution;

(b)   the money has been borrowed by a public utility company specified in Schedule 3 at a rate of interest not exceeding the rate specified by the Financial Secretary by notice in the Gazette;

(c)   the money has been borrowed from a person other than a financial institution or an overseas financial institution and the sums payable by way of interest are chargeable to tax under this Ordinance;

(d)   the money has been borrowed from a financial institution or an overseas financial institution and the repayment of the principal or interest is not secured or guaranteed either in whole or in part, and whether directly or indirectly, by any instrument executed or any undertaking given-

    (i)   by or on behalf of the borrower or any partner of the borrower;

    (ii)   where the borrower is a body of persons, whether corporate or unincorporate, by or on behalf of any shareholders, member, director or member of the board of management of the borrower; or

    (iii)   where the borrower is a corporation, by or on behalf of any associated corporation,

against a deposit made with that or any other financial institution or overseas financial institution where any sums payable by way of interest on the deposit are not chargeable to tax under this Ordinance;

(e)   the money has been borrowed wholly and exclusively to finance-

    (i)   capital expenditure incurred on the provision of machinery or plant which qualifies for an allowance under Part VI; or

(ii) the purchase of trading stock, and such stock is used by the borrower in the production of profits chargeable to tax under this Part,

and the lender is not-

(A) any partner of the borrower; or

(B) where the borrower is a body of persons, whether corporate or unincorporate, any shareholder, member, director or member of the board of management of the borrower; or

(C) where the borrower is a corporation, any associated corporation;

(f) the person chargeable to tax is a corporation and the deduction is in respect of interest payable by that corporation-

(i) on debentures;

(ii) to the holder of any instrument issued-

(A) bona fide and in the course of carrying on business and which is marketable in Hong Kong or in a major financial centre outside Hong Kong approved by the Commissioner for the purposes of this subparagraph; or

(B) in pursuance of any agreement or arrangements, where the issue of an advertisement or invitation to the public in respect of such agreement or arrangements, or any document which contains such an advertisement or invitation, has been authorized by the Securities and Futures Commission under section 4(2)(g) of the Protection of Investors Ordinance (Cap. 335); or

(iii) on moneys borrowed from an associated corporation, where the moneys borrowed in the hands of the associated corporation arise entirely from the proceeds of an issue by the associated corporation of debentures or of any such instrument as is described in subparagraph (ii), in an amount not exceeding the interest payable by the associated corporation to the holders of its debentures or of such instruments.

(3) For the purposes of subsection (2)-

(a) any reference in paragraph (d)(i) or (ii) or paragraph (e)(A) or (B) to-

(i) a borrower or partner of a borrower; or

(ii) a shareholder, member, director or member of the board of management,

who is a natural person, shall be deemed to extend to that person's parents, spouse, child, brother or sister (whether of the whole or half blood) and, in deducing such a relationship, an adopted child shall be deemed to be a child both of the natural parents and of the adopting parent and a step child to be the child both of the natural parents and of any step parent;

(b) an "associated corporation" means-

(i) a corporation over which the borrower has control;

(ii) a corporation which has control over the borrower; or

(iii) a corporation which is under the control of the same person as the borrower,

and, for the purposes of this definition, control shall have the same meaning as it has in section 2(2);

(ba) "debentures" means debentures listed on a stock exchange in Hong Kong or any other stock exchange recognized for the purposes of this paragraph by the Commissioner;

(c) an "overseas financial institution" means a person carrying on the business of banking or deposit-taking outside Hong Kong other than a person whom the Commissioner has, in accordance with the powers vested in him by subsection (4), determined shall not be recognized for the purposes of subsection (2) as an overseas financial institution.

(4) The Commissioner may for the purposes of subsection (2) determine that a person shall not be recognized as an overseas financial institution if he is of the opinion that that person's banking or deposit-taking business is not adequately supervised by a supervisory authority.

(5) The amendments to this section effected by the Inland Revenue (Amendment) Ordinance 1984 shall not have the effect of disallowing any deduction under subsection (1)(a) which could lawfully have been made immediately prior to the coming into force of that Ordinance where the deduction is in respect of sums payable prior to 1 April 1984.

(6) The Governor in Council may, by notice in the Gazette, amend Schedule 3.

Special payment under an approved retirement scheme allowable as a deduction

16A.(1) Subject to section 17(1)(k), where a person carrying on a trade, profession or business in Hong Kong makes a payment which is either -

> *(a)*   a contribution, other than an ordinary annual contribution, to a fund duly established under a recognized occupational retirement scheme; or

> *(b)*   a premium, other than an ordinary annual premium, in respect of a contract of insurance under a recognized occupational retirement scheme,

such payment shall, to the extent that it is made in respect of individuals employed by such person for the purposes of producing profits in respect of which he is chargeable to tax under this Part and that it is not excessive in view of all the relevant circumstances, be deemed to be an expense wholly and exclusively incurred in the production of such profits and shall be allowed as a deduction therefrom in accordance with subsection (2).

(2)   For the purpose of making the deduction provided for in subsection (1), one fifth part of the payment shall be deemed to have been expended during the basis period in which the payment was actually made and the remaining 4 parts shall be deemed to have been expended at the rate of one part in the basis period for each of the succeeding 4 years of assessment:

Provided that in no case shall the total amount of the deductions exceed the amount of the payment.

(3)   *(Repealed)*

Expenditure on scientific research

16B.(1) Notwithstanding anything in section 17, in ascertaining the profits from any trade or business in respect of which a person is chargeable to tax under this Part for any year of assessment there shall, subject to subsection (2), be deducted the following payments made, and expenditure incurred, by such person during the basis period for that year of assessment (other than any amount which is allowable as a deduction apart from this section), namely-

> *(a)*   payments to-

>> **(i)**   an approved research institute for scientific research related to that trade or business; or

>> **(ii)**   an approved research institute, the object of which is the undertaking of scientific research related to the class of trade or business to which that trade or business belongs; and

> *(b)*   expenditure on scientific research related to that trade or business, including capital expenditure except to the extent that it is expenditure on land or buildings or on alterations, additions or extensions to buildings.

(2)   Where any payment or expenditure to which this section refers is made or incurred outside Hong Kong and the trade or business in relation to which it is so made or incurred is carried on partly in and partly out of Hong Kong, the deduction allowable under this section shall be such part of the amount which would otherwise be allowable as is reasonable in the circumstances.

(3)   *(a)*   Where any plant or machinery, representing scientific research expenditure of a capital nature which pursuant to subsection (1)(b) has been allowed as a deduction in ascertaining the profits from a trade or business, ceases to be used by the person carrying on the trade or business for scientific research related to that trade or business and is then or thereafter sold by him, the proceeds of sale shall be treated as a trading receipt of the trade or business accruing at the time of the sale or, if the sale occurs on or after the date on which the trade or business is permanently discontinued, accruing immediately before the discontinuance.

   (b)   Where any such plant or machinery is destroyed, it shall for the purposes of paragraph (a) be treated as if it had been sold immediately before the destruction thereof and any insurance moneys or other compensation of any description received by the person carrying on the trade or business in respect of the destruction and any money received by him in respect of the remains of the plant or machinery shall be treated as if they were proceeds of that sale.

   (c)   The reference in paragraph (a) to the time of sale shall be construed as a reference to the time of completion or the time when possession is given, whichever is the earlier.

(4)   *(a)*   In this section-

   "an approved research institute" means any university, college, institute, association or organization which is approved in writing for the purposes of this section by the Director of Education as an institute, association or organization for undertaking scientific research which is or may prove to be of value to Hong Kong;

   "scientific research" means any activities in the fields of natural or applied science for the extension of knowledge.

   (b)   An approval for the purposes of paragraph (a) may-

      (i)   operate as from a date, whether before or after the date of approval, specified in the instrument of approval; and

      (ii)   be withdrawn at any time.

(5) In this section-

  (a) references to expenditure incurred on scientific research do not include any expenditure incurred in the acquisition of rights in, or arising out of, scientific research, but, save as aforesaid and subject to subsection (1)(b), include all expenditure incurred for the prosecution of, or the provision of facilities for the prosecution of, scientific research; and

  (b) references to scientific research related to a trade or business or class of trade or business shall be read as including a reference to-

    (i) any scientific research which may lead to or facilitate an extension, or an improvement in the technical efficiency, of that trade or business, or, as the case may be, of trades or businesses of that class; and

    (ii) any scientific research of a medical nature which is of special relation to the welfare of workers employed in that trade or business or, as the case may be, in trades or businesses of that class.

(6) For the purposes of this section-

  (a) expenditure shall not be regarded as incurred by a person in so far as it is, or is to be, met directly or indirectly by the Crown or by any government or public or local authority, whether in Hong Kong or elsewhere, or by any person other than the first-mentioned person; and

  (b) any expenditure of a capital nature incurred on scientific research related to any trade or business by a person about to carry on that trade or business shall be treated as if it had been incurred by that person on the first day upon which he does carry on that trade or business.

(7) The same sums paid, or expenditure incurred, shall not be taken into account for any of the purposes of this section in relation to more than one trade or business.

Payments for technical education

16C.(1) Notwithstanding anything in section 17, where a person carrying on a trade or business in Hong Kong makes any payment to be used for the purposes of technical education related to that trade or business at any university, university college, technical college or other similar institution which is approved in writing for the purposes of this section by the Director of Education (being an amount which is not otherwise allowable as a deduction under this Ordinance), the payment shall be deducted as an expense in ascertaining the profits from that trade or business for the year of assessment in the basis period of which the payment was made.

(2)   For the purposes of this section, technical education shall be deemed to be related to a trade or business, if, and only if, it is technical education of a kind specially requisite for persons employed in the class of trade or business to which that trade or business belongs.

(3)   An approval for the purposes of subsection (1) may-

        (a)   operate as from a date, whether before or after the date of approval, specified in the instrument of approval; and

        (b)   be withdrawn at any time.

Approved charitable donations

16D.(1) Subject to subsection (2), a person chargeable to tax under this Part may deduct the aggregate of approved charitable donations made by that person in the basis period for a year of assessment, if such aggregate is not less than $100, from what would otherwise have been the assessable profits of such person for that year of assessment.

(2)   A person shall not be entitled under subsection (1) to deduct for any year of assessment-

        (a)   any sum which is allowable as a deduction under section 12BA, 16, 16B or 16C;

        (b)   a sum in excess of 10% of such balance of that person's assessable profits after making any adjustment for the allowances and charges provided under Part VI.

Purchase and sale of patent rights, etc.

16E.(1) Notwithstanding anything in section 17, in ascertaining the profits from any trade, profession or business in respect of which a person is chargeable to tax under this Part for any year of assessment there shall, subject to subsections (2) and (6), be deducted any expenditure incurred by such person during the basis period for that year of assessment (other than any amount which is allowable as a deduction apart from this section) on the purchase of patent rights or rights to any know-how, for use in Hong Kong in the trade, profession or business in the production of such profits.

(2)   Where any rights of a kind referred to in subsection (1) are purchased partly for use in Hong Kong and partly for use outside Hong Kong the deduction allowable under this section shall be such part of the expenditure referred to in subsection (1) as is, having regard to the extent of the use in Hong Kong, reasonable and appropriate in the circumstances of the case.

(2A)   No deduction is allowable under subsection (1) in respect of patent rights or rights to any know-how purchased by a person wholly or partly from an associate.

(2B)   For the purposes of subsection (2A), rights of a kind referred to in subsection (1) that are purchased or sold by a trustee of a trust estate or a corporation controlled by such a trustee shall be deemed to have been purchased or sold, as the case may be, by each of the trustee, the corporation and the beneficiary under the trust.

(3)   Where any rights of a kind referred to in subsection (1) in respect of which a deduction has been allowed to any person under this section in ascertaining the profits from a trade, profession or business are thereafter sold by him-

> *(a)*   the proceeds of sale; or

> *(b)*   if the deduction was one to which subsection (2) applied, such part of the proceeds of sale as relates to the rights in respect of which a deduction was allowed under that subsection,

not being an amount otherwise chargeable to tax under this Part, shall, notwithstanding the exclusion relating to the sale of capital assets contained in section 14, be treated as a trading receipt of the trade, profession or business accruing at the time of sale, or if the sale occurs on or after the date on which the trade, profession or business is permanently discontinued, accruing immediately before the discontinuance.

(4)   In this section -

"associate", in relation to a person who purchases (including a person who is deemed to have purchased) rights of a kind referred to in subsection (1), means-

> *(a)*   where the purchaser is a natural person-

>> **(i)**   a relative of the purchaser;

>> **(ii)**   a partner of the purchaser and any relative of that partner;

>> **(iii)**   a partnership in which the purchaser is a partner;

>> **(iv)**   any corporation controlled by the purchaser, by a partner of the purchaser or by a partnership in which the purchaser is a partner;

>> **(v)**   any director or principal officer of any such corporation as is referred to in subparagraph (iv);

> *(b)*   where the purchaser is a corporation-

>> **(i)**   any associated corporation;

>> **(ii)**   any person who controls the corporation and any partner of such person, and, where either such person is a natural person, any relative of such person;

   (iii) any director or principal officer of that corporation or of any associated corporation and any relative of any such director or officer;

   (iv) any partner of the corporation and, where such partner is a natural person, any relative of such partner;

 (c) where the purchaser is a partnership-

   (i) any partner of the partnership and where such partner is a partnership any partner of that partnership, any partner with the partnership in any other partnership and where such partner is a partnership any partner of that partnership and where any partner of, or with, or in any of the partnerships mentioned in this subparagraph is a natural person, any relative of such partner;

   (ii) *(Repealed)*

   (iii) any corporation controlled by the partnership or by any partner thereof or, where such a partner is a natural person, any relative of such partner;

   (iv) any corporation of which any partner is a director or principal officer;

   (v) any director or principal officer of a corporation referred to in subparagraph (iii);

"associated corporation" means-

 (a) a corporation over which a person who purchases (including a person who is deemed to have purchased) rights of a kind referred to in subsection (1) has control;

 (b) a corporation which has control over such a purchaser, being a corporation; or

 (c) a corporation which is under the control of the same person as such a purchaser, being a corporation;

"beneficiary under the trust" means any person who benefits or is capable (whether by the exercise of a power of appointment or otherwise) of benefiting under a trust estate, either directly or through any interposed person, or who is able or might reasonably be expected to be able, whether directly or indirectly, to control the activities of the trust estate or the application of its corpus or income;

"control", in relation to a corporation, means the power of a person to secure-

> (*a*)   by means of the holding of shares or the possession of voting power in or in relation to that or any other corporation; or
>
> (*b*)   by virtue of any powers conferred by the articles of association or other document regulating that or any other corporation,

that the affairs of the first-mentioned corporation are conducted in accordance with the wishes of that person;

"know-how" means any industrial information or techniques likely to assist in the manufacture or processing of goods or materials;

"patent rights" means the right to do or authorize the doing of anything which would, but for that right, be an infringement of a patent;

"principal officer" means-

> (*a*)   a person employed by a corporation who, either alone or jointly with one or more other persons, is responsible under the immediate authority of the directors for the conduct of the business of the corporation; or
>
> (*b*)   a person so employed who, under the immediate authority of a director of the body corporate or a person to whom paragraph (a) applies, exercises managerial functions in respect of the body corporate;

"relative" means the spouse, parent, child, brother or sister of the relevant person, and, in deducing such a relationship, an adopted child shall be deemed to be a child both of the natural parents and the adopting parent and a step child to be the child of both the natural parents and of any step parent.

(5)   In this section, a reference to the purchase or sale of rights of a kind referred to in subsection (1) includes a reference to the purchase or sale of a share or interest in any such rights.

(6)   The amendments made to this section by the Inland Revenue (Amendment) Ordinance 1992 apply to patent rights or rights to any know-how purchased under contracts entered into on or after 18 April 1991 and the provisions of this section that were in force immediately before the commencement of that Ordinance continue to apply to patent rights or rights to any trade mark or design purchased under contracts entered into before 18 April 1991 and also to proceeds received from the sale of those rights whether before or after 18 April 1991 as if the amendments had not been enacted.

Deductions not allowed

17.(1) For the purpose of ascertaining profits in respect of which a person is chargeable to tax under this Part no deduction shall be allowed in respect of *(a)*   domestic or private expenses, including the cost of travelling between residence and place of business;

(b)   any disbursements or expenses not being money expended for the purpose of producing such profits;

(c)   any expenditure of a capital nature or any loss or withdrawal of capital;

(d)   the cost of any improvements;

(e)   any sum recoverable under an insurance or contract of indemnity;

(f)   rent of, or expenses in connection with, any premises or part of premises not occupied or used for the purpose of producing such profits;

(g)   any tax paid or payable under this Ordinance other than salaries tax paid in respect of employees' remuneration;

(h)   any sum paid by an employer being either an ordinary annual contribution to a fund duly established under a recognized occupational retirement scheme or an ordinary annual premium in respect of a contract of insurance under a recognized occupational retirement scheme, to the extent that the aggregate of such payments in respect of an employee under a recognized occupational retirement scheme or schemes exceeds 15% of the total emoluments of that employee for the period in respect of which the payment is made;

(i)   any provision made for the payment in respect of an employee of any sum referred to in paragraph (h), to the extent that the aggregate of such provision and any such payment as is referred to in that paragraph exceeds 15% of the total emoluments of that employee for the period in respect of which the provision is made;

(j)   any provision made in respect of an occupational retirement scheme other than for the payment of any sum referred to in paragraph (h);

(k)   any sum paid by an employer being either a contribution under an occupational retirement scheme or a premium in respect of a contract of insurance under an occupational retirement scheme, where-

    (i)   provision for the payment of such sum has been made in any prior year of assessment; and

    (ii)   a deduction has been allowed for such provision in any prior year of assessment; or

(2)   In computing the profits or losses of a person carrying on a trade, profession or business, nothing shall be deducted for salaries or other remuneration of, or for interest on capital or loans provided by, that person's spouse or, in the case of a partnership, any partner therein or any partner's spouse.

Basis for computing profits

18.(1) Save as provided in this section, the assessable profits for any year of assessment from any trade, profession or business carried on in Hong Kong shall be computed on the full amount of the profits therefrom arising in or derived from Hong Kong during the year preceding the year of assessment.

(2) Where the Commissioner is satisfied that the accounts of a trade, profession or business carried on in Hong Kong are usually made up to some day other than 31 March, he may direct that the assessable profits from that source be computed on the amount of the profits therefrom arising in or derived from Hong Kong during the year ending on that day in the year preceding the year of assessment. Where, however, the assessable profits from any trade, profession or business have been computed by reference to an account made up to a certain day, and no account is made up to the corresponding day in the year following, the assessable profits from that source both for the year of assessment in which such failure occurs and for the 2 years of assessment following shall be computed on such basis as the Commissioner in his discretion thinks fit.

(3) Subject to section 18C, where a person commences to carry on a trade, profession or business in Hong Kong on a day within a year of assessment, the assessable profits from that source for such year of assessment shall be computed on the amount of the profits therefrom arising in or derived from Hong Kong during the period beginning on the date of commencement and ending on the last day of that year of assessment.

(4) Where a person has commenced to carry on a trade, profession or business in Hong Kong on a day within the year preceding a year of assessment, the assessable profits from that source for that year of assessment shall be computed on the amount of the profits therefrom arising in or derived from Hong Kong for 1 year from such day:

Provided that such person may claim, by giving notice in writing to the Commissioner, to have the assessable profits from the source for that year of assessment and for the following year of assessment (but not for one or other of those years) recomputed on the basis of the actual profits therefrom arising in or derived from Hong Kong during each such year respectively, but where the commencement is in the year of assessment commencing on 1 April 1973, such claim for recomputation shall relate only to the year of assessment commencing on 1 April 1974.

(5) Where a person ceases to carry on a trade, profession or business in Hong Kong the assessable profits from that source for the year of assessment in which the cessation occurs shall be computed on the amount of the profits therefrom arising in or derived from Hong Kong during the period beginning on 1 April in that year and ending on the date of cessation:

Provided that where the profits arising in or derived from Hong Kong from that source during the year of assessment immediately preceding the year in which the cessation occurs exceed what would otherwise have been the assessable profits from that source for that preceding year such assessable profits shall be recomputed on the basis of the actual profits therefrom arising in or derived from Hong Kong during that preceding year and an additional assessment shall be made accordingly.

(6) Notwithstanding the provisions of section 70 a claim made for an adjustment of any assessment because of a change in the basis period required or authorized under the provisions of this section shall be entertained if it is made in writing within 2 years after the end of the relevant year of assessment or, where the claim has been made under the proviso to subsection (4), within 2 years after the end of the second of the 2 years of assessment referred to in such proviso. A claim so made shall be regarded as an objection to an assessment under section 64 for the purposes of Part XI.

(7) This section shall apply to the years of assessment up to and including the year of assessment commencing on 1 April 1974.

Assessable profits for the year of assessment 1974/5

18A.(1) Where the assessable profits for the year of assessment commencing on 1 April 1974 from any trade, profession or business fall to be computed under section 18(1) but the actual profits from that source for that year of assessment exceed those assessable profits as so computed, then, notwithstanding section 18, the assessable profits for the year of assessment commencing on 1 April 1974 shall be computed on the basis of those actual profits.

(2) Where the assessable profits for the year of assessment commencing on 1 April 1974 from any trade, profession or business fall to be computed under section 18(2) on the amount of profits from that source for the year ending on a day other than 31 March in the year preceding that year of assessment but the actual profits from that source-

> *(a)* for the year ending on the corresponding day in the year of assessment; or

> *(b)* if the accounts for that trade, profession or business were made up to more than 1 day in the year of assessment, for the year ending on such of those days as the Commissioner may direct,

exceed those assessable profits as so computed, then, notwithstanding section 18, the assessable profits for the year of assessment commencing on 1 April 1974 shall be computed on the basis of those actual profits.

(3) Where the assessable profits for the year of assessment commencing on 1 April 1974 from any trade, profession or business fall to be computed under section 18(4) but the lesser of the actual profits from that source for-

> *(a)* the year ending on the day in that year of assessment to which the accounts of that trade, profession or business were made up; or

    (b)   that year of assessment,

exceed those assessable profits as so computed, then notwithstanding section 18, the assessable profits for the year of assessment commencing on 1 April 1974 shall be computed on the basis of those actual profits.

(4)   For the purposes of applying this section there shall be disregarded any loss brought forward to the year of assessment commencing on 1 April 1974 under section 19(2).

Basis for computing assessable profit for years of assessment commencing on 1 April 1975

18B.(1) Subject to subsection (2) and to sections 18C, 18D and 18E, the assessable profits for any year of assessment commencing on or after 1 April 1975 from any trade, profession or business carried on in Hong Kong shall be computed on the full amount of the profits therefrom arising in or derived from Hong Kong during the year of assessment.

(2)   Subject to sections 18C, 18D and 18E, where the Commissioner is satisfied that the accounts of a trade, profession or business carried on in Hong Kong are made up to some day other than 31 March, he may direct that the assessable profits from that source for any year of assessment be computed on the full amount of profits therefrom arising in or derived from Hong Kong during the year ending on that day in the year of assessment.

Commencement of source of profits in years of assessment commencing on or after 1 April 1974

18C.(1) Subject to subsection (2) where a person commences to carry on a trade, profession or business in Hong Kong within any year of assessment commencing on or after 1 April 1974 and the Commissioner is satisfied that the first accounts of such trade, profession or business after its commencement are made up to some day other than 31 March, the assessable profits from that source for that year of assessment shall-

    (a)   if the first accounts are made up to a day within that year of assessment, be computed on the full amount of the profits from that source arising in or derived from Hong Kong during the period beginning on the day of commencement and ending on the day to which the accounts are made up; or

    (b)   if the first accounts are for a period in excess of a year and are made up to a day within a year of assessment following that in which the commencement occurred, be computed on such basis as the Commissioner thinks fit.

(2)   Where the first accounts of a trade, profession or business commenced in any year of assessment commencing on or after 1 April 1974 are for a period of 1 year or less and are made up to a day within the year of assessment following that in which the commencement occurred, there shall be deemed to be no assessable profits for the year of assessment in which the commencement occurred.

Cessation of source of profits in years of assessment commencing on 1 April 1975

18D.(1) Save as provided in this section, where, in any year of assessment commencing on or after 1 April 1975, a person ceases to carry on a trade, profession or business in Hong Kong, the assessable profits from that source for the year of assessment in which the cessation occurs shall be computed on the amount of the profits therefrom arising in or derived from Hong Kong during the period beginning on the day following the end of the basis period for the year preceding the year of assessment and ending on the date of cessation.

(2)   Where in any year of assessment commencing on or after 1 April 1975 a person ceases to carry on a trade, profession or business in Hong Kong which was commenced by him in Hong Kong before 1 April 1974, the assessable profits from that source for the year of assessment in which the cessation occurs shall be computed on the amount of the profits therefrom arising in or derived from Hong Kong during the period beginning on 1 April in that year and ending on the date of cessation:

Provided that where a person ceases to carry on such trade, profession or business in Hong Kong other than by reason of the death of an individual previously carrying on a trade, profession or business as the sole proprietor thereof, and the trade, profession or business, or any part thereof, is transferred to or carried on by any other person as his trade, profession or business, this subsection shall not apply, but the cessation shall, subject to subsection (3), be deemed to be a cessation for the purposes of subsection (1).

(2A)   Where a person ceases to carry on a relevant trade, profession or business on or after 1 April 1979, the following amount shall be treated as assessable profits therefrom for the year of assessment in which the cessation occurs and shall be in addition to the assessable profits therefrom which, apart from this subsection, fall to be computed for that year of assessment-

      (a)   in the case of an excepted trade, profession or business, the amount, if any, by which the relevant profits therefrom arising in or derived from Hong Kong during the relevant period exceed the transitional amount;

      (b)   in the case of any other relevant trade, profession or business, the full amount of any relevant profits therefrom arising in or derived from Hong Kong during the relevant period,

and, for the purposes of this subsection, profits are "relevant profits" if, but for subsection (2) and apart from Part VI, the assessable profits for that year of assessment would have included those profits, and

"excepted trade, profession or business" means a relevant trade, profession or business referred to in the definition in this subsection of "transitional amount";

"relevant period" means the period beginning on the day next following the end of the basis period for the year preceding the year of assessment in which the cessation occurs and ending on 31 March in the year preceding the year of assessment in which the cessation occurs;

"relevant trade, profession or business" means a trade, profession or business to which subsection (2) applies and in the case of which the basis period for the year preceding the year of assessment in which the cessation occurs ends on a day other than 31 March;

"transitional amount" means -

> *(a)* where the assessable profits from a relevant trade, profession or business for the year of assessment commencing on 1 April 1974 fell to be computed under section 18(2) on the amount of profits therefrom for the year ending on a day other than 31 March in the year preceding that year of assessment, the amount of profits from the relevant trade, profession or business arising in or derived from Hong Kong during the period beginning on the day next following the corresponding day in that year of assessment and ending on 31 March 1975;

> *(b)* where the assessable profits from a relevant trade, profession or business for the year of assessment commencing on 1 April 1974 fell to be computed under section 18A(2), the amount of profits from the relevant trade, profession or business arising in or derived from Hong Kong during the period beginning on the day next following the end of the basis period for that year of assessment and ending on 31 March 1975,

and where a loss was incurred in the carrying on of a relevant trade, profession or business referred to in paragraph (a) or (b) of this definition during the period therein referred to, "transitional amount", in relation to that trade, profession or business, shall be construed to mean a nil amount.

(3)-(4) *(Repealed)*

(5) Where a person who commenced to carry on a trade, profession or business in Hong Kong in a year of assessment commencing on or after 1 April 1975-

> *(a)* ceases to carry on such trade, profession or business in the year of assessment following that in which such commencement occurred; and

> *(b)* by virtue of section 18C(2), there has been deemed to be no assessable profits for the year of assessment in which the commencement occurred,

the assessable profits for the year of assessment in which the cessation occurs shall be recomputed on the basis of the actual profits arising in or derived from Hong Kong from the date of the commencement to the date of cessation.

(6) Notwithstanding section 70, where a person ceases to carry on a trade, profession or business in the circumstances described in subsection (4), a claim made by that person for an adjustment of any assessment in accordance with that subsection shall be entertained if it is made in writing within 2 years after the end of the year of assessment commencing on 1 April 1975.

(7) A claim made under subsection (6) shall be regarded as an objection to an assessment under section 64 for the purposes of Part XI.

Change of accounting date and apportionments

18E.(1) Where the assessable profits of a person from any trade, profession or business carried on in Hong Kong have been computed by reference to an account made up to a certain day in any year of assessment and either

> *(a)* that person fails to make up an account to the corresponding day in the following year of assessment; or
>
> *(b)* that person makes up accounts to more than one day in the following year of assessment,

then-

> **(i)** the assessable profits from that source for the year of assessment in which the circumstances described in either paragraph (a) or (b) prevail shall be computed on such basis as the Commissioner thinks fit; and
>
> **(ii)** the assessable profits for the year preceding that year of assessment shall be recomputed on such basis as the Commissioner thinks fit.

(2) For the purposes of subsection (1)-

> *(a)* where the accounts of any trade, profession or business are made up to the end of the Lunar year, the Commissioner may accept those accounts as being made up to a corresponding day in each year of assessment; and
>
> *(b)* in the case of a trade, profession or business which was commenced on or after 1 April 1974, the Commissioner may, if he considers it necessary, make a computation under subsection (1) in respect of a basis period which exceeds 12 months.

(3) For the purposes of this Part, where in the case of a trade, profession or business it is necessary in order to arrive at the assessable profits or the losses for any year of assessment to divide or apportion to specific periods the profits and losses for any period for which accounts have been made up, or to aggregate any such profits or losses or any apportioned parts thereof, it shall be lawful to make such division and apportionment or aggregation, and any such apportionment shall be made in proportion to the number of days or months in the respective periods unless the Commissioner, having regard to any special circumstances, otherwise directs.

(4) For the purposes of section 18D(2A), where in the case of a trade, profession or business it is necessary in order to arrive at the profits or losses for any period to divide or apportion to specific periods the profits and losses for any period for which accounts have been made up, or to aggregate any such profits or losses or any apportioned parts thereof, the Commissioner may make such division and apportionment or aggregation as he may deem proper in that case.

Adjustment of assessable profits

18F.(1) The amount of assessable profits for any year of assessment of a person chargeable to tax under this Part shall be increased by the amount of any balancing charge directed to be made on that person under Part VI and decreased by the allowances made to that person under Part VI for that year of assessment to the extent to which the relevant assets are used in the production of the assessable profits.

(2) When in any year of assessment the amount of the allowances made under Part VI to any person chargeable to tax under this Part exceeds the total amount of that person's assessable profits, as increased by any balancing charge, the amount of such excess shall, for the purposes of section 19C, be deemed to be a loss of that person for that year of assessment.

(3) This section shall apply to the year of assessment commencing on 1 April 1975 and to subsequent years of assessment.

Treatment of losses

19.(1) Subject to the provisions of subsection (3) where a loss is incurred in any year of assessment up to and including the year of assessment commencing on 1 April 1974 by a person chargeable to tax under this Part the amount of such loss attributable to activities in Hong Kong shall notwithstanding the provisions of section 70 be set off against what would otherwise have been the assessable profits of such person for that year of assessment.

(2) Where the amount of loss which may set off under subsection (1) is such that it cannot be wholly set off against the assessable profits of a person chargeable to tax under this Part for the year of assessment in which the loss occurred, the amount not so set off shall be carried forward and shall be set off against what would otherwise have been assessable profits of that person for the future years of assessment in succession:

Provided that-

    (a)   the amount of any such loss allowed to be set off in computing the assessable profits for any year of assessment shall not be set off in computing the assessable profits for any other year of assessment; and

    (b)   where a loss is set off under this subsection in respect of the year of assessment commencing on 1 April 1975 or any subsequent year of assessment, that loss shall be set off before the set off of any loss under section 19C.

(3)-(4) *(Repealed)*

19A.   *(Repealed)*

19B.   *(Repealed)*

Treatment of losses after 1 April 1975

19C.(1) Where in any year of assessment-

> *(a)*   an individual sustains a loss in any trade, profession or business carried on by him; and

> *(b)*   the individual or, in the case of a husband and wife, not being a wife living apart from her husband, the husband or wife does not elect for personal assessment under section 41 for that year of assessment,

the amount of that loss shall be carried forward and set off against the amount of his assessable profits from that trade, profession or business for subsequent years of assessment.

(2)   Where in any year of assessment-

> *(a)*   an individual incurs a share of a loss of a partnership in any trade, profession or business carried on by that partnership; and

> *(b)*   the individual or, in the case of a husband and wife, not being a wife living apart from her husband, the husband or wife does not elect for personal assessment under section 41 for that year of assessment,

the amount of that share of the loss shall be carried forward and set off against the amount of his share of assessable profits of the partnership from that trade, profession or business for subsequent years of assessment:

Provided that where at the end of the year of assessment commencing on 1 April 1983 a share of a loss to be carried forward under this subsection is one that was incurred by a husband and wife, not being a wife living apart from her husband, in partnership with each other, whether or not also with other persons-

> **(i)**   the share of the loss shall be deemed to be apportioned between the husband and wife in the proportions in which they were entitled to share profits between themselves as at the last day of the basis period for that year of assessment; and

> **(ii)**   each such portion of the share of the loss shall be carried forward and set off

against the husband's or, as the case may be, the wife's respective share of assessable profits of the partnership from that trade, profession or business for subsequent years of assessment.

(3)   Where in any year of assessment an individual has sustained a loss or has incurred a share of a loss of a partnership and-

> *(a)*   is personally assessed under Part VII; or

> *(b)*   in the case of a husband and wife, not being a wife living apart from her husband, the husband or wife is personally assessed under Part VII,

the amount of the loss or share of the loss shall be dealt with in accordance with that Part.

(4)   Where in any year of assessment a corporation or a person, who is not an individual, a partnership or a corporation, carrying on a trade, profession or business sustains a loss in that trade, profession or business, the amount of that loss shall be set off against the assessable profits of the corporation or person (including its share of the assessable profits of a partnership in which it is a partner) for that year of assessment and to the extent not so set off, shall be carried forward and set off against the corporation's or the person's assessable profits and its share of assessable profits of such a partnership for subsequent years of assessment.

(5)   Where-

> *(a)*   a trade, profession or business is carried on in Hong Kong by persons in partnership and any one of those persons is a corporation or is a person who is not an individual, a partnership or a corporation; and

> *(b)*   in any year of assessment a loss is incurred in that trade, profession or business,

then the corporation's or the person's share of that loss shall be set off against the assessable profits of the corporation or the person for the year of assessment in which the loss was incurred and to the extent not so set off, be carried forward and, for subsequent years of assessment, be set off first against the corporation's or the person's share of the assessable profits of such partnership and, to the extent not so set off, then against the assessable profits of the corporation or the person.

(6)   For the purposes of this section-

> *(a)*   the amount of any loss set off in computing the assessable profits for any year of assessment shall not be set off in computing the assessable profits for any other year of assessment;

> *(b)*   the amount of any loss carried forward to any year of assessment to be set off against the assessable profits for that year shall not be set off more than once in that year of assessment;

     (c)   the total amount set off against assessable profits shall not exceed the amount of the loss;

     (d)   the amount of any loss to be set off under this section shall be the loss attributable to activities in Hong Kong;

     (e)   the amount of any loss sustained in any trade, profession or business carried on for the benefit of a trust by a person in his capacity as trustee shall not be available for set off except against the assessable profits of that trust from that trade, profession or business for subsequent years of assessment.

(7)   For the purposes of this section-

     (a)   "partnership" does not include a partnership (other than a partnership referred to in section 345(2) of the Companies Ordinance (Cap. 32)) consisting at any time in the year of assessment of more than 20 partners;

     (b)   in calculating the number of partners in a partnership, there shall be included every partner in any other partnership which is itself a partner in the first-mentioned partnership.

(8)   This section shall apply to the year of assessment commencing on 1 April 1975 and to subsequent years of assessment.

Computation of losses after 1 April 1975

19D.(1) For the purposes of section 19C, the amount of loss incurred by a person chargeable to tax under this Part for any year of assessment shall be computed in like manner and for such basis period as the assessable profits for that year of assessment would have been computed.

(2) This section shall apply to the year of assessment commencing on 1 April 1975 and to subsequent years of assessment.

Adjustment of losses

19E.(1) For the purposes of section 19D, the amount of loss for any year of assessment of any person chargeable to tax under this Part shall be increased by the allowances made to that person under Part VI for that year of assessment to the extent to which the relevant assets are used in the production of the losses and decreased by the amount of any balancing charge directed to be made on that person under Part VI.

(2)   Where in any year of assessment the amount of the balancing charge made under Part VI to a person chargeable to tax under this Part exceeds the total amount of that person's losses, as increased by any allowances, the amount of such excess shall be deemed to be assessable profits of that person for that year of assessment.

(3)　　This section shall apply to the year of assessment commencing on 1 April 1975 and to subsequent years of assessment.

Liability of certain non-resident persons

20.(1)　For the purposes of this section-

> *(a)*　　a person is closely connected with another person where the Commissioner in his discretion considers that such persons are substantially identical or that the ultimate controlling interest of each is owned or deemed under this section to be owned by the same person or persons;

> *(b)*　　the controlling interest of a company shall be deemed to be owned by the beneficial owners of its shares, whether held directly or through nominees, and shares in one company held by or on behalf of another company shall be deemed to be held by the shareholders of the last-mentioned company.

(2)　　Where a non-resident person carries on business with a resident person with whom he is closely connected and the course of such business is so arranged that it produces to the resident person either no profits which arise in or derive from Hong Kong or less than the ordinary profits which might be expected to arise in or derive from Hong Kong, the business done by the non-resident person in pursuance of his connection with the resident person shall be deemed to be carried on in Hong Kong, and such non-resident person shall be assessable and chargeable with tax in respect of his profits from such business in the name of the resident person as if the resident person were his agent, and all the provisions of this Ordinance shall apply accordingly.

Persons chargeable on behalf of a non-resident

20A.(1)　A non-resident person shall be chargeable to tax either directly or in the name of his agent in respect of all his profits arising in or derived from Hong Kong from any trade, profession or business carried on in Hong Kong whether such agent has the receipt of the profits or not, and the tax so charged whether directly or in the name of the agent shall be recoverable by all means provided in this Ordinance out of the assets of the non-resident person or from the agent.　Where there are more agents than one they may be charged to tax jointly or severally in respect of the profits of the non-resident person and shall be jointly and severally liable for the tax thereon.

(2)　　Every person chargeable to tax as agent, or from whom tax is recoverable in respect of the profits of another person, shall retain out of any assets coming into his possession or control on behalf of such other person or in his capacity as agent so much thereof as shall be sufficient to produce the amount of such tax, and he shall be and is hereby indemnified against any person whomsoever in respect of his retention of such assets.

(3)　　Notwithstanding anything contained in subsections (1) and (2), any person who sells any goods in Hong Kong on behalf of a non-resident person shall furnish quarterly to the Commissioner a return showing the gross proceeds from such sales and shall at the same time pay to the Commissioner a sum equal to 1% of such proceeds or such lesser sum as may have been agreed with the Commissioner. On receipt of such sum the Commissioner shall issue a certificate in the form specified by the Board of Inland Revenue:

Provided that the Commissioner may exempt any such person from the provisions of this subsection on such conditions as he may consider fit.

Persons chargeable in respect of certain profits of a non-resident

20B.(1) Without prejudice to section 20A, this section applies in respect of a non-resident person who is chargeable to tax in respect of-

> *(a)* sums deemed by virtue of section 15(1)(a) or (b) to be receipts arising in or derived from Hong Kong from a trade, profession or business carried on in Hong Kong; or

> *(b)* sums received in respect of, or which in any way derive directly or indirectly from, the performance in Hong Kong by a non-resident entertainer or sportsman (whether or not he is the non-resident person who is so chargeable) of an activity in his character as entertainer or sportsman on or in connection with a commercial occasion or event, including-

> > **(i)** any appearance of the entertainer or sportsman by way of or in connection with the promotion of any such occasion or event; and

> > **(ii)** any participation by the entertainer or sportsman in or for sound recording, films, videos, radio, television or other similar transmissions (whether live or recorded).

(2) Where this section applies, the non-resident person is chargeable to tax in respect of the sums described in subsection (1) in the name of any person in Hong Kong who paid or credited those sums to that or any other non-resident person, and the tax so charged shall be recoverable by all means provided in this Ordinance from that person in Hong Kong.

(3) Where a person in Hong Kong from whom tax is recoverable by virtue of this section pays or credits to a non-resident person (whether or not he is the non-resident person who is chargeable to tax) sums described in subsection (1) he shall, at the time he makes the payment or credit, deduct from those sums so much thereof as is sufficient to produce the amount of such tax, and he is hereby indemnified against any person in respect of his deduction of such sum.

(4) In this section-

"commercial occasion or event" includes any description of occasion or event -

(*a*)   for which an entertainer or sportsman (or other person) might, by virtue of his performance of the activity, receive or become entitled to receive anything by way of cash or any other form of property; or

(*b*)   which is designed to promote commercial sales or activity by advertising, the endorsement of goods or services, sponsorship, or other promotional means of any kind;

"entertainer or sportsman" means a person, other than a corporation, who gives performances (whether alone or with others) in his character as entertainer or sportsman in any kind of entertainment or sport, including any activity of a physical kind which (whether in a live or recorded form) the public or any section of the public is or may be permitted (whether for payment or not) to see or hear.

Assessable profits of certain businesses to be computed on a percentage of the turnover

21.   Where the true amount of the assessable profits arising in or derived from Hong Kong of a non-resident person in respect of a trade, profession or business carried on in Hong Kong cannot be readily ascertained, such assessable profits may be computed on a fair percentage of the turnover of that trade or business in Hong Kong.

Computation of assessable profits from cinematograph films, patents, trademarks, etc.

21A.(1) The assessable profits of a person arising in or derived from Hong Kong in respect of a sum deemed by section 15(1)(a) or (b) to be a receipt arising in or derived from Hong Kong from a trade, profession or business carried on in Hong Kong shall, for the purposes of this Ordinance and notwithstanding any other provisions of this Part, be taken to be-

(*a*)   100% of the sum in the case of a sum derived from an associate:

Provided that this paragraph shall not apply in the case where the Commissioner is satisfied that no person carrying on a trade, profession or business in Hong Kong has at any time wholly or partly owned the property in respect of which the sum is paid; or

(*b*)   10% of the sum in any other case, including any case of the description mentioned in the proviso to paragraph (a).

(2)   For the purpose of ascertaining whether a sum was derived from an associate in the application of subsection (1), where the sum was derived from or by a trustee of a trust estate or a corporation controlled by such a trustee, that sum shall be deemed to have been derived from or by, as the case may be, each of the trustee, the corporation and the beneficiary under the trust.

(3)   In this section-

"associate" in relation to a person, means-

(a)   where the person is a natural person-

    (i)   a relative of the person;

    (ii)   a partner of the person and any relative of that partner;

    (iii)   a partnership in which the person is a partner;

    (iv)   any corporation controlled by the person, by a partner of the person or by a partnership in which the person is a partner;

    (v)   any director or principal officer of any such corporation as is referred to in subparagraph (iv);

(b)   where the person is a corporation-

    (i)   any associated corporation;

    (ii)   any person who controls the corporation and any partner of such person, and, where either such person is a natural person, any relative of such person;

    (iii)   any director or principal officer of that corporation or of any associated corporation and any relative of any such director or officer;

    (iv)   any partner of the corporation and, where such partner is a natural person, any relative of such partner;

(c)   where the person is a partnership-

    (i)   any partner of the partnership and where such partner is a partnership any partner of that partnership, any partner with the partnership in any other partnership and where such partner is a partnership any partner of that partnership and where any partner of, or with, or in any of the partnerships mentioned in this subparagraph is a natural person, any relative of such partner;

    (ii)   any corporation controlled by the partnership or by any partner thereof or, where such a partner is a natural person, any relative of such partner;

    (iii)   any corporation of which any partner is a director or principal officer;

    (iv)   any director or principal officer of a corporation referred to in subparagraph (ii);

"associated corporation", in relation to a person, means-

> *(a)*   a corporation over which the person has control;
>
> *(b)*   if the person is a corporation-
>
> > **(i)**   a corporation which has control over the person; or
> >
> > **(ii)**   a corporation which is under the control of the same person as is the first-mentioned person;

"beneficiary under the trust" means any person who benefits or is capable (whether by the exercise of a power of appointment or otherwise) of benefiting under a trust estate, either directly or through any interposed person, or who is able or might reasonably be expected to be able, whether directly or indirectly, to control the activities of the trust estate or the application of its corpus or income;

"control", in relation to a corporation, means the power of a person to secure-

> *(a)*   by means of the holding of shares or the possession of voting power in or in relation to that or any other corporation; or
>
> *(b)*   by virtue of any powers conferred by the articles of association or other document regulating that or any other corporation,

that the affairs of the first-mentioned corporation are conducted in accordance with the wishes of that person;

"principal officer" means-

> *(a)*   a person employed by a corporation who, either alone or jointly with one or more other persons, is responsible under the immediate authority of the directors for the conduct of the business of the corporation; or
>
> *(b)*   a person so employed who, under the immediate authority of a director of the corporation or a person to whom paragraph (a) applies, exercises managerial functions in respect of the corporation;

"relative" means the spouse, parent, child, brother or sister of the relevant person, and, in deducing such a relationship, an adopted child shall be deemed to be a child both of the natural parents and the adopting parent and a step child to be the child of both the natural parents and of any step parent.

Transitional

21B.(1) Subject to subsection (2), the amendments to section 21A effected by the Inland Revenue (Amendment) (No. 4) Ordinance 1993 shall apply to any sum received by or accrued to any person on or after 4 March 1993.

(2) The provisions of section 21A in force immediately prior to the coming into operation of the Inland Revenue (Amendment) (No. 4) Ordinance 1993 shall continue to apply to any sum received by or accrued to any person prior to 4 March 1993 as if that Ordinance had not been enacted.

Assessment of partnerships

22.(1) Where a trade, profession or business is carried on by 2 or more persons jointly the assessable profits therefrom shall be computed in one sum and the tax in respect thereof shall be charged in the partnership name.

(2) The precedent partner shall make and deliver a statement of the profits or losses of such trade, profession or business, on behalf of the partnership, ascertained in accordance with the provisions of this Part relating to the ascertainment of profits. Where no active partner is resident in Hong Kong the return shall be furnished by the manager or agent of the partnership in Hong Kong.

(3) If a change occurs in a partnership of persons carrying on any trade, profession or business, by reason of retirement or death, or the dissolution of the partnership as to one or more of the partners, or the admission of a new partner, in such circumstances that one or more of the persons who until that time were engaged in the trade, profession or business continue to be engaged therein, or if a person previously engaged in any trade, profession or business on his own account continues to be engaged in it, but as a partner in a partnership, the tax payable by the person or persons who carry on the trade, profession or business after that time shall, notwithstanding the change be computed on what would otherwise have been the assessable profits of such person or persons or the aggregation of such assessable profits as if no such change had occurred.

(4) Tax upon the partnership shall be recoverable by all means provided in this Ordinance out of the assets of the partnership, or from any partner.

(5) Tax may be assessed on the profits of a partnership notwithstanding the cessation or dissolution of such partnership and shall be recoverable from the former partners and from the assets of the partnership at the time of its cessation.

Ascertainment of share of partnership profits or losses

22A.(1) In order to ascertain the share of a partner of the assessable profits or losses of a partnership, such assessable profits or losses for the relevant year of assessment shall be apportioned amongst the persons who were partners during the basis period in the ratio in which the profits or losses of the basis period for that year of assessment were divided; and the profits or losses as so apportioned shall constitute the shares of the assessable profits and losses of the individual partners for that year of assessment.

(2) For the purposes of subsection (1), there shall be excluded from the assessable profits of a partnership any loss brought forward under section 19C.

(3) For the purposes of this section-

    (a) "partnership" does not include a partnership (other than a partnership referred to in section 345(2) of the Companies Ordinance (Cap. 32)) consisting at any time in the year of assessment of more than 20 partners;

    (b) in calculating the number of partners in a partnership, there shall be included every partner in any other partnership which is itself a partner in the first-mentioned partnership.

Limited partner loss relief

22B.(1) In this section-

"limited partner" means a person who is a partner in a partnership which is carrying on a trade, profession or business and that person is-

    (a) a limited partner in a limited partnership registered under the Limited Partnerships Ordinance (Cap. 37);

    (b) a general partner in a partnership in which he is not entitled to or does not take part in the management of the partnership but is entitled to have his liabilities, or his liabilities beyond a certain limit, for debts or obligations incurred by the partnership for the purposes of the trade, profession or business discharged or reimbursed by some other person; or

    (c) under the law of any place outside Hong Kong, not entitled to or does not take part in the management of the partnership and is not liable beyond a certain limit for debts or obligations incurred by the partnership for the purposes of the trade, profession or business;

"relevant sum" means the amount of the person's contribution to the partnership as at the end of the relevant year of assessment in which the loss is sustained, except that where the person ceased to be a partner in the partnership during that year of assessment it is the time when he so ceased.

(2) For the purposes of this section, a person's contribution to the partnership at any time is the aggregate of-

(*a*)   the amount which he has contributed to it as capital less the sum of-

    (**i**)   the amounts of capital that he has directly or indirectly drawn out or received back; and

    (**ii**)   anything that he is or may be entitled at any time while the partnership carries on the trade, profession or business to draw out, receive back or be reimbursed from another person, whether or not the entitlement is enforceable or is pursuant to an unenforceable undertaking or practice; and

(*b*)   the amount of any profits or gains of the partnership to which he is entitled but which he has not received in money or money's worth.

(**3**)   Notwithstanding section 19C, where in any year of assessment a person who is a limited partner in a partnership has incurred a share of a loss of that partnership the amount of the loss which may be set off against the assessable profits of the person is limited to the lesser of-

(*a*)   the amount of the loss; or

(*b*)   the relevant sum.

(**4**)   This section applies to years of assessment that commence on or after 1 April 1991 and to that part of any basis period for a year of assessment that occurs on or after 15 November 1990 but before 1 April 1991 but does not apply in respect of a share of a loss incurred under a transaction which was the subject of an application for advance clearance made to the Commissioner before 15 November 1990 and the Commissioner before or after that date expressed the opinion that the transaction would not fall within the terms of section 61A or, where no such application was made in respect of a loss incurred under a transaction entered into before that date, the transaction is, in the Commissioner's opinion, of the same type as any for which, in the circumstances prevailing as at 14 November 1990, he would have expressed the opinion that the transaction would not fall within the terms of section 61A.

Ascertainment of assessable profits of life insurance corporations

23.(**1**)   The assessable profits for any year of assessment of a corporation, whether mutual or proprietary, from the business of life insurance, shall-

(*a*)   be deemed to be 5% of the premiums from life insurance business in Hong Kong of the corporation during the basis period for that year; or

(*b*)   should the corporation so elect, be that part of the adjusted surplus ascertained in accordance with the provisions of subsections (2) to (7) deemed to arise in the basis period for that year less any dividend received which is required to be excluded by virtue of section 26(a):

Provided that-

(i)   any such election once made shall be irrevocable and in addition shall be deemed to apply to all future years of assessment; and

(ii)   until such part of the adjusted surplus is ascertained, the assessable profits shall be calculated provisionally in accordance with paragraph (a) of this subsection, and tax charged and collected as if no such election had been made.

(2)   A corporation which elects to be assessed in the manner provided in subsection (1)(b) shall submit to the Commissioner a certified true copy of the latest abstract of the report of the actuary submitted to the Insurance Authority under section 18 of the Insurance Companies Ordinance (Cap. 41) or, in the case of a corporation to which section 52(3) of that Ordinance applies, a copy of the latest such abstract submitted under that section.

(3)   Any election under subsection (1)(b) shall be effective only if the actuarial report is submitted not later than 2 years after the end of the period in respect of which it is made. Where an effective election has been made it shall be lawful to give effect to such election notwithstanding the provisions of section 70.

(4)   *(a)*   The surplus shall be the amount by which the life insurance fund exceeds the estimated liability of the corporation on the life insurance fund at the end of the period in respect of which any actuarial report is made.

          (b)   The adjusted surplus shall be ascertained by adding to the surplus-

          (i)   any deficit in respect of a period prior to the period in respect of which the relevant actuarial report is made where such deficit is included in such report;

          (ii)   any outgoing or expense charged against the life insurance fund in the relevant actuarial report which is not such that it would be allowed as a deduction in ascertaining assessable profits under the provisions of section 16;

          (iii)   any expense disbursement or loss charged against the life insurance fund in the relevant actuarial report which is such that it would not be allowed as a deduction in ascertaining assessable profits by reason of the provisions of section 17;

          (iv)   any income or profits of the corporation arising in the period in respect of which the relevant actuarial report is made, not being profits from the business of insurance other than life insurance, and not credited to the life insurance fund in such report;

    (v)   any appropriations of profits or transfers to reserve charged against the fund during the period in respect of which the relevant actuarial report is made, other than appropriations or transfers to policy holders in their capacity as such;

    (va)   the amount of a balancing charge directed to be made under Part VI,

and by deducting therefrom-

    (vi)   any surplus disclosed by a previous actuarial report which has been retained in the life insurance fund in the relevant actuarial report;

    (vii)   any transfer or appropriation to policy holders in their capacity as such, effected during the period in respect of which the relevant actuarial report is made where such transfer or appropriation has not been charged against the life insurance fund in such report;

    (viii) any outgoing or expenses not charged against the life insurance fund during the period in respect of which the relevant actuarial report is made which is such that it would be deducted in ascertaining assessable profits under the provisions of section 16;

    (ix)   any receipt of a capital nature, or transfer from reserve, credited to the life insurance fund during the period in respect of which the relevant actuarial report is made;

    (x)   the allowances provided by Part VI to the extent to which the relevant assets are used in the production of the adjusted surplus.

(5)   Notwithstanding anything contained in subsection (4) the adjusted surplus of a corporation which transacts life insurance business both within Hong Kong and elsewhere shall be the adjusted surplus ascertained in accordance with the provisions of the said subsection (4) less that portion of such adjusted surplus as is not deemed under the provisions of subsection (6) to be profits arising in or derived from Hong Kong.

(6)   Where a corporation transacts life insurance business both within Hong Kong and elsewhere, the portion of the adjusted surplus ascertained in accordance with the provisions of subsection (4) which shall be deemed to be profits arising in or derived from Hong Kong is the amount which bears the same proportion to the adjusted surplus so ascertained as the aggregate of the premiums from life insurance business in Hong Kong for the period of the relevant actuarial report bears to the aggregate of the premiums from the whole of the corporation's life insurance business for that period.

(7)   Any adjusted surplus ascertained in accordance with the foregoing provisions shall be deemed to arise during the years or other periods which make up the period in respect of which the relevant actuarial report is made in the proportion which the aggregate of the premiums from life insurance business in Hong Kong in each such period bears to the aggregate of such premiums for the total period in respect of which the relevant actuarial report is made.

(8)   *(a)*   Where the making of the adjustments required by subsection (4) results in a deficit, such deficit shall be deemed to be the loss sustained by the corporation during the period in respect of which the relevant actuarial report is made.

     (b)   In ascertaining for the purposes of sections 19 and 19C what part of such loss so calculated is attributable to activities in Hong Kong the provisions of subsections (5) and (6) shall apply mutatis mutandis.

     (c)   Any such loss attributable to activities in Hong Kong shall be deemed to have been sustained during the years which make up the period in respect of which the relevant actuarial report is made in the proportion which the aggregate of the premiums from life insurance business in Hong Kong in each such year bears to the aggregate of such premiums for the total period in respect of which the relevant actuarial report is made.

(9)   In this section-

"actuarial report" means any abstract referred to in subsection(2);

"life insurance business" means business of the following classes as specified in Part 2 of the First Schedule to the Insurance Companies Ordinance (Cap. 41)-

     A.   Life and annuity;

     B.   Marriage and birth;

     C.   Linked long term;

     D.   Tontines,

and references to a "life insurance fund" shall be construed accordingly;

"premiums from life insurance business in Hong Kong" includes-

     (a)   all premiums received or receivable in Hong Kong from both residents and non-residents; and

     (b)   all premiums receivable outside Hong Kong from residents of Hong Kong where such premiums are in respect of policies the proposals for which were received by the corporation in Hong Kong:

Provided that any such premiums returned to the insured and any corresponding premiums paid on reinsurance shall be deducted from the premiums so receivable.

Ascertainment of assessable profits of insurance corporations other than life insurance corporations

23A.(1) The assessable profits of a corporation, whether mutual or proprietary, from the business of insurance other than life insurance, shall be ascertained by taking the gross premiums from such insurance business in Hong Kong less any such premiums returned to the insured and any premiums paid on corresponding reinsurance and adding thereto any interest or other income arising in or derived from Hong Kong and the amount of any balancing charge directed to be made under Part VI, and deducting therefrom a reserve for unexpired risks at the percentage adopted by that corporation in relation to its operations as a whole for such risks at the end of the period for which such profits are ascertained, and adding thereto a reserve similarly calculated for unexpired risks outstanding at the commencement of such period, and from the amount so arrived at deducting the actual losses less the amount recoverable in respect thereof under reinsurance, the agency expenses in Hong Kong and the allowances provided under Part VI to the extent to which the relevant assets are used in the production of such profits, and a fair proportion of the expenses of the head office of the corporation:

Provided that where the Commissioner is satisfied that, by reason of the limited extent of such business transacted in Hong Kong by a non-resident insurance corporation it would be unreasonable to require such corporation to furnish the particulars necessary for the application of this section, he may permit the assessable profits of the corporation to be ascertained by reference to the proportion of the total profits and income of the corporation corresponding to the proportion which its premiums from insurance business in Hong Kong bear to its total premiums or on any other basis which appears to him to be equitable.

(2)   For the purposes of this section "premiums from insurance business in Hong Kong" shall include-

> *(a)*   all premiums in respect of contracts of insurance other than life insurance made in Hong Kong; and

> *(b)*   all premiums on contracts of insurance other than life insurance the proposals for which were made to the corporation in Hong Kong.

Mutual insurance corporations

23AA. For the purposes of this Part, a mutual insurance corporation shall be deemed to carry on an insurance business the surplus from which shall be ascertained in the manner provided in sections 23 and 23A for ascertaining assessable profits and shall be deemed to be assessable profits chargeable to tax under section 14.

Ascertainment of the assessable profits of a ship-owner
carrying on business in Hong Kong

23B.(1) Where a person carries on a business as an owner of ships and-

> *(a)*   the business is normally controlled or managed in Hong Kong; or

> *(b)*   the person is a company incorporated in Hong Kong,

that person shall be deemed to be carrying on that business in Hong Kong.

(2) Subject to subsection (6), where a person to whom subsection (1) does not apply carries on a business as an owner of ships, and any ship owned by that person calls at any location within the waters of Hong Kong, that person shall be deemed to be carrying on that business in Hong Kong.

(3) Subject to subsections (4) and (5), where a person is deemed to be carrying on a business as an owner of ships in Hong Kong under subsection (1) or (2), as the case may be, the assessable profits of that person from that business for a year of assessment shall be the sum bearing the same ratio to the aggregate of the relevant sums earned by or accrued to that person during the basis period for that year of assessment as that person's total shipping profits for the basis period bear to the aggregate of the total shipping income earned by or accrued to that person during that basis period for that year of assessment.

(4) Subject to subsection (5), where in the opinion of the assessor the provisions in subsection (3) for computing assessable profits cannot for any reason be satisfactorily applied in the case of a person to whom subsection (2) applies, the assessable profits of that person for any year of assessment may instead be computed on a fair percentage of the aggregate of the relevant sums earned by or accrued to that person during the basis period for that year of assessment.

(5) Notwithstanding section 70, where the assessable profits of any person have been computed for any year of assessment in accordance with subsection (4), the person shall, upon the submission to the assessor of accounts computed in accordance with the provisions of this Part relating to the ascertainment of assessable profits, be entitled to elect at any time within 2 years from the end of the year of assessment that his assessable profits for that year be re-computed in accordance with subsection (3).

(6) Where the Commissioner is satisfied that the call at any location within the waters of Hong Kong of any ship owned by a person to whom subsection (2) applies is of a casual nature, and that further calls at any location within those waters by that or any other ship in the same ownership are improbable, he may in his discretion direct that that person shall be deemed not to be carrying on a business as an owner of ships in Hong Kong under subsection (2) by reason of the casual call of that ship and accordingly, in the event of his making such a direction, that person shall be so deemed not to be carrying on that business.

(7) For the purposes of this section, it is declared that where a ship is operated during the basis period for a year of assessment by a person deemed to be carrying on a business as an owner of ships in Hong Kong under subsection (1) or (2), as the case may be-

(a) if the ship is a registered ship (in respect of which the definition of "exempt sums" applies) at any time during that basis period, only losses incurred by that person in respect of the operation of that ship while it is not such a registered ship shall be set off against the assessable profits of that person in accordance with section 19C;

(b) sections 18F and 19E shall apply in respect of the operation of the ship (treated as machinery or plant for the purposes of Part VI) by that person, and-

(i) subject to subsections (8) and (9), in the case of any initial allowance or annual allowance, as the case may be, that may be made to that person under Part VI, that allowance shall only be made in respect of that portion of the basis period during which the ship is not a registered ship (in respect of which the definition of "exempt sums" applies) to the extent that that ship is operated in that portion of that basis period for that year of assessment for the purpose of producing assess able profits;

(ii) in the case of any balancing allowance or balancing charge, as the case may be, that may be made to that person under Part VI, that allowance or charge shall be limited to a sum which is in the same proportion as the aggregate of the initial and annual allowances made to that person in computing his assessable profits since the acquisition of the ship bears to the aggregate of the initial and annual allowances that would have been made had the ship been operated by that person at all times since its acquisition for the purpose of producing assessable profits.

(8) Where in the basis period for any year of assessment a registered ship (in respect of which the definition of "exempt sums" applies) ceases to be a registered ship, any allowances that may be made under Part VI in respect of the operation of that ship (treated as machinery or plant for the purposes of that Part) for that year of assessment and subsequent years, shall be computed on the reducing value of the ship after taking into account the amounts of-

(a) any initial allowance made under section 37(1), 37A(I) or 39B(1); and

(b) subject to subsection (9), any annual allowance that would have been made under section 37(2), 37A(2) or 39B(2) had the ship, since its acquisition by a person deemed to be carrying on a business as an owner of ships in Hong Kong under subsection (1) or (2), as the case may be, been operated for the purpose of producing assessable profits.

(9)   For the purposes of subsections (7)(b)(i) and (8)(b)-

    (a)   in the case of subsection (7)(b)(i), the reference to Part VI (which Part contains sections 37(2) and 37A(2) amongst others); and

    (b)   in the case of subsection (8)(b), the reference to sections 37(2) and 37A(2),

shall, in both cases, be construed as if the words "at the end of the basis period" (in the first place where they appear in section 37(2), and where they appear in section 37A(2)) read "during the basis period"

(10)   For the purposes of this section, any sums earned by or accrued to the owner of a ship under a charter-party that does not, or does not purport to, extend to the whole of that ship shall, to the extent that those sums are derived from, attributable to, or in respect of, any voyage or voyages of that ship commencing from any location within the waters of Hong Kong, be deemed to be derived from, attributable to, or in respect of, any relevant carriage shipped in Hong Kong.

(11)   A copy of, or extract from, the register of ships in legible form issued and certified under the Merchant Shipping (Registration) Ordinance (Cap. 415) shall-

    (a)   in relation to any year of assessment, be proof that a ship was a registered ship or was not a registered ship, or be proof that a ship had commenced to be a registered ship or had ceased to be a registered ship, as the case may be; and

    (b)   in relation to the date of the provisional registration of that ship under that Ordinance, be proof that that registered ship was so registered from that date of provisional registration.

(12)   In this section-

"bill of lading" has the same meaning as in the Import and Export Ordinance (Cap. 60), but does not include a bill of lading which describes any port or other location within the waters of Hong Kong as the port of origin or the port of destination;

"business as an owner of ships" means a business of chartering or operating ships, but does not include dealing in ships or agency business in connection with shipping;

"charter hire" means any sums earned by or accrued to an owner of a ship under a charter-party in respect of the operation of the ship, but does not include any sums so earned or accrued where that charter-party does not, or does not purport to, extend to the whole of that ship;

"exempt sums" means any sums derived from, attributable to, or in respect of-

> *(a)*   any relevant carriage shipped aboard a registered ship at any location within the waters of Hong Kong and proceeding to sea from that or any other location within those waters; or

> *(b)*   any towage operation undertaken by a registered ship proceeding to sea from any location within the waters of Hong Kong;

"goods" includes livestock and mails;

"goods in transit", in relation to the shipment of goods aboard a ship, means goods-

> *(a)*   specified in a bill of lading;

> *(b)*   brought to Hong Kong by sea solely for the purpose of the onward carriage of those goods; and

> *(c)*   in respect of which any freight charges for that onward carriage are not paid or payable in Hong Kong;

"operation", in relation to a ship, includes the use or possession of the ship, and "operated" shall be construed accordingly;

"owner", in relation to a ship, includes a charterer of the ship under a charter-party;

"passengers" does not include re-embarking passengers;

"re-embarking passengers", in relation to a voyage of a ship, means passengers whose passenger tickets in respect of the voyage do not specify Hong Kong as the place of departure or as the place of destination;

"registered ship" means a ship registered under the Merchant Shipping (Registration) Ordinance (Cap. 415);

"relevant carriage", in relation to a ship, means the carriage by sea of passengers or goods, or both passengers and goods, as the case may be, but does not include the carriage of goods in transit;

"relevant limited partnership" means a limited partnership-

> *(a)*   registered in accordance with the provisions of the Limited Partnerships Ordinance (Cap. 37) on or before 2 December 1990 and continuing to be so registered after that date; and

> *(b)*   whose principal assets include any ship, or any interest therein, acquired by or on behalf of that partnership on or before that date;

"relevant sums" means-

(a)   any sums derived from, attributable to, or in respect of-

  (i)   any relevant carriage shipped in Hong Kong;

  (ii)   any towage operation undertaken by a ship within the waters of Hong Kong, or any towage operation undertaken by that ship commencing from any location within those waters, as the case may be;

  (iii)   any dredging operation undertaken by a ship within the waters of Hong Kong;

  (iv)   any charter hire in respect of-

    (A)   the operation of a ship navigating solely or mainly within the waters of Hong Kong; or

    (B)   a charter-party where one of the parties thereto is a relevant limited partnership;

(b)   one half of any sums derived from, attributable to, or in respect of, any charter hire in respect of the operation of a ship navigating between any location within the waters of Hong Kong and any location within river trade waters,

but does not include exempt sums;

"river trade waters" means the waters contained within river trade limits other than the waters of Hong Kong contained within those limits;

"sea", except in relation to relevant carriage, means the waters of the sea other than those contained within river trade limits;

"ship" includes any dynamically supported craft within the meaning of the Shipping and Port Control Ordinance (Cap. 313);

"shipped", in the case of passengers, means embarked;

"shipped in Hong Kong", in relation to the shipment of relevant carriage, means shipped aboard a ship at any location within the waters of Hong Kong;

"total shipping income", in relation to any basis period, means the worldwide income of a person from the person's business as an owner of ships, and indicated as such by that person's accounts for that period;

"total shipping profits", in relation to any basis period, means the worldwide profits of a person from the person's business as an owner of ships, and indicated as such by that person's accounts for that period.

Ascertainment of the assessable profits of a resident aircraft-owner

23C.(1) Where a person carries on a business as an owner of aircraft and-

> *(a)*   the business is normally controlled or managed in Hong Kong; or

> *(b)*   the person is a company incorporated in Hong Kong,

that person shall be deemed to be carrying on that business in Hong Kong.

(2)   Where a person is deemed to be carrying on a business as an owner of aircraft in Hong Kong under this section the assessable profits from that business for any year of assessment shall be the sum bearing the same ratio to the aggregate of the relevant sums earned by or accrued to that person during the basis period for that year of assessment as that person's total aircraft profits for the basis period bear to the aggregate of the total aircraft income earned by or accrued to that person during that basis period for that year of assessment.

(3)   For the purposes of this section, any sums earned by or accrued to the owner of an aircraft under a charter-party (whether by demise or not) that does not, or does not purport to, extend to the whole of that aircraft shall, to the extent that those sums are derived from, attributable to, or in respect of, any outward flight or flights of that aircraft commencing from any aerodrome or airport within Hong Kong, be deemed to be derived from, attributable to, or in respect of, any relevant carriage shipped in Hong Kong.

(4)   For the purposes of this section, the following sums earned by or accrued to an owner of aircraft under a charter-party otherwise than by demise shall be deemed to be derived from, attributable to, or in respect of, any relevant carriage shipped in Hong Kong-

> *(a)*   in the case of a charter-party which is a flight charter, any sums earned by or accrued to that owner under that charter-party and derived from, attributable to, or in respect of, any outward flight or flights of that aircraft commencing from any aerodrome or airport within Hong Kong;

> *(b)*   in the case of a charter-party which is a time charter, the sum bearing the same ratio to the aggregate of the sums earned by or accrued to that owner under that charter-party as the total number of flying hours of that aircraft flown in respect of all outward flights of that aircraft commencing from any aerodrome or airport within Hong Kong to the final destinations of those flights bear to the aggregate of the total number of flying hours of that aircraft flown in respect of all flights of that aircraft under that charter-party.

(5)   In this section-

"aerodrome or airport" includes any helipad;

"air waybill" has the same meaning as in the Import and Export Ordinance (Cap. 60), but does not include an air waybill which describes any aerodrome or airport in Hong Kong as the aerodrome or airport of departure or the aerodrome or airport of destination;

"aircraft" includes a helicopter;

"business as an owner of aircraft" means a business of chartering or operating aircraft, but does not include dealing in aircraft or agency business in connection with air transport;

"charter hire" means any sums earned by or accrued to an owner of an aircraft under a charter-party by demise in respect of the operation of the aircraft, but does not include any sums so earned or accrued where that charter-party does not, or does not purport to, extend to the whole of that aircraft;

"goods" includes livestock and mails;

"goods in transit", in relation to the shipment of goods aboard an aircraft, means goods

    (a)   specified in an air waybill (issued by or on behalf of an owner of aircraft) or a post office delivery bill;

    (b)   brought to Hong Kong by air solely for the purpose of the onward carriage of those goods; and

    (c)   in respect of which any freight charges for that onward carriage are not paid or payable in Hong Kong;

"operation", in relation to an aircraft, includes the use or possession of the aircraft;

"owner", in relation to an aircraft, includes a charterer of the aircraft under a charter-party;

"passengers" does not include passengers in transit;

"passengers in transit", in relation to a flight of an aircraft, means passengers-

    (a)   whose passenger tickets in respect of the flight do not specify Hong Kong as the place of departure or as the place of destination; or

    (b)   who-

        (i)   travel to Hong Kong in any aircraft owned by an owner of aircraft and leave Hong Kong in that or any other aircraft in the same ownership; and

(ii)   not more than 24 hours after travelling to and arriving at Hong Kong, leave Hong Kong for a destination other than the one from which they had travelled;

"permanent establishment" means a branch, management or other place of business, but does not include an agency unless the agent has, and habitually exercises, a general authority to negotiate and conclude contracts on behalf of his principal;

"post office delivery bill", in relation to the carriage of mails, means any document (whether referred to as an "AV7 bill" or otherwise) which does not describe Hong Kong, or the General Post Office of Hong Kong, as the office of origin or the office of destination in respect of those mails;

"relevant carriage", in relation to an aircraft, means the carriage by air of passengers or goods, or both passengers and goods, as the case may be, but does not include the carriage of goods in transit;

"relevant charter hire" means charter hire other than charter hire attributable to a permanent establishment maintained outside Hong Kong by a person deemed to be carrying on a business as an owner of aircraft in Hong Kong under this section, but does not include-

(a)   charter hire in respect of the operation of an aircraft flying between aerodromes or airports within Hong Kong; or

(b)   charter hire in respect of the operation of an aircraft flying between any aerodrome or airport within Hong Kong and any aerodrome or airport within Macau;

"relevant sums" means-

(a)   any sums derived from, attributable to, or in respect of-

       (i)   any relevant carriage shipped in Hong Kong;

       (ii)   any relevant charter hire;

       (iii)   any charter hire in respect of the operation of an aircraft flying between aerodromes or airports within Hong Kong;

(b)   one half of any sums derived from, attributable to, or in respect of, any charter hire in respect of the operation of an aircraft flying between any aerodrome or airport within Hong Kong and any aerodrome or airport within Macau;

"shipped", in the case of passengers, means embarked;

"shipped in Hong Kong", in relation to the shipment of relevant carriage, means shipped aboard an aircraft at any aerodrome or airport within Hong Kong;

"total aircraft income", in relation to any basis period, means the worldwide income of a person from the person's business as an owner of aircraft, and indicated as such by that person's accounts for that period;

"total aircraft profits", in relation to any basis period, means the worldwide profits of a person from the person's business as an owner of aircraft, and indicated as such by that person's accounts for that period.

Ascertainment of the assessable profits of a non-resident aircraft-owner

23D.(1) Subject to subsection (5), where a person to whom section 23C does not apply carries on a business as an owner of aircraft, and any aircraft owned by that person lands at any aerodrome or airport within Hong Kong, that person shall be deemed to be carrying on that business in Hong Kong.

(2) Subject to subsections (3) and (4), where a person is deemed to be carrying on a business as an owner of aircraft under this section the assessable profits of that person from that business for any year of assessment shall be the sum bearing the same ratio to the aggregate of the relevant sums earned by or accrued to that person during the basis period for that year of assessment as that person's total aircraft profits for the basis period bear to the aggregate of the total aircraft income earned by or accrued to that person during that basis period for that year of assessment.

(3) Subject to subsection (4), where in the opinion of the assessor the provisions in subsection (2) for computing assessable profits cannot for any reason be satisfactorily applied in the case of a person to whom this section applies, the assessable profits of that person for any year of assessment may instead be computed on a fair percentage of the aggregate of the relevant sums earned by or accrued to that person during the basis period for that year of assessment.

(4) Notwithstanding section 70, where the assessable profits of any person have been computed for any year of assessment in accordance with subsection (3), the person shall, upon the submission to the assessor of accounts computed in accordance with the provisions of this Part relating to the ascertainment of assessable profits, be entitled to elect at any time within 2 years from the end of the year of assessment that his assessable profits for that year be re-computed in accordance with subsection (2).

(5) Where the Commissioner is satisfied that the landing at any aerodrome or airport within Hong Kong of any aircraft owned by a person to whom this section applies is of a casual nature, and that further landings at any aerodrome or airport within Hong Kong by that or any other aircraft in the same ownership are improbable, he may in his discretion direct that that person shall be deemed not to be carrying on a business as an owner of aircraft in Hong Kong under this section by reason of the casual landing of that aircraft and accordingly, in the event of his making such a direction, that person shall be so deemed not to be carrying on that business.

(6)   For the purposes of this section, any sums earned by or accrued to the owner of an aircraft under a charter-party (whether by demise or not) that does not, or does not purport to, extend to the whole of that aircraft shall, to the extent that those sums are derived from, attributable to, or in respect of, any outward flight or flights of that aircraft commencing from any aerodrome or airport within Hong Kong, be deemed to be derived from, attributable to, or in respect of, any relevant carriage shipped in Hong Kong.

(7)   For the purposes of this section, the following sums earned by or accrued to an owner of an aircraft under a charter-party otherwise than by demise shall be deemed to be derived from, attributable to, or in respect of, any relevant carriage shipped in Hong Kong-

> *(a)*   in the case of a charter-party which is a flight charter, any sums earned by or accrued to that owner under that charter-party and derived from, attributable to, or in respect of, any outward flight or flights of that aircraft commencing from any aerodrome or airport within Hong Kong;

> *(b)*   in the case of a charter-party which is a time charter, the sum bearing the same ratio to the aggregate of the sums earned by or accrued to that owner under that charter-party as the total number of flying hours of that aircraft flown in respect of all outward flights of that aircraft commencing from any aerodrome or airport within Hong Kong to the final destinations of those flights bear to the aggregate of the total number of flying hours of that aircraft flown in respect of all flights of that aircraft under that charter-party.

(8)   In this section-

"aerodrome or airport" includes any helipad;

"air waybill" has the same meaning as in the Import and Export Ordinance (Cap. 60), but does not include an air waybill which describes any aerodrome or airport in Hong Kong as the aerodrome or airport of departure or the aerodrome or airport of destination;

"aircraft" includes a helicopter;

"business as an owner of aircraft" means a business of chartering or operating aircraft, but does not include dealing in aircraft or agency business in connection with air transport;

"charter hire" means any sums earned by or accrued to an owner of an aircraft under a charter-party by demise in respect of the operation of the aircraft, but does not include any sums so earned or accrued where that charter-party does not, or does not purport to, extend to the whole of that aircraft;

"goods" includes livestock and mails;

"goods in transit" in relation to the shipment of goods aboard an aircraft, means goods -

> *(a)*   specified in an air waybill (issued by or on behalf of an owner of aircraft) or a post office delivery bill;
>
> *(b)*   brought to Hong Kong by air solely for the purpose of the onward carriage of those goods; and
>
> *(c)*   in respect of which any freight charges for that onward carriage are not paid or payable in Hong Kong;

"operation", in relation to an aircraft, includes the use or possession of the aircraft;

"owner", in relation to an aircraft, includes a charterer of the aircraft under a charter-party;

"passengers" does not include passengers in transit;

"passengers in transit" in relation to a flight of an aircraft, means passengers -

> *(a)*   whose passenger tickets in respect of the flight do not specify Hong Kong as the place of departure or as the place of destination; or
>
> *(b)*   who-
>
> > **(i)**   travel to Hong Kong in any aircraft owned by an owner of aircraft and leave Hong Kong in that or any other aircraft in the same ownership; and
> >
> > **(ii)**   not more than 24 hours after travelling to and arriving at Hong Kong, leave Hong Kong for a destination other than the one from which they had travelled;

"permanent establishment" means a branch, management or other place of business, but does not include an agency unless the agent has, and habitually exercises, a general authority to negotiate and conclude contracts on behalf of his principal;

"post office delivery bill" in relation to the carriage of mails, means any document (whether referred to as an "AV7 bill" or otherwise) which does not describe Hong Kong, or the General Post Office of Hong Kong, as the office of origin or the office of destination in respect of those mails;

"relevant carriage", in relation to an aircraft, means the carriage by air of passengers or goods, or both passengers and goods, as the case may be, but does not include the carriage of goods in transit;

"relevant charter hire" means charter hire attributable to a permanent establishment maintained in Hong Kong by a person deemed to be carrying on a business as an owner of aircraft in Hong Kong under this section, but does not include-

    (a)   charter hire in respect of the operation of an aircraft flying between aerodromes or airports within Hong Kong; or

    (b)   charter hire in respect of the operation of an aircraft flying between any aerodrome or airport within Hong Kong and any aerodrome or airport within Macau;

"relevant sums" means-

    (a)   any sums derived from, attributable to, or in respect of-

        (i)   any relevant carriage shipped in Hong Kong;

        (ii)   any relevant charter hire;

        (iii)   any charter hire in respect of the operation of an aircraft flying between aerodromes or airports within Hong Kong;

    (b)   one half of any sums derived from, attributable to, or in respect of, any charter hire in respect of the operation of an aircraft flying between any aerodrome or airport within Hong Kong and any aerodrome or airport within Macau;

"shipped", in the case of passengers, means embarked;

"shipped in Hong Kong", in relation to the shipment of relevant carriage, means shipped aboard an aircraft at any aerodrome or airport within Hong Kong;

"total aircraft income" in relation to any basis period, means the worldwide income of a person from the person's business as an owner of aircraft, and indicated as such by that person's accounts for that period;

"total aircraft profits", in relation to any basis period, means the worldwide profits of a person from the person's business as an owner of aircraft, and indicated as such by that person's accounts for that period.

Alternative computation of "total shipping profits" and "total aircraft profits"

23E.   Where total shipping profits within the meaning of section 23B(12) or total aircraft profits within the meaning of section 23C(5) or 23D(8), as the case may be, have been computed on a basis which differs materially from that provided for in this Part for the ascertainment of assessable profits in respect of which a person is chargeable to tax, those profits may be adjusted so as to correspond as nearly as may be to the sum that would have been arrived at had they been computed in accordance with the provisions of this Part relating to the ascertainment of assessable profits in respect of which a person is chargeable to tax.

Clubs, trade associations, etc.

24.(1)   Where a person carries on a club or similar institution which receives from its members not less than half of its gross receipts on revenue account (including entrance fees and subscriptions), such person shall be deemed not to carry on a business; but where less than half of its gross receipts are received from members, the whole of the income from transactions both with members and others (including entrance fees and subscriptions) shall be deemed to be receipts from a business, and such person shall be chargeable in respect of the profits therefrom.

(2)   Where a person carries on a trade, professional or business association in such circumstances that more than half its receipts by way of subscriptions are from persons who claim or would be entitled to claim that such sums were allowable deductions for the purposes of section 16, such person shall be deemed to carry on a business, and the whole of the income of such association from transactions both with members and others (including entrance fees and subscriptions) shall be deemed to be receipts from business, and such person shall be chargeable in respect of the profits therefrom.

(3)   In this section, "members" means those persons entitled to vote at a general meeting of the club, or similar institution, or trade, professional or business association.

Deduction of property tax from profits tax

25.   Where property tax is payable for any year of assessment under Part II in respect of any land or buildings owned by a person carrying on a trade, profession or business, any profits tax payable by such person in respect of that year of assessment shall be reduced by a sum not exceeding the amount of such property tax paid by him:

Provided that-

> *(a)*   no reduction shall be allowed unless either the profits derived from such property are part of the profits of the trade, profession or business carried on by such person or the property is occupied or used by him for the purposes of producing profits in respect of which he is chargeable to tax under this Part;

> *(b)*   if the amount of property tax paid for a year of assessment exceeds the profits tax payable, the amount so paid in excess shall be refunded in accordance with the provisions of section 79;

> *(c)*   where property tax for the year of assessment commencing on 1 April 1960, or earlier years, exceeded the profits tax payable for such years the amount of the excess shall be set off against the profits tax payable for the year of assessment commencing on 1 April 1961, after deduction of the property tax paid for that year and any balance left over shall be carried forward and set off in like manner against the profits tax payable for the next succeeding years.

Exclusion of certain dividends and profits from the assessable profits of other persons

26.   For the purposes of this Part-

> *(a)*   a dividend from a corporation which is chargeable to tax under this Part shall not be included in the profits in respect of which any other person is chargeable to tax under this Part; and

> *(b)*   save as otherwise provided no part of the profits or losses of a trade, profession or business carried on by a person who is chargeable to tax under this Part shall be included in ascertaining the profits in respect of which any other person is chargeable to tax under this Part.

Exclusion of certain profits from tax

26A.(1) For the purposes of this Part-

> *(a)*   interest paid or payable on a Tax Reserve Certificate issued by the Commissioner;

> *(b)*   interest paid or payable on a bond issued under the Loans Ordinance (Cap. 61) or the Loans (Government Bonds) Ordinance (Cap. 64);

> *(c)*   any profit on the sale or other disposal or on the redemption on maturity or presentment of such a bond;

> *(d)*   interest paid or payable on an Exchange Fund debt instrument;

> *(e)*   any profit on the sale or other disposal or on the redemption on maturity or presentment of such an Exchange Fund debt instrument;

> *(f)*   interest paid or payable on a Hong Kong dollar denominated multilateral agency debt instrument; and

> *(g)*   any profit on the sale or other disposal or on the redemption or maturity or presentment of such a Hong Kong dollar denominated multilateral agency debt instrument,

shall not be included in the profits of any corporation or other person chargeable to tax under this Part.

(1A)   For the purposes of this Part, sums received by or accrued to an authorized mutual fund corporation or trustees of an authorized unit trust by way of-

(*a*)   gains or profits arising from the sale or other disposal or on the redemption on maturity or presentment of securities;

(*b*)   gains or profits under a foreign exchange contract or futures contract; and

(*c*)   interest,

shall not be included in the profits of the corporation or trustees (as the case may be).

(2)   In this section-

"authorized" means authorized under section 15 of the Securities Ordinance (Cap. 333);

"computer" means any device for storing, processing or retrieving information;

"Exchange Fund" means the fund of that name established under section 3(1) of the Exchange Fund Ordinance (Cap. 66);

"Exchange Fund debt instrument" means any instrument (whether described as an "Exchange Fund Bill" or otherwise) issued under the Exchange Fund Ordinance (Cap. 66) evidencing the deposit of a sum of money in Hong Kong currency with the Monetary Authority for the account of the Exchange Fund, being an instrument which recognizes an obligation to pay a stated amount, with or without interest, and which is transferable in a manner specified by that Authority;

"foreign exchange" means the exchange of different currencies;

"futures contract" has the same meaning as in section 2(1) of the Commodities Trading Ordinance (Cap. 250);

"instrument" includes-

(*a*)   every written document;

(*b*)   any information recorded in the form of an entry in a book of account; and

(*c*)   any information which is recorded (whether by means of a computer or otherwise) in a non-legible form but is capable of being reproduced in a legible form;

"multilateral agency debt instrument" means an instrument specified in Part I of Schedule 6 issued by a body specified in Part II of that Schedule;

"mutual fund corporation" has the same meaning as in section 2(1) of the Securities Ordinance (Cap. 333);

"securities" includes-

(a)   any negotiable receipt or other negotiable certificate or instrument evidencing the deposit of a sum of money, or any rights or interests arising under any such receipt, certificate of instrument;

(aa)   any prescribed instrument within the meaning of section 137B of the Banking Ordinance (Cap. 155); and

(b)   any bill of exchange within the meaning of section 3 of the Bills of Exchange Ordinance (Cap. 19),

but otherwise has the same meaning as in section 2(1) of the Securities Ordinance (Cap. 333);

"unit trust" has the same meaning as in section 2(1) of the Securities Ordinance (Cap.333).

(3)   The Legislative Council may by resolution amend Schedule 6.

PART V - Allowances

Allowances, general provisions

27.(1) This Part prescribes the allowances which shall be granted to persons chargeable to tax under Parts III and VII and the circumstances in which such allowances are grantable.

(2) Every person who claims an allowance under this Part shall make his claim in the specified form and an allowance shall be granted only if the claim contains such particulars and is supported by such proof as the Commissioner may require.

(3) In this Part-

"adopted" means adopted in any manner recognized by the laws of Hong Kong;

"allowance" means an allowance granted under this Part;

"child" means any child of a person chargeable to tax or of his or her spouse or former spouse whether or not born in wedlock and includes the adopted or step child of either or both of them;

"person" means a person chargeable to tax under Part III or, as the case may be, Part VII

"prescribed amount" and "prescribed percentage" mean the amount and percentage specified in the second column of the Fourth Schedule in relation to the provisions of this Part specified in the first column of that Schedule.

Basic allowance

28.(1) The following allowance ("basic allowance") shall be granted in any year of assessment-

    (a)   an allowance of the prescribed amount;

    (b)   an additional allowance of the prescribed amount, but this allowance shall be reduced by the prescribed percentage of the sum, if any, by which-

        (i)   in the case of a person who is chargeable to salaries tax under Part III, the net assessable income of that person, as reduced under section 12BA by approved charitable donations, exceeds the prescribed amount; and

        (ii)   in the case of a person who has elected to be assessed under Part VII, the total income of that person, as reduced under section 42(2) and (5), exceeds the prescribed amount referred to in subparagraph (i).

(2)   No person may be granted-

> *(a)*   both a basic allowance and a married person's allowance; or
>
> *(b)*   a basic allowance where his or her spouse has claimed a married person's allowance.

Married person's allowance

29.(1) An allowance ("married person's allowance") shall be granted under this section in any year of assessment if a person is, at any time during that year, married and-

> *(a)*   the spouse of that person did not have assessable income in the year of assessment; or
>
> *(b)*   that person and his or her spouse have made, in relation to the year of assessment, an election under section 10(2); or
>
> *(c)*   that person has elected to be assessed under Part VII.

(2)   Where an election has been made under section 10(2) a married person's allowance shall be granted to the person chargeable to salaries tax under section 10(3).

(3)   A married person's allowance grantable under this section is-

> *(a)*   an allowance of the prescribed amount;
>
> *(b)*   an additional allowance of the prescribed amount, but this allowance shall be reduced by the prescribed percentage of the amount, if any, by which-
>
>> **(i)**   in the case of a person who is chargeable to salaries tax under section 10(3), the aggregate of the net assessable incomes of that person and of his or her spouse as reduced by approved charitable donations provided for under section 12BA, exceeds the prescribed amount;
>>
>> **(ii)**   in the case of a person assessable to salaries tax who is entitled to married person's allowance because he or she has such a wife or husband as is described in subsection (1)(a), the net assessable income as reduced by approved charitable donations provided for under section 12BA, exceeds the prescribed amount; and
>>
>> **(iii)**   in the case of a person who has elected personal assessment under Part VII, the total income (as reduced under section 42(2) and (5)) of that person and his or her spouse exceeds the prescribed amount.

(4)   Where husband and wife are living apart a married person's allowance shall only be granted where the spouse claiming the allowance is maintaining or supporting the other.

(5)   Where a married person's allowance is granted in respect of a husband and wife living apart, the husband and wife shall be treated as not living apart for the purposes of Part VII.

(6)   Any claim to an allowance to which subsection (4) applies may be revoked by the claimant within the year of assessment in respect of which it was made or within 6 years after the expiration of that year.

Dependent parent allowance

30.(1) An allowance ("dependent parent allowance") shall be granted under this section in any year of assessment if the person or his or her spouse, not being a spouse living apart from that person, maintains a parent or a parent of his or her spouse in the year of assessment and that parent at any time in that year was-

     (a)   ordinarily resident in Hong Kong; and

     (b)   aged 60 or more or, being under the age of 60, was eligible to claim an allowance under the Government's Disability Allowance Scheme.

(2) A dependent parent allowance may be granted in respect of each such parent who is so maintained.

(3) A dependent parent allowance grantable under this section is-

     (a)   an allowance of the prescribed amount;

     (b)   an additional allowance of the prescribed amount if a parent in respect of whom the person is eligible to claim an allowance under paragraph (a) for the year of assessment was residing, otherwise than for full valuable consideration, with the person continuously throughout the year of assessment.

(4) For the purposes of this section-

     (a)   a parent shall only be treated as being maintained by a person or his or her spouse if-

          (i)   the parent resides, otherwise than for full valuable consideration, with that person and his or her spouse for a continuous period of not less than 6 months in the year of assessment; or

          (ii)   the person or his or her spouse contributes not less than the prescribed amount in money towards the maintenance of that parent in the year of assessment;

     (b)   "parent or parent of his or her spouse" means, in relation to any person -

    (i)   a parent of whose marriage, the person or his or her spouse is the child;

    (ii)   a parent by whom the person or his or her spouse was adopted;

    (iii)   a step parent of the person or of his or her spouse;

    (iv)   the natural father or mother of the person or his or her spouse; or

    (v)   in the case of a deceased spouse a person who would have been the parent of the person's spouse by reason of subparagraphs (i) to (iv) if the spouse had not died.

Dependent grandparent allowance

30A.(1) An allowance ("dependent grandparent allowance") shall be granted under this section in any year of assessment if a person or his or her spouse, not being a spouse living apart from that person, maintains a grandparent or a grandparent of his or her spouse in the year of assessment and that grandparent at any time in that year was-

    (a)   ordinarily resident in Hong Kong; and

    (b)   aged 60 or more or, being under the age of 60, was eligible to claim an allowance under the Government's Disability Allowance Scheme.

(2) A dependent grandparent allowance may be granted in respect of each such grandparent who is so maintained.

(3) A dependent grandparent allowance grantable under this section is-

    (a)   an allowance of the prescribed amount;

    (b)   an additional allowance of the prescribed amount if a grandparent in respect of whom the person is eligible to claim an allowance under paragraph (a) for the year of assessment was residing, otherwise than for full valuable consideration, with the person continuously throughout the year of assessment.

(4) For the purposes of this section-

    (a)   a grandparent shall only be treated as being maintained by a person or his or her spouse if-

        (i)   the grandparent resides, otherwise than for full valuable consideration, with that person and his or her spouse for a continuous period of not less than 6 months in the year of assessment; or

(ii)   the person or his or her spouse contributes not less than the prescribed amount in money towards the maintenance of that grandparent in the year of assessment;

(b)   "grandparent or grandparent of his or her spouse" means, in relation to any person-

(i)   a natural grandfather or grandmother of the person or his or her spouse;

(ii)   an adoptive grandparent of the person or his or her spouse (whether an adoptive parent of a natural parent, adoptive parent or step parent of the person or his or her spouse, or a natural parent of an adoptive parent of the person or his or her spouse);

(iii)   a step grandparent of the person or his or her spouse (whether a step parent of a natural parent, adoptive parent or step parent of the person or his or her spouse, or a natural parent of a step parent of the person or his or her spouse);

(iv)   in the case of a deceased spouse a person who would have been the grandparent of the person's spouse by reason of subparagraphs (i) to (iii) if the spouse had not died.

Child allowance

31.(1) An allowance ("child allowance") shall be granted under this section in the prescribed amount in any year of assessment if the person had living and was maintaining at any time during the year of assessment an unmarried child who was-

(a)   under the age of 18;

(b)   of or over the age of 18 years but under the age of 25 years and was receiving full time education at a university, college, school or other similar educational establishment; or

(c)   of or over the age of 18 years and was, by reason of physical or mental disability, incapacitated for work.

(2)   Subject to subsection (3), where more than one person is entitled to claim a child allowance under this section in respect of the same child for the same year of assessment, the allowance due shall be apportioned on such basis as the Commissioner may decide having regard to the contributions made by each individual to the maintenance and education of the child during the year of assessment.

(3)   In the case of a husband and wife, not being a husband and wife living apart, chargeable to salaries tax under Part III-

> *(a)*   all child allowances grantable under this section shall be claimed by one spouse; and
>
> *(b)*   the claim shall be made by such spouse as the spouses may nominate.

(4)   A nomination under subsection (3)(b) made in relation to any year of assessment shall not be revoked save with the consent of the Commissioner whose decision in the matter shall be final and not subject to objection or appeal.

(5)   The total of the child allowances granted to a person in respect of his or her children shall not exceed the prescribed amount.

Single parent allowance

32.(1) An allowance ("single parent allowance") of the prescribed amount shall be granted if at any time during the year of assessment the person had the sole or predominant care of a child in respect of whom the person was entitled during the year of assessment to be granted a child allowance.

(2) A person shall not be entitled to claim single parent allowance-

> *(a)*   if at any time during the year of assessment the person was married and not living apart from his or her spouse;
>
> *(b)*   by reason only that the person made contributions to the maintenance and education of the child during the year of assessment; or
>
> *(c)*   in respect of any 2nd or subsequent child.

(3)   Where 2 or more persons are entitled to claim single parent allowance in respect of the same child for the same year of assessment, the allowance due shall be apportioned on such basis as the Commissioner may decide-

> *(a)*   having regard to the respective periods for which each person had the sole or predominant care of the child during the year of assessment; or
>
> *(b)*   if, in the opinion of the Commissioner, those periods are uncertain, on such basis as the Commissioner may decide as being just.

Provisions supplementary to sections 30, 30A and 31

33.(1) Subject to section 31(2), a dependent parent allowance, a dependent grandparent allowance or a child allowance shall not be given to more than one person in any year of assessment in respect of the same parent, grandparent or child.

(1A)   A dependent parent allowance and a dependent grandparent allowance shall not both be given in any year of assessment in respect of the same dependent person.

(2)   Subject to section 31(2) and (3), where the Commissioner has reason to believe that 2 or more persons are eligible to claim such an allowance in respect of the same parent, grandparent or child for the same year of assessment, the Commissioner shall not consider any claim until he is satisfied that the claimants have agreed which of them shall be entitled to claim in that year.

(3)   Where a dependent parent allowance, a dependent grandparent allowance or a child allowance has been granted-

>   *(a)*   otherwise than under section 31(2) to 2 or more persons in respect of the same parent, grandparent or child; or

>   *(b)*   to both a husband and wife, contrary to section 31(3); or

>   *(c)*   to a person and, within 6 months of such allowance being granted, another person appears to the Commissioner to be eligible to be granted that allowance in respect of the same parent, grandparent or child for the same year of assessment,

the Commissioner shall invite the persons to whom the allowance has been granted and any other individual who appears to the Commissioner to be eligible to be granted the allowance to agree which of them is to have the allowance (being an agreement consistent with the provisions of this Part) and the Commissioner may in consequence of such agreement, or if the individuals do not so agree within a reasonable time, within the period specified in section 60, raise additional assessments under that section.

(3A)   Where the Commissioner has reason to believe that there are persons eligible to claim, respectively, a dependent parent allowance and a dependent grandparent allowance in respect of the same dependent person for the same year of assessment, the Commissioner shall not consider any claim until he is satisfied that the claimants have agreed which of the allowances shall be claimed in that year.

(3B)   Where a dependent parent allowance and a dependent grandparent allowance have both been granted in respect of the same dependent person contrary to subsection (1A), the Commissioner shall invite the persons to whom the allowances have been granted to agree which of the allowances is to be given (being an agreement consistent with the provisions of this Part) and the Commissioner may in consequence of such agreement, or if the individuals do not so agree within a reasonable time, within the period specified in section 60, raise additional assessments under that section.

(3C)   Where-

>   *(a)*   a dependent parent allowance or a dependent grandparent allowance has been granted to a person in respect of a dependent person; and

>   *(b)*   within 6 months of that allowance being granted, another person appears to the Commissioner to be eligible to be granted the other allowance in respect of the same dependent person for the same year of assessment,

the Commissioner shall invite the person to whom the allowance has been granted and any other individual who appears to the Commissioner to be eligible to be granted the other allowance in respect of the same dependent person to agree which of the allowances is to be granted (being an agreement consistent with the provisions of this Part) and the Commissioner may in consequence of such agreement, or if the individuals do not so agree within a reasonable time, within the period specified in section 60, raise additional assessments under that section.

(4)   The Commissioner shall exercise his powers under this section in such manner as may appear to him to be just having regard to such information only as may be in his possession at the time when he exercises those powers.

PART VI - Depreciation, Etc.

Initial and annual allowances, industrial buildings and structures

34.(1) Where a person incurs capital expenditure on the construction of a building or structure which is to be an industrial building or structure occupied for the purposes of a trade there shall be made to the person who incurred the expenditure for the year of assessment in the basis period for which the expenditure was incurred an allowance to be known as an "initial allowance" equal to one-fifth thereof.

Provided that-

(a) no initial allowance shall be made for the 8 successive years of assessment commencing on 1 April in each of the years 1957 to 1964;

(b) where any initial allowance has been made in relation to capital expenditure on a building or structure under this subsection before such building or structure comes to be used and when it first comes to be used it is not an industrial building or structure, such allowance shall be disallowed and such additional assessments as may be necessary consequent thereon shall be made.

(2) *(a)* Where any person is, at the end of the basis period for any year of assessment, entitled to an interest in a building or structure which is an industrial building or structure and where that interest is the relevant interest in relation to the capital expenditure incurred on the construction of that building or structure an allowance for depreciation by wear and tear, to be known as an "annual allowance", equal to one-twenty-fifth of that expenditure shall be made to him for that year of assessment.

(b) Where the interest in a building or structure, which is the relevant interest in relation to any expenditure, is sold while the building or structure is an industrial building or structure the annual allowance, in the years of assessment the basis periods for which end after the time of that sale shall be computed by reference to the residue of expenditure immediately after the sale and shall be the fraction of the said residue the numerator of which is 2, where the building or structure was first used before the commencement of the basis period for the year of assessment commencing on 1 April 1965, and one, where the building or structure was first used on or after the commencement of such basis period, and the denominator of which is the number of years of assessment comprised in the period which-

(i) begins with the first year of assessment for which the buyer is entitled to an annual allowance or would be so entitled if the building or structure had at all material times continued to be an industrial building or structure; and

(ii) ends with the year of assessment which, where the building or structure was first used before the commencement of the basis period for the year of assessment commencing on 1 April 1965, is the 50th year after the year in which the building or structure was first used, and where the building or structure was first used on or after such basis period, is the 25th year after the year of assessment in which the building or structure was first used, and so on for any subsequent sales.

(c) Notwithstanding anything in the preceding provisions of this section, in no case shall the amount of an annual allowance for any year of assessment in respect of any expenditure exceed such as, apart from the writing off falling to be made by reason of the making of that allowance, would be the residue of that expenditure at the end of his basis period for that year of assessment.

Balancing allowances and charges, industrial buildings and structures

35.(1) Where any capital expenditure has been incurred on the construction of a building or structure and any of the following events occurs while the building or structure is an industrial building or structure, that is to say -

(a) the relevant interest in the building or structure is sold; or

(b) that interest, being a leasehold interest, comes to an end otherwise than on the person entitled thereto acquiring the interest which is reversionary thereon; or

(c) the building or structure is demolished or destroyed or, without being demolished or destroyed, ceases altogether to be used,

an allowance or charge, to be known as a "balancing allowance" or a "balancing charge" shall, in the circumstances mentioned in this section, be made to or, as the case may be, on the person entitled to the relevant interest immediately before that event occurs for the year of assessment in his basis period for which that event occurs:

Provided that no balancing allowance shall be made to any person where the building or structure is demolished for purposes unconnected with or not in the ordinary course of conduct of the trade or business for the purposes of which the building or structure was used in circumstances qualifying for annual allowances under section 34.

(2) Where there are no sale, insurance, salvage or compensation moneys, or where the residue of the expenditure immediately before the event exceeds those moneys, a balancing allowance shall be made and the amount thereof shall be the amount of the said residue or, as the case may be, of the excess thereof over the said moneys.

(3)   If the sale, insurance, salvage or compensation moneys exceed the residue, if any, of the expenditure immediately before the event, a balancing charge shall be made and the amount on which it is made shall be an amount equal to the excess or, where the residue is nil, to the said moneys.

(4)   Notwithstanding anything in subsection (3), in no case shall the amount on which a balancing charge is made on a person exceed the aggregate of the following amounts, that is to say-

> *(a)*   the amount of the initial allowance, if any, made to him in respect of the expenditure in question;

> *(b)*   the amount of the annual allowances, if any, made to him in respect of the expenditure in question.

Special provisions on termination of leasehold interest

35A.   Where, on the termination of a leasehold interest-

> *(a)*   a lessee of any building or structure remains in possession thereof with the consent of the lessor without a new lease being granted to him, the leasehold interest shall be deemed for the purposes of this Part to continue so long as he so remains in possession;

> *(b)*   a new lease is granted to the lessee either by way of regrant or in pursuance of an option available to him under the terms of the first lease, this Part shall have effect as if the second lease were a continuation of the first lease.

Buildings and structures bought unused

35B.   Where capital expenditure is incurred on the construction of a building or structure and, before that building or structure is used, the relevant interest therein is sold-

> *(a)*   the expenditure actually incurred on the construction thereof shall be left out of account for the purposes of this Part and any initial allowance made under section 34 shall be disallowed and such additional assessments as may be necessary consequent thereon shall be made; but

> *(b)*   **(i)**   in a case where the person who sells that interest incurred that expenditure and made that sale in the course of a trade which consists, in whole or part, in the construction or development of buildings or structures for the purpose of sale, the person who buys that interest shall be deemed for those purposes to have incurred, on the date when the purchase price becomes payable, capital expenditure on the construction thereof equal to the net price paid by him for that interest; and

> **(ii)** in any other case, the person who buys that interest shall be deemed, for those purposes to have incurred, on the date when the purchase price becomes payable, capital expenditure on the construction thereof equal to the expenditure actually incurred on the construction of the building or structure or to the net price paid by him for that interest, whichever is the less:

> Provided that-

> *(a)* where in a case to which paragraph (b)(i) applies the relevant interest in the building or structure is sold more than once before the building or structure is used, only the person who buys that interest on the occasion of the last of those sales shall be deemed to have incurred capital expenditure on the construction of the building or structure and that capital expenditure shall be equal to the net price paid on the first sale or the net price paid by him, whichever is the less;

> *(b)* where in a case to which paragraph (b)(ii) applies the relevant interest in the building or structure sold more than once before the building or structure is used, that paragraph shall have effect only in relation to the last of those sales.

Rebuilding allowance for a commercial building or structure

36. Where at the end of the basis period for any year of assessment a person is entitled to an interest in a commercial building or structure and where that interest is the relevant interest in relation to the capital expenditure incurred on the construction of that building or structure, an allowance to be known as a "rebuilding allowance" equal to 2% of the capital expenditure incurred on the construction of such building or structure shall be made to him for that year of assessment.

Application of provisions to machinery or plant

36A.(1) Except where otherwise provided, in relation to the initial and annual allowances on machinery or plant-

> *(a)* sections 37, 37A, 38 and 39 shall apply to the years of assessment up to and including the year of assessment commencing on 1 April 1979; and

> *(b)* sections 39B, 39C and 39D shall apply to the year of assessment commencing on 1 April 1980 and to subsequent years of assessment.

(2) Where in relation to any machinery or plant the Commissioner is satisfied that in respect of any year of assessment commencing on or after 1 April 1980 the application of any of the provisions of the sections referred to in subsection (1)(b) is impracticable or inequitable, he may direct that the provisions of the sections referred to in subsection (1)(a) shall apply to the extent and for the duration specified in the direction.

(3) Where under subsection (2) the Commissioner directs that the provisions of section 37 shall apply to any machinery or plant in respect of-

  (a) the year of assessment commencing on 1 April 1980, the initial allowance shall be equal to 35% of the expenditure referred to in subsection (1) of that section;

  (b) any year of assessment commencing on or after 1 April 1981, the initial allowance shall be equal to 55% of the expenditure referred to in subsection (1) of that section;

  (c) any year of assessment commencing on or after 1 April 1989, the initial allowance shall be equal to 60% of the expenditure referred to in subsection (1) of that section.

Initial and annual allowances, machinery or plant

37.(1) Where a person carrying on a trade, profession or business incurs capital expenditure on the provision of machinery or plant for the purposes of producing profits chargeable to tax under Part IV then, except where such expenditure is expenditure of a kind described in section 16B(1)(b), there shall be made to him, for the year of assessment in the basis period for which the expenditure is incurred, an allowance, to be known as an "initial allowance".

(1A) For the purposes of subsection (1), the initial allowance shall be-

  (a) in respect of a year of assessment up to and including the year of assessment commencing on 1 April 1973, equal to one-fifth of the expenditure referred to in subsection (1); and

  (b) in respect of the year of assessment commencing on 1 April 1974 and all subsequent years of assessment up to and including the year of assessment commencing on 1 April 1979, equal to one-quarter of such expenditure.

(2) Where at the end of the basis period for any year of assessment a person owns and has in use machinery or plant for the purposes of producing profits chargeable to tax under Part IV there shall be made to him in respect of that year of assessment an allowance to be known as an "annual allowance" for depreciation by wear and tear of those assets. The allowance shall be calculated at the rates prescribed by the Board of Inland Revenue and shall be computed on the reducing value of the asset, which shall be the cost of the asset reduced by-

  (a) any initial allowance computed in accordance with the provisions of this section; and

   (b) the annual allowances computed under the provisions of this section:

Provided that-

   (a) where the asset was acquired before the basis period in respect of the year of assessment 1947/48 the value at the end of the basis period shall be computed by deducting from the amount paid for the asset by its present owner annual allowances as if this subsection had been in force during the whole period of ownership of the asset excluding any period during which the owner was deprived of the use of the asset by reason of enemy occupation;

   (b) the Commissioner may in his discretion allow a higher rate than that prescribed by the Board of Inland Revenue.

(2A) For the purposes of subsection (2), in any case where machinery or plant is owned and used by a person for any period immediately before he uses it for the purposes of producing profits chargeable to tax under Part IV, "cost of the asset" means the sum computed by deducting from the actual cost the notional amount of the annual allowances which would have been made under subsection (2) to the owner if since acquiring the asset he had used it for the purpose of producing profits chargeable to tax under Part IV.

(3) Nothing in subsection (2) shall apply in respect of any machinery or plant owned and used by a person for the purposes of his trade or business where such machinery or plant represents scientific research expenditure of a capital nature which pursuant to section 16B(1)(b) has been allowed as a deduction in ascertaining the profits from such trade or business in respect of which such person is chargeable to tax under Part IV for any year of assessment.

(4) If a person succeeds to any trade, profession or business which immediately before the succession-

   (a) was carried on by another person; and

   (b) made use of machinery or plant for the purpose of producing profits chargeable to tax under Part IV,

and, immediately after the succession, such machinery or plant, without being sold to the successor, is in use in that trade, profession or business for the same purpose, the reduced value of such machinery or plant shall, for the purpose of computing annual allowances under subsection (2), be taken to be the reduced value thereof still unallowed to that other person as at the time of the succession.

(5) Notwithstanding subsection (4), no initial allowance shall be made under this Part by virtue of subsection (4).

Initial and annual allowances in respect of machinery and plant acquired under hire purchase agreement

37A.(1) Where a person carrying on a trade, profession or business incurs capital expenditure under a hire purchase agreement on the provision of machinery or plant for the purposes of producing profits chargeable to tax under Part IV then, except where such expenditure is expenditure of a kind described in section 16B(1)(b), there shall be made to him for each year of assessment in the basis period for which he has made an instalment payment under such agreement, an initial allowance.

(1A) For the purposes of subsection (1), the initial allowance shall be-

      (a)   in respect of a year of assessment up to and including the year of assessment commencing on 1 April 1973, equal to one-fifth of the capital portion only of the instalment payment referred to in subsection (1);

      (b)   in respect of the year of assessment commencing on 1 April 1974 and all subsequent years of assessment up to and including the year of assessment commencing on 1 April 1979, equal to one-quarter of the capital portion only of such payment;

      (c)   in respect of the year of assessment commencing on 1 April 1980 equal to 35% of the capital portion only of such payment;

      (d)   in respect of the year of assessment commencing on 1 April 1981 and all subsequent years of assessment up to and including the year of assessment commencing on 1 April 1988, equal to 55% of the capital portion only of such payment; and

      (e)   in respect of any year of assessment commencing on or after 1 April 1989, equal to 60% of the capital portion only of such payment.

(2) Where at the end of the basis period for any year of assessment a person has in use for the purposes of producing profits chargeable to tax under Part IV, machinery or plant acquired by him under a hire purchase agreement there shall be made to him in respect of that year of assessment an annual allowance for depreciation by wear and tear on such machinery or plant.

(3) An annual allowance under this section shall be calculated at rates prescribed by the Board of Inland Revenue and shall be computed on the reducing value of such machinery or plant which shall be the full cost thereof, excluding any interest which may be included in such cost under the terms of the agreement and reduced by any initial or previous annual allowances computed under this section:

Provided that the Commissioner may in his discretion allow a higher rate than that prescribed by the Board of Inland Revenue.

(4)   Nothing in subsection (2) shall apply in respect of any machinery or plant used by a person for the purposes of his trade or business where such machinery or plant represents scientific research expenditure of a capital nature which pursuant to section 16B(1)(b) has been allowed as a deduction in ascertaining the profits from such trade or business in respect of which such person is chargeable to tax under Part IV for any year of assessment.

Balancing allowances and charges, machinery or plant

38.(1) Where any of the following events occurs in the case of any machinery or plant in respect of which an initial allowance or an annual allowance has been made for any year of assessment to a person carrying on a trade, profession or business, that is to say, either-

> *(a)*   the machinery or plant is sold, whether while still in use or not; or

> *(b)*   the machinery or plant is destroyed; or

> *(c)*   the machinery or plant is put out of use as being worn out or obsolete or otherwise useless or no longer required,

and the event in question occurs either whilst the person is carrying on his trade, profession or business or at the time when he ceases so to do, an allowance or charge, to be known as a "balancing allowance" or a "balancing charge", shall in the circumstances mentioned in this section, be made to or, as the case may be, on that person for the year of assessment in his basis period for which that event occurs.

(2) Where there are no sale, insurance, salvage or compensation moneys or where the amount of the capital expenditure of the person in question on the provision of the plant or machinery still unallowed as at the time of the event exceeds those moneys, a balancing allowance shall be made, and the amount thereof shall be the amount of the expenditure still unallowed as aforesaid or, as the case may be, the excess thereof over the said moneys; but in a case where an annual allowance has been computed on the cost of the asset as determined in accordance with section 37(2A), the cost of the asset as computed in accordance with that subsection shall be deemed to be the capital expenditure for the purposes of this subsection and in a case where an annual allowance has been computed in accordance with section 37(4), the reduced value used for the purpose of that subsection shall be deemed to be the capital expenditure for the purposes of this subsection.

(3) If the sale, insurance, salvage or compensation moneys exceed the amount, if any, of the said expenditure still unallowed as at the time of the event, a balancing charge shall be made, and the amount on which it is made shall be an amount equal to the excess or, where the said amount still unallowed is nil, to the said moneys.

(4) Where by reason of a person ceasing to carry on his trade, profession or business, machinery or plant in respect of which an initial or an annual allowance has been made is put out of use, such person shall be deemed to have received immediately prior to such cessation, sale moneys for such machinery or plant of such an amount as the Commissioner may consider it would have realized had it been sold in the open market at the time of cessation:

Provided that if such person sells such machinery or plant within 12 months of the date of cessation he may claim the adjustment of any balancing allowance or charge which may have been made to or on him as if such sale had taken place immediately prior to the date of cessation and notwithstanding the provisions of section 70 an assessor shall make any necessary correction to any assessment.

(5) Notwithstanding anything contained in this section, in no case shall the amount on which a balancing charge is made on a person exceed the aggregate of the following amounts, that is to say-

> *(a)*   the amount of the initial allowance, if any, made to him in respect of the expenditure in question;

> *(b)*   the amount of the annual allowances, if any, made to him in respect of the expenditure in question, including any allowance computed under proviso (b) to section 37(2) at a rate higher than that prescribed by the Board of Inland Revenue.

Determination of cost of individual assets sold together for one price

38A.   Where assets which qualify for initial or annual allowances under this Part are sold together or with other assets in pursuance of one bargain the Commissioner shall for the purposes of the calculation of the allowances and charges provided for in this Part, and having regard to all the circumstances of the transaction allocate a purchase price to each individual asset.

Commissioner's power to determine the true value of an asset on sale

38B.   Where an asset which qualifies for initial or annual allowances is sold, and-

> *(a)*   the buyer is a person over whom the seller has control; or

> *(b)*   the seller is a person over whom the buyer has control; or

> *(c)*   both the seller and the buyer are persons over both of whom some other person has control; or

> *(d)*   the sale is between a husband and wife, not being a wife living apart from her husband,

the Commissioner shall, if he is of the opinion that the sale price of such asset does not represent its true market value at the time of such sale, determine such true market value and the amount so determined shall be deemed to be the sale price of such asset for the purpose of calculating the allowances and charges provided for in this Part.

Special provision as to allowances on a change in partnership

38C.   Where a change occurs in a partnership of persons carrying on any trade, profession or business and an application made in accordance with the provisions of the proviso to section 22(3) has been properly received by an assessor the provisions of this Part shall apply as if no such change had occurred except that any annual and rebuilding allowances in respect of assets of the old partnership acquired by the new partnership granted for the year of assessment in which such assets were acquired by the new partnership, shall be apportioned pro rata between the old and the new partnership.

Replacement of machinery or plant

39.   Where machinery or plant in the case of which any of the events mentioned in section 38(1) has occurred is replaced by the owner thereof and a balancing charge falls to be made on him by reason of that event or, but for the provisions of this section, would have fallen to be made on him by reason thereof, then, if by notice in writing to the Commissioner he so elects, the following provisions shall have effect, that is to say-

> *(a)*   if the amount on which the charge would have been made is greater than the capital expenditure on providing the new machinery or plant-
>
> > **(i)**   the charge shall be made only on an amount equal to the difference; and
> >
> > **(ii)**   no initial allowance, no balancing allowance and no annual allowance shall be made or allowed in respect of the new machinery or plant or the expenditure on the provision thereof; and
> >
> > **(iii)**   in considering whether any, and, if so, what balancing charge fails to be made in respect of the expenditure on the new machinery or plant, there shall be deemed to have been made in respect of that expenditure an initial allowance equal to the full amount of that expenditure;
>
> *(b)*   if the capital expenditure on providing the new machinery or plant is equal to or greater than the amount on which the charge would have been made-
>
> > **(i)**   the charge shall not be made; and
> >
> > **(ii)**   the amount of any initial allowance in respect of the said expenditure shall be calculated as if the expenditure had been reduced by the amount on which the charge would have been made; and
> >
> > **(iii)**   in considering what annual allowance is to be made in respect of the new machinery or plant, there shall be left out of account a proportion of the machinery or plant equal to the proportion which the amount on which the charge would have been made bears to the amount of the said expenditure; and
> >
> > **(iv)**   in considering whether any and, if so, what balancing allowance or

108

balancing charge falls to be made in respect of the new machinery or plant, the initial allowance in respect thereof shall be deemed to have been increased by an amount equal to the amount on which the charge would have been made.

Reduction of allowances not to affect calculation of subsequent allowances

39A.   Where, by virtue of section 12(2), 18F(1) or 19E(1), the amount of any allowance provided for under this Part is reduced, such reduction shall not affect the calculation of subsequent allowances which shall be computed in the first place as if the full amount of the allowance had been granted and shall then where appropriate be apportioned in relation to the extent to which the relevant assets are or have been used in the production of assessable income or assessable profits.

Initial and annual allowances on machinery or plant under the pooling system

39B.(1) Where a person carrying on a trade, profession or business incurs capital expenditure on the provision of machinery or plant for the purposes of producing profits chargeable to tax under Part IV then, except where such expenditure is expenditure of a kind described in section 16B(1)(b), there shall be made to him, for the year of assessment in the basis period for which the expenditure is incurred, an allowance, to be known as an "initial allowance".

(1A)   For the purposes of subsection (1), the initial allowance shall be equal to the following percentages of the expenditure referred to in that subsection-

> *(a)*   for the year of assessment commencing on 1 April 1980, 35%;

> *(b)*   for the year of assessment commencing on 1 April 1981 and all subsequent years of assessment up to and including the year of assessment commencing on 1 April 1988, 55%;

> *(c)*   for any year of assessment commencing on or after 1 April 1989, 60%.

(2)   Where during the basis period for any year of assessment or during the basis period for any earlier year of assessment a person owns or has owned and has in use or has had in use any machinery or plant for the purposes of producing profits chargeable to tax under Part IV, there shall be made to him in respect of each class of machinery or plant for that year of assessment an allowance, to be known as an "annual allowance", for depreciation by wear and tear of such machinery or plant.

(3)   The annual allowance shall be calculated at the rates of depreciation prescribed by the Board of Inland Revenue and shall be computed on the reducing value of each class of machinery or plant.

(4)   Subject to subsections (5), (6) and (7), the reducing value of a class of machinery or plant shall be the aggregate capital expenditure incurred on the provision of the machinery or plant belonging to that class reduced by-

(a)   the aggregate of any initial allowances computed in accordance with section 37 in respect of any machinery or plant belonging to that class;

(b)   the aggregate of any annual allowances computed in accordance with section 37 in respect of any machinery or plant belonging to that class;

(c)   the aggregate of any initial allowances computed in accordance with this section in respect of any machinery or plant belonging to that class;

(d)   any annual allowance computed in accordance with this section;

(e)   any sale, insurance, salvage or compensation moneys received in respect of any machinery or plant belonging to that class; and

(f)   any reducing value of machinery or plant excluded from the total reducing value of a class of machinery or plant under section 39C(3).

(5)   Where, prior to the commencement of the Inland Revenue (Amendment) (No. 4) Ordinance 1980, any machinery or plant has been the subject of a balancing allowance or balancing charge computed in accordance with section 38, such machinery or plant shall, for the purposes of subsection (4), be excluded from the class of machinery or plant.

(6)   Where any machinery or plant is owned and used by a person for any period immediately before he uses it for the purposes of producing profits chargeable to tax under Part IV, the capital expenditure incurred on the provision of the machinery or plant for the purposes of subsection (4) shall be computed by deducting from the actual cost the notional amount of the annual allowances which would have been made under section 37 to the owner if since acquiring the machinery or plant he had used it for the purpose of producing profits chargeable to tax under Part IV.

(7)   If a person succeeds to any trade, profession or business which immediately before the succession-

(a)   was carried on by another person; and

(b)   the machinery or plant that was used at any time by that other person for the purpose of producing profits chargeable to tax under Part IV is not sold to the successor,

the reducing value of such machinery or plant shall, for the purpose of computing annual allowances under subsection (3), be taken to be the reducing value thereof still unallowed to that other person as at the time of succession.

(8)   Notwithstanding subsection (7), no initial allowance shall be made under this Part by virtue of subsection (7).

(9)   No annual allowance shall be made where the reductions made under subsection (4) exceed the aggregate capital expenditure incurred on the provision of the class of machinery or plant.

(10)   Nothing in subsection (2) shall apply in respect of any machinery or plant owned and used by a person for the purposes of his trade or business where such machinery or plant represents scientific research expenditure of a capital nature which pursuant to section 16B(1)(b) has been allowed as a deduction in ascertaining the profits from such trade or business in respect of which such person is chargeable to tax under Part IV for any year of assessment.

(11)   The Commissioner may in his discretion allow a higher rate of depreciation in respect of any class of machinery or plant than that prescribed by the Board of Inland Revenue.

Pooling system when not to apply

39C.(1)   The provisions of this Part which applied immediately prior to the commencement of the Inland Revenue (Amendment) (No. 4) Ordinance 1980 shall continue to apply-

> *(a)*   subject to subsection (2), in respect of machinery or plant to which section 37A applies;
>
> *(b)*   in respect of machinery or plant to which section 39A applies.

(2)   Where, pursuant to the terms and conditions of a hire purchase agreement, machinery or plant to which section 37A applies passes into the ownership of the person carrying on a trade, profession or business who incurred the capital expenditure under the hire purchase agreement, the reducing value of such machinery or plant computed in accordance with that section shall be included in the class of machinery or plant for the purposes of section 39B for the years of assessment following the year of assessment during the basis period for which the machinery or plant passed into the ownership of that person.

(3)   Where any machinery or plant which is included in a class of machinery or plant for the purposes of section 39B and which was used wholly and exclusively in the production of profits chargeable to tax under Part IV is subsequently not so used wholly and exclusively in the production of such profits, the provisions of this Part which applied immediately prior to the commencement of the Inland Revenue (Amendment) (No. 4) Ordinance 1980 shall apply to such machinery or plant in respect of the year of assessment during the basis period for which the machinery or plant is subsequently not used wholly and exclusively in the production of profits chargeable to tax under Part IV, and the reducing value of such machinery or plant shall be deemed to be such an amount as the Commissioner may consider it would have realized had it been sold in the open market at the time it ceased to be used wholly and exclusively in the production of such profits, and such reducing value shall be excluded from the total reducing value of that class of machinery or plant.

(4)   For the purposes of subsection (2), in the application of section 37A, subsection (2) of that section shall be read as if "during the basis period" was substituted for "at the end of the basis period".

Balancing allowances and charges under the pooling system

39D.(1) Where at the end of a basis period for a year of assessment the aggregate reductions made under section 39B(4) in respect of a class of machinery or plant exceed the aggregate capital expenditure incurred by a person on the provision of machinery or plant belonging to that class-

> *(a)*   a charge, to be known as a "balancing charge", shall be made on him, and the amount on which it is made shall be an amount equal to the excess; and

> *(b)*   the reducing value at the end of the basis period for that year of assessment shall be nil.

(2)   Subject to subsection (3) and except where subsection (4) applies, where a person ceases to carry on his trade, profession or business in a year of assessment, the aggregate of the sale, insurance, salvage or compensation moneys, if any, of the machinery or plant in respect of which an initial allowance or annual allowance has been made shall be compared with the amount of the reducing value of the class of machinery or plant at the end of the basis period for that year of assessment and-

> *(a)*   where there are no sale, insurance, salvage or compensation moneys, or where the amount of the reducing value exceeds the aggregate of such moneys, an allowance, to be known as a "balancing allowance", shall be made to him, and the amount thereof shall be the amount of the reducing value or, as the case may be, the excess thereof over the aggregate of the said moneys; or

> *(b)*   where there are sale, insurance, salvage or compensation moneys, and the aggregate of such moneys exceeds the amount, if any, of the reducing value, a charge, to be known as a "balancing charge", shall be made on him, and the amount on which it is made shall be an amount equal to the excess or, where the reducing value is nil, to the aggregate of the said moneys.

(3)   Subsection (2) shall not apply on the occasion on which any machinery or plant, to which section 39B(7) applies, passes by way of succession.

(4)   Where by reason of a person ceasing to carry on his trade, profession or business machinery or plant in respect of which an initial allowance or annual allowance has been made is put out of use and there are no sale, insurance, salvage or compensation moneys, such person shall, subject to subsection (5), be deemed to have received immediately prior to such cessation, sale moneys for such machinery or plant of such an amount as the Commissioner may consider it would have realized had it been sold in the open market at the time of cessation.

(5)   If a person sells any machinery or plant referred to in subsection (4) within 12 months of the date of cessation he may claim the adjustment of any balancing allowance or balancing charge which may have been made to or on him as if such sale had taken place immediately prior to the date of cessation and notwithstanding section 70 an assessor shall make any necessary correction to any assessment.

(6)   Notwithstanding anything contained in this section, where the aggregate of any sale, insurance, salvage or compensation moneys in respect of any machinery or plant exceeds the capital expenditure incurred on the provision of that machinery or plant, the aggregate of such moneys shall-

> *(a)*   for the purposes of calculating a balancing charge under subsection (2)(b); and

> *(b)*   in calculating the reducing value of the class of machinery or plant under section 39B(4),

not exceed the capital expenditure incurred on the provision of that machinery or plant.

(7)   For the purposes of subsection (6), the capital expenditure incurred on the provision of the machinery or plant shall be taken as-

> *(a)*   in a case where section 37(2A) applies, the "cost of the asset" computed in accordance with that section;

> *(b)*   in a case where section 39B(6) applies, the capital expenditure computed in accordance with that section; or

> *(c)*   in any other case, the aggregate capital expenditure incurred by the person in question on the provision of the machinery or plant for the purposes of producing profits chargeable to tax under Part IV.

Allowances under this Part in respect of capital expenditure on leased machinery and plant

39E.(1) Notwithstanding anything to the contrary in this Part, a person (in this section referred to as "the taxpayer") who incurs capital expenditure on the provision of machinery or plant, being machinery or plant acquired by the taxpayer under a contract entered into after the commencement of the Inland Revenue (Amendment) Ordinance 1986, for the purpose of producing profits chargeable to tax under Part IV shall not have made to him the initial or annual allowances prescribed in section 37, 37A or 39B if, at a time when the machinery or plant is owned by the taxpayer, a person holds rights as lessee under a lease of the machinery or plant, and-

> *(a)*   the machinery or plant was, prior to its acquisition by the taxpayer, owned and used by that person (whether alone or with others), or any associate of that person (which person or any such associate is hereinafter referred to as "the end-user"); or

> *(b)*   the machinery or plant, not being a ship or aircraft or any part thereof, is while the lease is in force-

> > **(i)**   used wholly or principally outside Hong Kong by a person other than the taxpayer; or

    (ii)   the whole or a predominant part of the cost of the acquisition or construction of the machinery or plant was financed directly or indirectly by a non-recourse debt; or

    (iii)   the machinery or plant is a ship or aircraft or any part thereof and-

        (i)   the person holding rights as lessee is not an operator of a Hong Kong ship or aircraft; or

        (ii)   the whole or a predominant part of the cost of acquisition or construction of the ship or aircraft or the part thereof was financed directly or indirectly by a non-recourse debt.

(2)   Subsection (1)(a) shall not apply where-

    (a)   the machinery or plant was acquired by the taxpayer on payment from the end-user at not more than the price which the end-user paid to the supplier (not being a supplier who is himself an end-user); and

    (b)   no initial or annual allowances have at any time prior to the acquisition of the machinery or plant by the taxpayer been made under section 37, 37A or 39B to the end-user in respect of such machinery or plant.

(3)   For the purposes of subsection (2) an allowance shall be deemed not to have been made if the end-user, by notice in writing to the Commissioner within 3 months of the date on which the capital expenditure on the provision of machinery or plant giving rise to the allowance is incurred, or within such further time as the Commissioner may, in any particular case, permit, disclaims such allowance.

(4)   For the purposes of this section, where a trustee of a trust estate or a corporation controlled by such a trustee owns machinery or plant or holds rights as a lessee under a lease of machinery or plant, the trustee, the corporation and the beneficiary under the trust shall each be deemed to be the owner or holder, as the case may be, of rights as a lessee of the machinery or plant.

(5)   In this section-

"acquisition" means acquisition by a person as owner and includes holding or hiring under a hire-purchase agreement or, if the hire-purchase agreement is a conditional sale agreement, holding as purchaser;

"arrangement" includes-

    (a)   any agreement, arrangement, understanding, promise or undertaking, whether express or implied, and whether or not enforceable, or intended to be enforceable, by legal proceedings; and

(b) any scheme, plan, proposal, action or course of action or course of conduct;

"associate", in relation to a person holding rights as lessee under any lease of machinery or plant (including a person who is deemed to be holding such rights), means-

(a) where the person holding such rights is a natural person-

    (i) a relative of the person holding such rights;

    (ii) a partner of the person holding such rights and any relative of that partner;

    (iii) a partnership in which the person holding such rights is a partner;

    (iv) any corporation controlled by the person holding such rights, by a partner of the person holding such rights or by a partnership in which the person holding such rights is a partner;

    (v) any director or principal officer of any such corporation as is referred to in subparagraph (iv);

(b) where the person holding such rights is a corporation-

    (i) any associated corporation;

    (ii) any person who controls the corporation and any partner of such person, and, where either such person is a natural person, any relative of such person;

    (iii) any director or principal officer of that corporation or of any associated corporation and any relative of any such director or officer;

    (iv) any partner of the corporation and, where such partner is a natural person, any relative of such partner;

(c) where the person holding such rights is a partnership-

    (i) any partner of the partnership and where such partner is a partnership any partner of that partnership, any partner with the partnership in any other partnership and where such partner is a partnership any partner of that partnership and where any partner of, or with, or in any of the partnerships mentioned in this subparagraph is a natural person, any relative of such partner;

    (ii) *(Repealed)*

> **(iii)** any corporation controlled by the partnership or by any partner thereof or, where such a partner is a natural person, any relative of such partner;
>
> **(iv)** any corporation of which any partner is a director or principal officer;
>
> **(v)** any director or principal officer of a corporation referred to in subparagraph (iii);

"associated corporation" means-

> *(a)* a corporation over which the person holding rights under any lease of machinery or plant (including a person who is deemed to be holding such rights) has control;
>
> *(b)* a corporation which has control over such person holding rights, being a corporation;
>
> *(c)* a corporation which is under the control of the same person as such person holding rights, being a corporation;

"beneficiary under the trust" means any person who benefits or is capable (whether by the exercise of a power of appointment or otherwise) of benefiting under a trust estate, either directly or through any interposed person, or who is able or might reasonably be expected to be able, whether directly or indirectly, to control the activities of the trust estate or the application of its corpus or income;

"conditional sale agreement" means an agreement for the sale of goods under which the purchase price or part of it is payable by instalments, and the property in the goods remains in the seller (notwithstanding that the buyer is to be in possession of the goods) until such conditions as to the payment of instalments or otherwise as may be specified in the agreement are fulfilled;

"control", in relation to a corporation, means the power of a person to secure-

> *(a)* by means of the holding of shares or the possession of voting power in or in relation to that or any other corporation; or
>
> *(b)* by virtue of any powers conferred by the articles of association or other document regulating that or any other corporation,

that the affairs of the first-mentioned corporation are conducted in accordance with the wishes of that person;

> "lend-user" means any person (whether alone or with others) holding rights as lessee under a lease of machinery or plant or any associate of such person;

"held for use" includes installed ready for use and held in reserve;

"lease" includes-

    (a)   any arrangement under which a right to use machinery or plant is granted by the owner of the machinery or plant to another person; and

    (b)   any arrangement under which a right to use machinery or plant, being a right derived directly or indirectly from a right referred to in paragraph (a), is granted by a person to another person,

but does not include a hire-purchase agreement or a conditional sale agreement unless, in the opinion of the Commissioner, the right under the agreement to purchase or obtain the property in the goods would reasonably be expected not to be exercised;

"non-recourse debt", in relation to the financing of the whole or a predominant part of the cost of the acquisition or construction of any machinery or plant, means a debt where the rights of the creditor in the event of default in the repayment of principal or payment of interest-

    (a)   are limited wholly or predominantly to any or all of the following-

        (i)   rights (including a right to moneys payable) in relation to the machinery or plant or the use of the machinery or plant;

        (ii)   rights (including rights to moneys payable) in relation to goods produced, supplied, carried, transmitted or delivered, or services provided, by means of the machinery or plant;

        (iii)   rights (including a right to moneys payable) in relation to the loss or disposal of the whole or a part of the machinery or plant or of the taxpayer's interest in the machinery or plant;

        (iv)   any conjunction of such rights as are referred to in subparagraphs (i), (ii) and (iii);

        (v)   rights in respect of a mortgage or other security over the machinery or plant; or

        (vi)   rights arising out of any arrangement relating to the financial obligations of the end-user of the machinery or plant towards the taxpayer, being financial obligations in relation to the machinery or plant;

    (b)   are in the opinion of the Commissioner capable of being limited as described in paragraph (a), having regard to either or both of the following-

> **(i)** the assets of the taxpayer;
>
> **(ii)** any arrangement to which the taxpayer is a party; or

(c) where paragraphs (a) and (b) do not apply, are limited by reason that not all of the assets of the taxpayer (not being assets that are security for a debt of the taxpayer other than a debt arising in relation to the financing of the whole or part of the cost of the acquisition of the machinery or plant) would be available for the purpose of the discharge of the whole of the debt so arising (including the payment of interest) in the event of any action or actions by the creditor or creditors against the taxpayer arising out of the debt;

"operator of a Hong Kong aircraft" means a person who-

(a) holds an air operators' certificate issued under the Air Navigation (Overseas Territories) Order 1977 by the Governor of Hong Kong; and

(b) carries on business as an operator of aircraft and the business is controlled and managed in Hong Kong;

"operator of a Hong Kong ship" means a person who-

(a) is responsible for defraying all or a substantial portion of the expenses of operating the ship and the ship operates mainly in the waters of Hong Kong or between the waters of Hong Kong and waters within the river trade limits; and

(b) carries on business as an operator of ships and the business is controlled and managed in Hong Kong;

"principal officer" means-

(a) a person employed by a corporation who, either alone or jointly with one or more other persons, is responsible under the immediate authority of the directors for the conduct of the business of the corporation; or

(b) a person so employed who, under the immediate authority of a director of the body corporate or a person to whom paragraph (a) applies, exercises managerial functions in respect of the body corporate;

"relative" means the spouse, parent, child, brother or sister of the relevant person, and, in deducing such a relationship, an adopted child shall be deemed to be a child both of the natural parents and the adopting parent and a step child to be the child of both the natural parents and of any step parent;

"used" includes held for use.

(6)   The amendments made to this section by section 4(b) and (d)(iv) of the Inland Revenue (Amendment) Ordinance 1992 apply to capital expenditure on the provision of machinery or plant under a transaction entered into on or after 15 November 1990 except expenditure under a transaction which was the subject of an application for advance clearance made to the Commissioner before 15 November 1990 and the Commissioner before or after that date expressed the opinion that the transaction would not fall within the terms of section 61A or, where no such application was made in respect of a transaction entered into before 15 November 1990 under which expenditure was incurred on or after 15 November 1990, the transaction under which the expenditure was made is, in the Commissioner's opinion, of the same type as any for which, in the circumstances prevailing as at 14 November 1990, he would have expressed the opinion that the transaction would not fall within the terms of section 61A.

Interpretation

40.(1) In this Part-

"basis period" has the meaning assigned to it by section 2 except that-

> *(a)*   where 2 basis periods overlap the period common to both shall be deemed to fall in the first basis period only; and

> *(b)*   where there is an interval between the end of the basis period for one year of assessment and the beginning of the basis period for the next year of assessment the interval shall be deemed to fall in the second basis period but where, in respect of salaries tax, the interval is the year ending on 31 March 1973, that interval shall not be deemed to fall in the second basis period;

"capital expenditure"

> *(a)*   includes interest paid and commitment fees incurred in respect of a loan made for the sole purpose of financing the provision of an industrial building or structure or commercial building or structure or machinery or plant; but

> *(b)*   does not include expenditure which is reimbursed by way of or attributable to any grant, subsidy or similar financial assistance and in relation to the person incurring the expenditure does not include any expenditure which is allowed to be deducted in ascertaining for the purpose of Part IV the profits of a trade or business carried on by that person;

"capital expenditure on the provision of machinery or plant" includes capital expenditure on alterations to an existing building incidental to the installation of that machinery or plant for the purposes of the trade, profession or business;

"class of machinery or plant" means the items of machinery or plant for which the same rate of depreciation is prescribed by the Board of Inland Revenue;

"commercial building or structure" means any building or structure or part of any building or structure used by the person entitled to the relevant interest for the purposes of his trade, profession or business other than an industrial building or structure;

"hire-purchase agreement" means an agreement for the bailment of goods under which the bailee may buy the goods, or under which the property in the goods will or may pass to the bailee;

"industrial building or structure" means any building or structure or part of any building or structure used-

    (a)   for the purposes of a trade carried on in a mill, factory or other similar premises; or

    (b)   for the purposes of a transport, tunnel, dock, water, gas or electricity undertaking or a public telephonic or public telegraphic service; or

    (c)   for the purposes of a trade which consists of the manufacture of goods or materials or the subjection of goods or materials to any process; or

    (d)   for the purposes of a trade which consists in the storage.

        (i)   of goods or materials which are to be used in the manufacture of other goods or materials; or

        (ii)   of goods or materials which are to be subjected in the course of a trade to any process; or

        (iii)   of goods or materials on their arrival into Hong Kong; or

    (e)   for the purposes of the business of farming;

    (f)   for the purposes of scientific research in relation to any trade or business,

and, in particular, the said expression includes any building or structure or part of any building or structure used by a person carrying on a trade, undertaking or business specified in paragraphs (a) to (e) of this definition and provided by him for the welfare of workers employed in his trade, undertaking or business and in use for that purpose:

Provided that-

        (i)   where part of the whole of a building or structure is, and part thereof is not, an industrial building or structure, and the capital expenditure which has been incurred on the construction of the second mentioned part is not more than one-tenth of the total capital expenditure which has been incurred on the construction of the whole building or structure, the whole building or structure and every part thereof shall be treated as an industrial building or structure; and

(ii) subject to the provisions of paragraph (i) of this proviso but notwithstanding anything else contained in the foregoing provisions of this definition, the expression "industrial building or structure" shall not include any building or structure or part of any building or structure used as a dwelling house (other than as a dwelling house for the housing of manual workers), retail shop, showroom, hotel or office;

"relevant interest" means, in relation to any expenditure incurred on the construction of a building or structure the interest in that building or structure to which the person who incurred the expenditure was entitled when he incurred it;

"residue of expenditure" means the amount of the capital expenditure incurred in the construction of a building or structure reduced by-

(a) the amount of any initial allowance made;

(b) any annual allowance made;

(c) any balancing allowance granted,

and increased by any balancing charges made:

Provided that in computing the residue of expenditure there shall be written off, in respect of any year in which no initial or annual allowance fell to be made, an amount of one-fiftieth of the capital expenditure in the case of a year prior to the year of assessment commencing on I April 1965, and one-twenty-fifth of the capital expenditure in the case of such or any subsequent year of assessment, and for the purposes of this proviso "year" means the period which would have comprised a year of assessment in respect of which an initial or annual allowance would have fallen to be made if the building or structure had then been in use as an industrial building or structure and the provisions of section 34 had then been in force.

(2) For the purposes of this Part, any capital expenditure incurred for the purposes of a trade, profession or business by a person about to carry on such trade, profession or business shall be treated as if it had been incurred by that person on the first day upon which he does carry on such trade, profession or business.

(3) References in this Part to capital expenditure incurred on the construction of a building or structure do not include any expenditure incurred on the acquisition of, or of rights in or over, any land.

40A. *(Repealed)*

PART VII - Personal Assessment

Interpretation

40B.   In this Part, unless the context otherwise requires-

"income", in relation to any person, means income derived beneficially by that person;

"individual" means a person electing or who has elected to be chargeable to tax under this Part;

"joint total income" means joint total income calculated in accordance with section 42A;

"loss" and "losses" do not include a loss sustained by a person acting in his capacity as trustee of a trust.

Election for personal assessment

41.(1) Subject to subsection (1A), an individual-

> *(a)*   of or above the age of 18 years, or under that age if both his or her parents are dead; and

> *(b)*   who is or, if he or she is married, whose spouse is either a permanent or temporary resident,

may elect for personal assessment on his or her total income in accordance with this Part.

(1A)   Where-

> *(a)*   an individual is married and not living apart from his or her spouse; and

> *(b)*   both that individual and his or her spouse-

>> **(i)**   have income assessable under this Ordinance; and

>> **(ii)**   are eligible to make an election under subsection (1),

then that individual may not make such an election unless his or her spouse does so too.

(2)   Where an individual is deceased an executor shall have the same right to elect for personal assessment on the total income of the deceased as the deceased would have if he were alive.

(2A)   Where-

> *(a)*   a deceased individual, or his executor on his behalf, elected to be personally assessed for the year of assessment in which the deceased died; and

  (b) that individual was a partner in a partnership; and

  (c) that individual had a share of the partnership assessable profits or losses in the year of assessment following that in which he died,

then his executor may claim to have that share of such assessable profits or losses computed in accordance with Part IV included in the deceased's total income for the year of assessment in which he died.

(3) Any election under this section shall be made in writing and lodged with the Commissioner not later than 2 years after the end of the year of assessment in respect of which the election is made or 1 month after an assessment of income or profits forming part of the individual's total income for such year of assessment becomes final and conclusive under section 70 or within such further period, if any, as the Commissioner may allow as being reasonable in the particular circumstances, whichever is the later.

(4) In this section-

"permanent resident" means an individual who ordinarily resides in Hong Kong;

"temporary resident" means an individual who stays in Hong Kong for a period or a number of periods amounting to more than 180 days during the year of assessment in respect of which the election is made or for a period or periods amounting to more than 300 days in 2 consecutive years of assessment one of which is the year of assessment in respect of which the election is made.

Calculation of total income

42.(1) For the purposes of this Part the total income of an individual for any year of assessment shall, subject to subsection (8), be the aggregate of the following amounts-

  (a) **(i)** *(Repealed)*

      (ii) in respect of the years of assessment commencing on or after 1 April 1983, the sum equivalent to the net assessable value as ascertained in accordance with sections 5(1A) and 5B:

      Provided that where an individual is a joint owner or co-owner of property, that individual's share of the net assessable value shall be computed by apportioning the value ascertained in accordance with section 5(1A) or 5B-

        (a) in the case of joint ownership, between the joint owners equally; and

        (b) in the case of ownership in common, between the owners in common each in proportion to his share in such ownership;

> *(b)*   the net assessable income of the individual for that year of assessment; and
>
> *(c)*   the assessable profits of the individual for that year of assessment computed in accordance with Part IV:
>
> *(d)*   *(Repealed)*

Provided that there shall be deducted from that part of the total income arising from paragraph (a) the amount of any interest payable on any money borrowed for the purpose of producing that part of the total income where the amount of such interest has not been allowed and deducted under Part IV.

(2)   There shall be deducted from the total income of an individual for any year of assessment-

> *(a)*   subject to subsections (3) and (4), the aggregate of approved charitable donations which are made during the year of assessment by the individual and his or her spouse, if such aggregate of donations is not less than $100; and
>
> *(b)*   the amount of the individual's loss or share of loss for that year of assessment computed in accordance with Part IV.

(3)   An individual shall not be entitled under subsection (2)(a) to deduct for any year of assessment any sum which is allowable as a deduction under section 16, 16B, 16C or 16D or which has been allowed to the individual's spouse against total income that is required to be aggregated with that of the individual under section 42A(1).

(4)   The total amount-

> *(a)*   of any sum which is allowable as a deduction under subsection (2)(a); and
>
> *(b)*   any sum which is allowable as a deduction under section 16D,

shall not exceed 10% of the total amount of-

> **(i)**   the total income of the individual for the year of assessment; and
>
> **(ii)**   any sum which is allowable as a deduction under section 16D.

(5)   Where in any year of assessment the amount of an individual's loss under subsection (2)(b) exceeds that individual's total income, after making the deductions under subsection (2)(a), the amount of such excess shall be carried forward and set off against the individual's total income for future years of assessment:

Provided that, in a case where the total incomes of spouses are required to be aggregated under section 42A(1), any such excess for either spouse shall, before being carried forward and set off under this subsection, be reduced as far as can be done by being set off against the total income of the other spouse as reduced under subsection (2).

(6) The proviso to subsection (5) shall apply, with any necessary modifications, in relation to an individual who has elected to be personally assessed under this Part and to his or her spouse where-

> *(a)* by reason of the application of section 41(1A), that individual could not have so elected unless his or her spouse did so too, had his or her spouse had income assessable under this Ordinance; and

> *(b)* for this reason only he or she was able so to elect,

as if the total income of both spouses had been required to be aggregated under section 42A(1).

(7) The amount of any excess set off under subsection (5) against an individual's total income or that of the individual's spouse for any year of assessment shall not be set off for any other year of assessment.

(8) For the purposes of this Part the total income of an individual for any year of assessment shall not include the profits or losses or share of profits or losses of that individual as a member of any partnership (other than a partnership referred to in section 345(2) of the Companies Ordinance (Cap. 32)) consisting, at any time in that year of assessment, of more than 20 partners.

(9) For the purposes of subsection (8), in calculating the number of partners in a partnership there shall be included every partner in any other partnership which is itself a partner in the first-mentioned partnership.

(10) Where an election is made by a husband and wife under section 41(1A) the total income (as reduced under subsections (2) and (5)) of each of them shall be separately calculated under this section before both incomes are aggregated under section 42A.

Assessment to tax

42A.(1) In giving effect to an election under section 41 the assessor shall make a single assessment-

> *(a)* in the sum of the total income, as reduced under section 42(2) and (5), of the individual making the election; or

> *(b)* in the case of an election under section 41(1A), in the sum of the joint total income resulting from the aggregation of the total income of the one spouse, as so reduced, with that of the other, as also so reduced,

as reduced in each case by such of the allowances prescribed in Part V as may be appropriate.

(2) In the case of an election under section 41(1A) by a husband and wife who married one another in the year of assessment to which the election relates, they shall be deemed for the purpose of ascertaining their joint total income under subsection (1)(b) to have married at the commencement of that year.

42B.   *(Repealed)*

Rates of charge

43.(1) Tax shall be charged on the amount of the assessment referred to in section 42A(1) at the rates specified in Schedule 2-

> *(a)*   on the individual; or

> *(b)*   in the case of a husband and wife making an election under section 41(1A) on both of them subject to apportionment in the manner prescribed by subsection (2B).

(1A)   Notwithstanding subsection (1), the amount of tax charged under that subsection shall not in any case exceed the amount which would have been chargeable had the standard rate been charged on the total income (as reduced under section 42(2) and (5)) or, as the case may be, the joint total income.

(2)   Any property tax, any salaries tax and any profits tax paid under the provisions of Parts II, III and IV respectively shall, where the relevant amounts on which such taxes were calculated are included in the total income of the person who paid the tax, be set off for the purposes of collection against the tax charged under this Part on that person.

(2A)   *(Repealed)*

(2B)   Any tax chargeable on a husband and wife under subsection (1)(b) in any year of assessment shall be apportioned between them so that each spouse shall, in respect of that year, be charged such proportion of the tax as the total income of that spouse (as reduced under section 42(2) and (5)) bears to joint total income of the husband and wife:

Provided that where an additional assessment is issued under section 60, the whole of the tax payable shall be charged on the individual assessed in respect of that income under Part II, III or IV.

(2C)   *(Repealed)*

(3)   Where the aggregate of the taxes which may be set off under subsection (2) exceeds the amount of tax charged under this Part, the Commissioner shall, on receipt of a claim from the person charged in the specified form and on being satisfied that the claim is in order, refund such excess to that person.

43A.   *(Repealed)*

PART VIII - Double Taxation Relief

44.   (Repealed)

Relief in respect of Commonwealth income tax

45.(1) If any person resident in Hong Kong who has paid, by deduction or otherwise, or is liable to pay, tax under this Ordinance for any year of assessment on any part of his income, proves to the satisfaction of the Commissioner that he has paid, by deduction or otherwise, or is liable to pay, Commonwealth income tax for that year in respect of the same part of his income, he shall be entitled to relief from tax in Hong Kong paid or payable by him on that part of his income at a rate thereon to be determined as follows-

> *(a)*   if the Commonwealth rate of tax does not exceed one-half of the rate of tax appropriate to his case under this Ordinance in Hong Kong the rate at which relief is to be given shall be the Commonwealth rate of tax;

> *(b)*   in any other case the rate at which relief is to be given shall be half the rate of tax appropriate to his case under this Ordinance.

(2)   If any person not resident in Hong Kong who has paid, by deduction or otherwise, or is liable to pay, tax under this Ordinance for any year of assessment on any part of his income proves to the satisfaction of the Commissioner that he has paid, by deduction or otherwise, or is liable to pay Commonwealth income tax for that year of assessment in respect of the same part of his income, he shall be entitled to relief from tax paid or payable by him under this Ordinance on that part of his income at a rate thereon to be determined as follows-

> *(a)*   if the Commonwealth rate of tax appropriate to his case does not exceed the rate of tax appropriate to his case under this Ordinance, the rate at which relief is to be given shall be one-half of the Commonwealth rate of tax;

> *(b)*   if the Commonwealth rate of tax appropriate to his case exceeds the rate of tax appropriate to his case under this Ordinance, the rate at which relief is to be given shall be equal to the amount by which the rate of tax appropriate to his case under this Ordinance exceeds one-half of the Commonwealth tax.

(3)   For the purposes of this section, Commonwealth income tax means any income tax charged under any law in force in any part of the Commonwealth (other than the United Kingdom or Hong Kong) if the legislature of that part or place has provided for relief in respect of tax charged on income both in that part or place and Hong Kong in a manner similar to that provided in this section.

(4)   For the purpose of this section the expression "rate of tax" when applied to tax paid or payable under this Ordinance means the rate determined by dividing the amount of the tax paid or payable for the year (before the deduction of the relief granted under this section) by the amount of the income in respect of which the tax paid or payable under this Ordinance has been charged for that year and the Commonwealth rate of tax shall be computed in a similar manner.

(5) Where a person is for any year of assessment resident both in Hong Kong and in a part or place in which Commonwealth income tax is charged, he shall for the purposes of this section be deemed to be resident where during that year he resides for the longer period.

(6) The expression "income" in this section shall mean income or profits.

Official secrecy

46. Where, under any law in force in any part of the Commonwealth provision is made for the allowance of relief from income tax in respect of the payment of tax under this Ordinance, the obligation as to secrecy imposed by section 4 of this Ordinance shall not prevent the disclosure to the authorized officers of the government in that part of the Commonwealth of such facts as may be necessary to enable the proper relief to be given in cases where relief is claimed from tax under this Ordinance or from income tax in that part or place aforesaid.

47-48. (*Repealed*)

Double taxation arrangements

49.(1) If the Governor in Council by order declares that arrangements specified in the order have been made with the Government of any territory outside Hong Kong with a view to affording relief from double taxation in relation to income tax and any tax of a similar character imposed by the laws of that territory, and that it is expedient that those arrangements should have effect, the arrangements shall have effect in relation to tax under this Ordinance notwithstanding anything in any enactment.

(2) (*Repealed*)

(3) On the making of an order under this section with respect to arrangements relating to any territory forming part of the Commonwealth (other than the United Kingdom or Hong Kong), section 45 shall cease to have effect as respects that territory except in so far as the arrangements otherwise provide.

(4) Any order made under this section may be revoked by a subsequent order.

(5) Where any arrangements have effect by virtue of this section, the obligation as to secrecy imposed by section 4 shall not prevent the disclosure to any authorized officer of the government with which the arrangements are made of such information as is required to be disclosed under the arrangements.

(6) The Governor in Council may make rules for carrying out the provisions of any arrangements having effect under this section.

Tax credits

50.(1) The provisions of this section shall have effect where, under arrangements having effect under section 49, tax payable in respect of any income in the territory with the Government of which the arrangements are made is to be allowed as a credit against tax payable in respect of that income in Hong Kong; and in this section the expression "foreign tax" means any tax payable in that territory which under the arrangements is to be so allowed and the expression "tax" means tax chargeable under this Ordinance.

(2) The amount of the tax chargeable in respect of the income shall be reduced by the amount of the credit:

Provided that credit shall not be allowed against tax for any year of assessment unless the person entitled to the income is resident in Hong Kong for that year.

(3) The credit shall not exceed the amount which would be produced by computing the amount of the income in accordance with the provisions of this Ordinance and then charging it to tax at a rate ascertained by dividing the tax chargeable (before allowance of credit under any arrangements having effect under section 49) on the total income of the person entitled to the income by the amount of his total income.

(4) Without prejudice to the provisions of subsection (3), the total credit to be allowed to a person for any year of assessment for foreign tax under all arrangements having effect under section 49 shall not exceed the total tax payable by him for that year of assessment.

(5) In computing the amount of the income-

> *(a)* no deduction shall be allowed in respect of foreign tax (whether in respect of the same or any other income);

> *(b)* where the tax chargeable depends on the amount received in Hong Kong, the said amount shall be increased by the appropriate amount of the foreign tax in respect of the income;

> *(c)* where the income includes a dividend and under the arrangements foreign tax not chargeable directly or by deduction in respect of dividend is to be taken into account in considering whether any, and if so what, credit is to be given against tax in respect of the dividend the amount of the income shall be increased by the amount of the foreign tax not so chargeable which falls to be taken into account in computing the amount of the credit,

but notwithstanding anything in the preceding provisions of this subsection a deduction shall be allowed of any amount by which the foreign tax in respect of the income exceeds the credit therefor.

(6) Subsection (5)(a) and (b) (but not the remainder thereof) shall apply to the computation of total income for the purposes of determining the rate mentioned in subsection (3), and shall apply thereto in relation to all income in the case of which credit falls to be given for foreign tax under arrangements for the time being in force under section 49.

(7) Where-

(a)   the arrangements provide, in relation to dividends of some classes, but not in relation to dividends of other classes, that foreign tax not chargeable directly or by deduction in respect of dividends is to be taken into account in considering whether any, and if so what, credit is to be given against tax in respect of the dividends; and

(b)   a dividend is paid which is not of a class in relation to which the arrangements so provide,

then, if the dividend is paid to a company which controls, directly or indirectly not less than one-half of the voting power in the company paying the dividend, credit shall be allowed as if the dividend were a dividend of a class in relation to which the arrangements so provide.

(8) Credit shall not be allowed under the arrangements against tax chargeable in respect of the income of any person for any year of assessment if he elects that credits shall not be allowed in the case of his income for that year.

(9) Any claim for an allowance by way of credit shall be made not later than 2 years after the end of the year of assessment, and in the event of any dispute as to the amount allowable the claim shall be subject to objection and appeal in like manner as an assessment.

(10)   Where the amount of a credit given under the arrangement is rendered excessive or insufficient by reason of any adjustment of the amount of any tax payable either in Hong Kong or elsewhere, nothing in this Ordinance limiting the time for the making of assessments or claims for relief shall apply to any assessment or claim to which the adjustment gives rise, being an assessment or claim made not later than 2 years from the time when all such assessments, adjustments and other determinations have been made, whether in Hong Kong or elsewhere, as are material in determining whether any and if so what credit falls to be given.

PART IX - Returns, Etc.

Returns and information to be furnished

51.(1) An assessor may give notice in writing to any person requiring him within a reasonable time stated in such notice to furnish any return which may be specified by the Board of Inland Revenue for-

> *(a)*   property tax, salaries tax or profits tax; or

> *(b)*   property tax, salaries tax and profits tax,

under Parts II, III, IV, XA, XB and XC, containing such particulars and in such form as may be specified by the Board of Inland Revenue.

(2) Every person chargeable to tax for any year of assessment shall inform the Commissioner in writing that he is so chargeable not later than 4 months after the end of the basis period for that year of assessment unless he has already been required to furnish a return under the provisions of subsection (1).

(2A) An assessor shall give notice to any individual who has elected to be personally assessed under Part VII requiring that individual within a reasonable time stated in the notice to furnish a return in the specified form of his total income assessable under this Ordinance.

(2B)   Where a notice is required to be given under subsection (2A) to an individual who is married and not living apart from his or her spouse-

> *(a)*   such notice shall be given to both that individual and his or her spouse; and

> *(b)*   they shall be required to furnish a return of their joint total income assessable under this Ordinance.

(2C)   For the purposes of this section, compliance by a person, and his or her spouse when they have jointly elected to be personally assessed, with the requirements of a notice issued under subsection (1) shall be deemed to be compliance with the requirements of a notice issued under subsection (2A) or (2B).

(3) An assessor may give notice in writing to any person when and as often as he thinks necessary requiring him within a reasonable time stated in such notice to furnish fuller or further returns respecting any matter of which a return is required or prescribed by this Ordinance.

(4) For the purposes of obtaining full information in regard to any matter which may affect any liability, responsibility or obligation of any person under this Ordinance-

> *(a)*   an assessor or an inspector may give notice in writing to such person, or to any other person whom he considers may be in possession of information or

documents in regard to any such matter as aforesaid, requiring him within such reasonable time as is stated in the notice to furnish all information in his possession respecting any such matter, and to produce for examination any deeds, plans, instruments, books, accounts, trade lists, stock lists, vouchers, bank statements or other documents which the assessor or inspector giving the notice considers are or may be relevant for the purpose aforesaid:

Provided that in the case of a notice under this paragraph requiring the production of any account kept by a solicitor and relating to the affairs of any client or clients of his, production of a copy of all relevant entries therein respecting any matter upon which information is sought shall be a sufficient compliance with the aforesaid requirement of the notice if the copy is certified by the solicitor as being a correct copy of all relevant entries in such account respecting the matter aforesaid;

> *(b)* an assistant commissioner may give notice in writing to such person, or to such other person, requiring him, at a time and place to be named by the assistant commissioner, to attend and be examined, and upon such examination to answer truthfully all questions put to him, respecting any such matter as aforesaid.

(4A) For the avoidance of doubt it is hereby declared that the powers conferred by subsection (4) include the power to require information from, and to require the attendance for the purpose of being examined of,-

> *(a)* any person, or any employee of any person, who was a party to any particular land or property transaction;

> *(b)* any person, or any employee of any person, who has acted for or is acting for any party to any particular land or property transaction;

> *(c)* any person who either paid or received, directly or indirectly, any consideration, brokerage, commission or fee in respect of or in connection with any particular land or property transaction; and

> *(d)* any person, or any employee of any person, who was concerned in the passing of any consideration, brokerage, commission or fee, or in the clearing or collection of any cheque or other instrument of exchange, respecting any particular land or property transaction,

as to any of the following matters, that is to say-

> **(i)** the full names (including aliases) and addresses of any of the persons referred to in paragraphs (a) to (d) and any other information in his possession which may be helpful in identifying or locating any such persons;

    (ii)   any consideration, brokerage, commission or fee paid or received in respect of or in connection with any such land or property transaction; and

    (iii)   the terms and conditions of any such land or property transaction,

and the existence in respect of any communication, whether oral or written, of privilege from disclosure shall not constitute any excuse for the non-disclosure of information as to any of the matters specified in paragraphs (i) to (iii) where disclosure thereof is required from any of the persons referred to in paragraphs (a) to (d), but except as aforesaid nothing in subsection (4) shall require disclosure by counsel or solicitor of any privileged information or communication given or made to him in that capacity.

(4B)   *(a)*   Any person who without reasonable excuse, the burden of proof whereof shall lie upon him, fails to comply with the requirements of a notice given to him under subsection (4)(a) or fails to attend in answer to a notice issued under subsection (4)(b) or having attended fails to answer any questions put to him, being questions which under that paragraph may be put to him, shall be liable to a penalty of $5,000 recoverable under section 75 as a civil debt due to the crown:

    Provided that-

    (i)   the Commissioner may compound any such penalty and may before judgment in proceedings therefor stay or compound such proceedings, or may refuse to accept payment of such penalty or any part thereof except under a judgment of the court in proceedings for the recovery thereof;

    (ii)   the court before which any proceedings for such penalty are brought may, if it thinks fit, give judgment for a less amount.

    (b)   In addition to giving judgment for the penalty or any less amount as aforesaid, the court may order the person against whom the proceedings were brought to do, within a time specified in the order, the act which he has failed to do.

(5) A return, statement, or form purporting to be furnished under this Ordinance by or on behalf of any person shall for all purposes be deemed to have been furnished by that person or by his authority, as the case may be, unless the contrary is proved, and any person signing any such return, statement, or form shall be deemed to be cognizant of all matters therein.

(6) Any person who ceases to carry on any trade, profession or business or who ceases to own any source of income or to be the owner of any land or buildings or land and buildings in respect of which tax is chargeable under the provisions of Part II, III, IV or VII shall so inform the Commissioner in writing within 1 month of such cessation.

(7) Any person chargeable to tax under Part III, IV or VII who is about to leave Hong Kong for any period exceeding 1 month shall give notice in writing to the Commissioner of his expected date of departure, and if he intends to return to Hong Kong the approximate date of his return. Such notice shall be given not later than 1 month before the expected date of departure:

Provided that-

(a)   the Commissioner may accept such shorter notice as he may deem reasonable; and

(b)   this subsection shall not apply in the case of an individual who is required in the course of his employment, business or profession to leave Hong Kong at frequent intervals.

(8) Any person chargeable to tax under Part II, III, IV or VII who changes his address shall within 1 month inform the Commissioner in writing of the particulars of the change.

(9)   *(Repealed)*

Power to require statement of assets and liabilities, etc.

51A.(1) Where the Commissioner or the deputy commissioner is personally of the opinion that a person has made an incorrect return or supplied false information having the effect of understating his income or profits chargeable to tax and has done so without reasonable excuse and not through an innocent oversight or omission, the Commissioner may, with the consent of the Board of Review, give notice in writing to such person requiring him to furnish within the time limited by such notice, not being less than 30 days from the date of service of the notice, a statement containing particulars of-

(a)   all assets which the person or his spouse possessed in Hong Kong, including any possessed jointly or severally with any other person, at such times as may be specified in the notice; and

(b)   all liabilities to which the person or his spouse was subject in Hong Kong, including any to which he was subject jointly or severally with any other person, at such times as may be specified in the notice; and

(c)   all expenditure or disbursements from funds in Hong Kong, including remittances overseas and gifts, incurred or made by the person or his spouse during such periods as may be specified in the notice; and

(d)   all sums, including remittances, gifts and legacies received in Hong Kong by the person or his spouse during such periods as may be specified in the notice.

(2) A notice given under subsection (1) shall not specify any time or period earlier than 7 years before the commencement of the year of assessment in which it is given.

(3) An application for the consent of the Board of Review shall be made in writing by the Commissioner to the clerk of the Board and shall be accompanied by a statement of the material on the basis of which it is proposed to exercise the powers of the Commissioner or deputy commissioner under subsection (1).

(4) Upon receipt of an application under subsection (3), the Chairman of the Board of Review shall appoint 3 members from the panel of the Board of Review, one of whom shall be the Chairman or a deputy chairman, to consider the application.

(5) When the Board is considering an application, the Commissioner or his authorized representative may attend, but the person in respect of whom the application is made may not attend.

(6) Subject to subsection (7), neither in the application nor on the consideration thereof shall the identity of the person in respect of whom the application is made be revealed to the Board of Review.

(7) If the person on whom a notice under subsection (1) has been given so requests, the Commissioner shall furnish him with a certificate from the Chairman or deputy chairman of the Board of Review certifying that the Board's consent to the issue of the notice was given, and for the purpose of obtaining such a certificate the Commissioner shall reveal to the Chairman or deputy chairman the identity of that person.

(8) The decision of the Board of Review to grant or refuse consent shall be final.

Power to issue search warrant

51B.(1) If the Commissioner, or an officer of the Inland Revenue Department not below the rank of chief assessor authorized in writing by the Commissioner for the purpose (in this section referred to as the authorized officer), satisfies a magistrate, by statement made on oath,-

    (a)   that there are reasonable grounds for suspecting that a person has made an incorrect return or supplied false information having the effect of understating his income or profits chargeable to tax and has done so without reasonable excuse and not through an innocent oversight or omission; or

    (b)   that a person has failed to comply with an order of a court made under section 80(1) or (2A) directing him to comply with the requirements of a notice given to him under section 51(1) or (3),

the magistrate may by warrant authorize the Commissioner or authorized officer to exercise the following powers-

    (i)   without previous notice at any reasonable time during the day, to enter and have free access to any land, buildings, or place where he suspects there to be any books, records, accounts or documents of that person, or of any other person, which may afford evidence material in assessing the liability of the first-mentioned person for tax, and there to search for and examine any books, records, accounts or documents;

(ii) in carrying out any such search, to open or cause to be removed and opened, any article in which he suspects any books, records, accounts or documents to be contained;

(iii) to take possession of any books, records, accounts or documents of that person or that person's spouse, and to make copies of such parts of any books, records, accounts or documents of any other person, as may afford evidence material in assessing the liability of the first-mentioned person for tax;

(iv) to retain any such books, records, accounts or documents for as long as they may be reasonably required for any assessment to be made or for any proceedings under this Ordinance to be completed:

Provided that if the Commissioner or authorized officer shall retain any book, record, account or document for a period of more than 14 days, the person aggrieved may apply in writing to the Board of Review for an order directing the return thereof and the Board of Review, after hearing the applicant or his authorized representative and the Commissioner or his representative, may so order, either unconditionally or subject to any condition which the Board may consider it proper to impose.

(1A) Any officer of the Inland Revenue Department under the direction of the Commissioner or an authorized officer may assist the Commissioner or an authorized officer in the execution of a warrant issued under subsection (1) and may exercise any of the powers referred to in subsection (1)(i), (ii) and (iii).

(2) When exercising any power under subsection (1), the Commissioner or authorized officer shall produce on demand the warrant issued to him under that subsection.

(3) The person to whose affairs any books, records, accounts or documents taken possession of under subsection (1) relate shall be entitled to examine and make extracts from them at such times and under such conditions as the Commissioner may determine.

(4) Any person who obstructs or hinders the Commissioner or an authorized officer acting in the discharge of his duty under subsection (1) or an officer assisting him under subsection (1A) shall be guilty of an offence: Penalty a fine of $5,000 and imprisonment for 6 months.

Business records to be kept

51C.(1) Subject to subsection (2), every person carrying on a trade, profession or business in Hong Kong shall keep sufficient records in the English or Chinese language of his income and expenditure to enable the assessable profits of such trade, profession or business to be readily ascertained and shall retain such records for a period of not less than 7 years after the completion of the transactions, acts or operations to which they relate.

(2)   Subsection (1) shall not require the preservation of any records-

        (a)   which the Commissioner has specified need not be preserved; or

        (b)   of a corporation which has been dissolved.

Rent records to be kept

51D.(1) Subject to subsection (2), every person who is the owner of land or buildings or land and buildings situated in Hong Kong shall keep sufficient records in the English or Chinese languages of the consideration, in money or money's worth, payable or deemed to be payable to him, to his order or for his benefit on or after 1 April 1983 in respect of the right of use of that land or buildings or land and buildings to enable the assessable value of that land or buildings or land and buildings to be readily ascertained and shall retain such records for a period of not less than 7 years after the completion of the transactions, acts or operations to which they relate.

(2)   Subsection (1) shall not require the preservation of any records-

        (a)   which the Commissioner has specified need not be preserved; or

        (b)   of a corporation which has been dissolved.

Information to be furnished by officials and employers

52.(1) The Commissioner may give notice in writing to any officer in the employment of the Government or of any public body requiring him within a reasonable time stated in such notice to furnish any particulars which he may require for the purposes of this Ordinance which may be in the possession of such officer:

Provided that no such officer shall by virtue of this section be obliged to disclose any particulars as to which he is under any express statutory obligation to observe secrecy.

(2) Every person who is an employer shall, when required to do so by notice in writing given by an assessor, furnish within a reasonable time stated in such notice a return containing the names and places of residence and the full amount of the remuneration, whether in cash or otherwise, for the period specified in the notice, of-

        (a)   all persons employed by him in receipt of remuneration in excess of a minimum figure to be fixed by the assessor; and

        (b)   any other person employed by him named by the assessor.

(3) For the purposes of this section, any director of a company, or person engaged in the management of a company, shall be deemed to be a person employed by the company.

(4) Where any person who is an employer commences to employ in Hong Kong an individual who is or is likely to be chargeable to tax under Part III, or any married person, he shall give notice thereof in writing to the Commissioner not later than 3 months after the date of commencement of such employment, stating the full name and address of the individual, the date of commencement and the terms of employment.

(5) Where any person who is an employer ceases or is about to cease to employ in Hong Kong an individual who is or is likely to be chargeable to tax under Part III, or any married person, he shall give notice thereof in writing to the Commissioner not later than 1 month before such individual ceases to be employed in Hong Kong, stating the name and address of the individual and the expected date of cessation:

Provided that the Commissioner may accept such shorter notice as he may deem reasonable.

(6) The employer of any individual who is chargeable to tax under Part III and is about to leave Hong Kong for any period exceeding 1 month shall give notice in writing to the Commissioner of the expected date of departure of such individual. Such notice shall be given not later than 1 month before the expected date of departure:

Provided that-

(a) the Commissioner may accept such shorter notice as he may deem reasonable; and

(b) this subsection shall not apply in the case of an individual who is required in the course of his employment to leave Hong Kong at frequent intervals.

(7) An employer who is required by subsection (6) to give notice to the Commissioner of the expected departure of an individual shall not, in the case of an individual whom he has ceased, or is about to cease, to employ in Hong Kong, except with the consent in writing of the Commissioner or in the case of money paid to the Commissioner on the direction of the individual, make any payment of money or money's worth to or for the benefit of the individual for a period of 1 month from the date on which he gave the notice; and compliance with this subsection shall constitute a defence in any proceedings against an employer in respect of his failure to make any payment to or for the benefit of the individual during the said period.

(8) Notwithstanding anything to the contrary in subsections (4) and (5) an employer shall not be required to give notice under those subsections in respect of a married person if he has reasonable grounds for believing that neither that person nor his or her spouse are, or are likely to be, chargeable to tax under Part III.

Who may act for incapacitated or non-resident persons

53. An act or thing required by or under this Ordinance to be done by any person shall, if such person is an incapacitated or non-resident person, be deemed to be required to be done by the trustee of such incapacitated person or by the agent of such non-resident person, as the case may be.

Liability of executor of deceased taxpayer

54. The executor of a deceased person shall be chargeable with the tax for all periods prior to the date of such person's death with which the said person would be chargeable if he were alive, and shall be liable to do all such acts, matters or things as the deceased person if he were alive would be liable to do under this Ordinance:

Provided that-

> *(a)*   no proceedings, other than an assessment to additional tax under section 82A, shall be instituted against the executor under the provisions of Part XIV in respect of any act or default of the deceased person;

> *(b)*   no assessment or additional assessment, other than an assessment to additional tax under section 82A, in respect of a period prior to the date of such person's death shall be made after the expiry of 1 year from such date of death, or 1 year from the date of filing any affidavit required under the Estate Duty Ordinance (Cap. III), whichever is the later.

55.   *(Repealed)*

Precedent partner to act on behalf of partnership

56.(1) Wherever 2 or more persons in partnership act as agents, or are employers, or are persons in receipt of profits or act in any other capacity whatever, either on behalf of themselves or of any other person, the precedent partner of such partnership shall be answerable for doing all such acts, matters and things as would be required to be done under the provisions of this Ordinance by an individual acting in such capacity:

Provided that any person to whom a notice has been given under the provisions of this Ordinance as precedent partner of a partnership shall be deemed to be the precedent partner thereof unless he proves that he is not a partner in such partnership, or that some other person resident in Hong Kong is the precedent partner thereof.

(2) Where 2 or more persons who are not in partnership act jointly in any capacity mentioned in subsection (1), they shall be jointly and severally answerable for doing all such acts, matters, and things as would be required to be done under the provisions of this Ordinance by an individual acting in such capacity.

Joint owners and co-owners

56A.(1) Where 2 or more persons are joint owners or owners in common of any land or buildings or land and buildings, any of those persons appearing from any deed, conveyance, judgment or other instrument in writing registered in the Land Registry under the Land Registration Ordinance (Cap. 128) to be such an owner shall be answerable for doing all such acts, matters and things as would be required to be done under the provisions of this Ordinance by a sole owner.

(2) Nothing in subsection (1) shall relieve any person of any obligation under this Ordinance or affect any right and obligation of joint owners or owners in common as between themselves.

(3) Where any person pays property tax under subsection (1) and that person is not, apart from that subsection, liable to that tax or part of it, that person may recover from any other person that tax or part of it to which that other person, apart from that subsection, is liable under this Ordinance.

Principal officer to act on behalf of a corporation or body of persons

57.(1) The secretary, manager, any director or the liquidator of a corporation and the principal officer of a body of persons shall be answerable for doing all such acts, matters, or things as are required to be done under the provisions of this Ordinance by such corporation or body of persons.

(2) If no secretary, manager, director or liquidator of a corporation or no principal officer of a body of persons is ordinarily resident in Hong Kong, the corporation or body of persons, as the case may be, shall inform the Commissioner, and keep him so informed at all times, of the name and address of an individual ordinarily resident in Hong Kong who shall be answerable for doing all such acts, matters, or things as are required to be done under the provisions of this Ordinance by such corporation or body of persons.

Signature and service of notices

58.(1) Every notice to be given by the Commissioner, an assistant commissioner, an assessor or an inspector under this Ordinance shall bear the name of the Commissioner, assistant commissioner, assessor or inspector, as the case may be, and every such notice shall be valid if the name of the Commissioner, assistant commissioner, assessor or inspector is duly printed or signed thereon.

(2) Every notice given by virtue of this Ordinance may be served on a person either personally or by being delivered at, or sent by post to, his last known postal address, place of abode, business or employment or any place at which he is, or was during the year to which the notice relates, employed or carrying on business or the land or buildings or land and buildings in respect of which he is chargeable to tax under Part II.

(3) Any notice sent by post shall be deemed, unless the contrary is shown, to have been served on the day succeeding the day on which it would have been received in the ordinary course by post.

(4) In proving service by post it shall be sufficient to prove that the letter containing the notice was duly addressed and posted.

(5) Every name printed or signed on any notice or signed on any certificate given or issued for the purposes of this Ordinance which purports to be the name of the person authorized to give or issue the same shall be judicially noticed.

(6) If a notice given under this Part requires something to be done within a time stated in the notice, the Commissioner or, in the case of a notice given by an assessor, an assessor may by notice in writing extend the time for complying with the notice.

58A.   (*Repealed*)

PART X - Assessments

Assessor to make assessments

59.(1) Every person who is in the opinion of an assessor chargeable with tax under this Ordinance shall be assessed by him as soon as may be after the expiration of the time limited by the notice requiring him to furnish a return under section 51 (1):

Provided that the assessor may assess any person at any time if he is of opinion that such person is about to leave Hong Kong, or that for any other reason it is expedient to do so.

(1A) Notwithstanding subsection (1), where an assessor is of the opinion that an election by an individual under section 41 for personal assessment on his total income would result in a refund becoming due of the whole of the amount which be might lawfully be assessed for property tax if such amount were paid, the assessor shall not be obliged to proceed to make an assessment in respect of that tax.

(1B) Notwithstanding subsection (1),where an assessor is satisfied that-

> *(a)* an individual or his or her spouse, not being a spouse living apart from that individual, carries on (not jointly with another person) a trade, profession or business in Hong Kong and the individual is eligible to elect under section 41 for personal assessment on his total income; and

> *(b)* the assessable profits of that individual in respect of his trade, profession or business in Hong Kong for any year of assessment do not exceed the amount specified in the second column of item 1 (c) of the Fourth Schedule; and

> *(c)* the individual, and his or her spouse, not being a spouse living apart from that individual, has no income, property, or profits chargeable to tax under this Ordinance for that year of assessment, other than in respect of such trade, profession or business,

the assessor shall not be obliged to proceed to make an assessment of profits tax in respect of such assessable profits.

(1C) Notwithstanding subsection (1), where an assessor is satisfied that-

> *(a)* an individual or his or her spouse, not being a spouse living apart from that individual, carries on a trade, profession or business in Hong Kong, either solely or jointly with another person, and the individual is eligible to elect under section 41 for personal assessment on his total income; and

> *(b)* the individual, and his or her spouse, not being a spouse living apart from that individual, has no income, property or profits chargeable to tax under this Ordinance for any year of assessment, other than in respect of such trade, profession or business; and

    (c)   the assessable profits of the individual or his or her spouse, not being a spouse living apart from that individual, in respect of such trade, profession or business for such year of assessment, or his or her share of those profits if he or she is a partner in the trade, profession or business, are such that if there were an election for personal assessment under section 41 and after taking into account the allowances that would have to be deducted under Part V, no tax would be charged on either of them,

the assessor shall not be obliged to proceed to make an assessment of profits tax in respect of such assessable profits and, if he has made such an assessment, he may notwithstanding section 70, annul the assessment or in case of assessment of a partnership may reduce it insofar as it relates to the share of profits of such individual or his or her spouse.

(2) Where a person has furnished a return in accordance with the provisions of section 51 the assessor may either-

    (a)   accept the return and make an assessment accordingly; or

    (b)   if he does not accept the return, estimate the sum in respect of which such person is chargeable to tax and make an assessment accordingly or

    (c)   *(Repealed)*

(3) Where a person has not furnished a return and the assessor is of the opinion that such person is chargeable with tax, he may estimate the sum in respect of which such person is chargeable to tax and make an assessment accordingly, but such assessment shall not affect the liability of such person to a penalty by reason of his failure or neglect to deliver a return.

(4) In the case of profits from a trade or business, if accounts of such trade or business have not been kept in a satisfactory form, the assessor may assess the profits or income of such trade or business on the basis of the usual rate of net profit on the turnover of such trade or business, and the Board of Inland Revenue may prescribe the amounts of such usual rates of profits in particular classes of trade or business.

59A.   *(Repealed)*

Additional assessments

60.(1) Where it appears to an assessor that for any year of assessment any person chargeable with tax has not been assessed or has been assessed at less than the proper amount, the assessor may, within the year of assessment or within 6 years after the expiration thereof, assess such person at the amount or additional amount at which according to his judgment such person ought to have been assessed, and the provisions of this Ordinance as to notice of assessment, appeal and other proceedings shall apply to such assessment or additional assessment and to the tax charged thereunder:

Provided that-

(a)   (*Repealed*)

(b)   where the non-assessment or under-assessment of any person for any year of assessment is due to fraud or willful evasion, such assessment or additional assessment may be made at any time within 10 years after the expiration of that year of assessment.

(2) Where it appears to an assessor that the whole or part of any tax repaid to a person (otherwise than in consequence of an assessment having been determined on objection or appeal) has been repaid by mistake, whether of fact or law, the assessor may, within the year of assessment to which the repayment relates or within 6 years after the expiration thereof, assess such person in the amount of tax so repaid by mistake, and the provisions of this Ordinance as to notice of assessment, objection, appeal and other proceedings shall apply to such assessment and to the tax charged thereunder.

(3) No assessment shall be made under subsection (2) if the repayment was in fact made on the basis of, or in accordance with, the practice generally prevailing at the time when the repayment was made.

Certain transactions and dispositions to be disregarded

61. Where an assessor is of opinion that any transaction which reduces or would reduce the amount of tax payable by any person is artificial or fictitious or that any disposition is not in fact given effect to, he may disregard any such transaction or disposition and the person concerned shall be assessable accordingly.

Transactions designed to avoid liability for tax

61A.(1) This section shall apply where any transaction has been entered into or effected after the commencement of the Inland Revenue (Amendment) Ordinance 1986 (other than a transaction in pursuance of a legally enforceable obligation incurred prior to such commencement) and that transaction has, or would have had but for this section, the effect of conferring a tax benefit on a person (in this section referred to as "the relevant person"), and, having regard to-

(a)   the manner in which the transaction was entered into or carried out;

(b)   the form and substance of the transaction;

(c)   the result in relation to the operation of this Ordinance that, but for this section, would have been achieved by the transaction;

(d)   any change in the financial position of the relevant person that has resulted, will result, or may reasonably be expected to result, from the transaction;

    (e)   any change in the financial position of any person who has, or has had, any connection (whether of a business, family or other nature) with the relevant person, being a change that has resulted or may reasonably be expected to result from the transaction;

    (f)   whether the transaction has created rights or obligations which would not normally be created between persons dealing with each other at arm's length under a transaction of the kind in question; and

    (g)   the participation in the transaction of a corporation resident or carrying on business outside Hong Kong,

it would be concluded that the person, or one of the persons, who entered into or carried out the transaction, did so for the sole or dominant purpose of enabling the relevant person, either alone or in conjunction with other persons, to obtain a tax benefit.

(2) Where subsection (1) applies, the powers conferred upon an assessor under Part X shall be exercised by an assistant commissioner, and such assistant commissioner shall, without derogation from the powers which he may exercise under that Part, assess the liability to tax of the relevant person-

    (a)   as if the transaction or any part thereof had not been entered into or carried out; or

    (b)   in such other manner as the assistant commissioner considers appropriate to counteract the tax benefit which would otherwise be obtained.

(3) In this section-

"tax benefit" means the avoidance or postponement of the liability to pay tax or the reduction in the amount thereof;

"transaction" includes a transaction, operation or scheme whether or not such transaction, operation or scheme is enforceable, or intended to be enforceable, by legal proceedings.

Utilization of losses to avoid tax

61B.   Where the Commissioner is satisfied that-

    (a)   any change in the shareholding in any corporation, as a direct or indirect result of which profits have been received by or accrued to that corporation during any year of assessment, has been effected by any person after the commencement of the Inland Revenue (Amendment) Ordinance 1986; and

    (b)   the sole or dominant purpose of the change was for the purpose of utilizing any loss or any balance of any loss sustained in a trade, profession or business

carried on by the corporation, in order to avoid liability on the part of that corporation or any other person for the payment of any tax or to reduce the amount thereof,

the set off of any such loss or balance of loss against any such profits shall be disallowed.

Notice to be issued by Commissioner

62.(1) The Commissioner shall give a notice of assessment to each person who has been assessed stating the amount assessed, the amount of tax charged, and such due date for payment thereof as may be fixed by the Commissioner.

(2) *(Repealed)*

(3) Where by reason of an amendment of the law it is necessary to vary the amount of tax charged in any notice of assessment the Commissioner may give such notification as may be necessary to the person assessed in that notice of assessment, and any notification so given shall, as regards any particulars of the assessment contained in the notification which have not been included in the notice of assessment, have effect as if the notification were a notice of assessment.

Validity of assessments, etc.

63. No notice, assessment, certificate, or other proceeding purporting to be in accordance with the provisions of this Ordinance shall be quashed, or deemed to be void or voidable, for want of form, or be affected by reason of a mistake, defect, or omission therein, if the same is in substance and effect in conformity with or according to the intent and meaning of this Ordinance, and if the person assessed or intended to be assessed or affected thereby is designated therein according to common intent and understanding.

Appointment of agent in the United Kingdom

63A. For the purposes of facilitating the assessment of the income or profits of a person residing in the United Kingdom the Governor may appoint an agent in the United Kingdom who may exercise in respect of any United Kingdom resident who may apply to be dealt with through him all the powers conferred by this Ordinance on an assistant commissioner. The agent appointed under this section shall report to the Commissioner the amount of the assessable income or profits of any such person ascertained in accordance with the provisions of this Ordinance and shall forward to the Commissioner the accounts and computations upon which his assessment is based:

Provided that nothing in this section shall affect the right of objection or appeal under Part XI.

PART XA - Provisional Salaries Tax

Liability for provisional salaries tax

63B.(1) Every person who is chargeable to salaries tax under Part III in respect of any year of assessment shall be liable to pay provisional salaries tax in respect of that year of assessment in accordance with this Part.

(2) In the case of a husband and wife, where either the husband or wife is assessed to salaries tax under section 10(3) on the aggregate of their net chargeable incomes in respect of the year of assessment preceding that in respect of which provisional salaries tax is payable-

> *(a)* such provisional salaries tax shall be payable on the net chargeable income adjusted as necessary under section 63C(1); and

> *(b)* the person who is assessed to salaries tax in respect of that preceding year of assessment shall be solely liable to pay that provisional salaries tax.

Amount of provisional salaries tax

63C.(1) Subject to subsections (2) and (3), provisional salaries tax in respect of any year of assessment shall be payable at the rates specified in Schedule 2 for that year of assessment by reference to the amount of the net chargeable income for the preceding year of assessment adjusted, for the purposes of this section, as follows-

> *(a)* any loss set off under section 12A in calculating the net assessable income, or net assessable incomes, on which that net chargeable income is based, shall be added;

> *(b)* any loss which may be set off under section 12A in the year of assessment shall be set off against that amount:

Provided that-

> **(i)** in respect of the year of assessment up to and including the year of assessment commencing on 1 April 1984, in no case shall the amount of provisional salaries tax charged on any person under this subsection exceed the amount which would have been chargeable on him had the standard rate for the year of assessment been charged on the whole of his assessable income for the preceding year of assessment as reduced by the outgoings, expenses and allowances provided for in section 12(1) and any excess set off under section 12A; and

> **(ii)** in respect of the year of assessment commencing on 1 April 1985 and subsequent years of assessment, in no case shall the amount of provisional

salaries tax charged under this subsection exceed the amount which would have been chargeable had the standard rate been charged on the whole of-

(A)   the net assessable income for the preceding year of assessment as reduced by approved charitable donations provided for under section 12BA; or

(B)   in the case of a husband and wife to whom section 63B(2) applies, the aggregate of their net assessable incomes for the preceding year of assessment as reduced by approved charitable donations provided for under section 12BA.

(1A)   *(Repealed)*

(2) If a person commences to derive income from a source on a day within any year of assessment, an assessor may estimate the sum in respect of which provisional salaries tax is payable in that year and the succeeding year of assessment.

(3) If a person ceases to derive income from a source within any year of assessment an assessor may estimate the sum in respect of which provisional salaries tax is payable for that year of assessment and for the year preceding that year of assessment.

(4) If a person is liable to pay provisional salaries tax, an assessor shall, as soon as may be after the expiration of the time limited by the notice requiring that person to furnish a return under section 51(1), assess or estimate the amount of the provisional salaries tax which he is liable to pay.

(5) Notwithstanding subsection (4), an assessor may assess or estimate the amount of provisional salaries tax which any person is liable to pay if he is of the opinion that the person is about to leave Hong Kong or that for any other reason it is expedient to do so.

(6) When an assessor has assessed or estimated the amount of provisional salaries tax which a person is liable to pay, the Commissioner shall give a notice to that person stating the amount of provisional salaries tax to be paid, and such due date for payment thereof as may be fixed by the Commissioner.

(6A)   Where in any year of assessment a notice for payment of provisional salaries tax has been given under subsection (6) and thereafter any rate specified in Schedule 2, or any allowance provided for in Part V, for that year of assessment is amended, the amount of provisional salaries tax stated in the notice shall nevertheless be payable.

(7) For the purposes of Part XII, provisional salaries tax shall be deemed to be a tax charged under the provisions of this Ordinance and a notice under subsection (6) shall be deemed to be a notice of assessment.

Demands for provisional salaries tax

63D.(1) In any year of assessment, a notice for payment of provisional salaries tax may be-

> *(a)*   given separately to any person liable to pay provisional salaries tax; or

> *(b)*   included in a notice of assessment to salaries tax.

(2)(*Repealed*)

Holding over of payment of provisional salaries tax

63E.(1) Where in relation to any year of assessment a person is liable to pay provisional salaries tax, he may, by notice in writing lodged with the Commissioner not later than-

> *(a)*   28 days before the day by which the provisional salaries tax is to be paid; or

> *(b)*   14 days after the date of the notice for payment of provisional salaries tax under section 63C(6),

whichever is the later, apply to the Commissioner on any of the grounds specified in subsection (2) to have the payment of the whole or part of such tax held over until he is required to pay salaries tax for that year of assessment or, in the case of an application on the ground set out in subsection (2)(d), until-

> **(i)**   the determination of the objection or settlement thereof under section 64(3); or

> **(ii)**   he is required to pay salaries tax for that year of assessment,

whichever is the sooner.

(2)   The grounds referred to in subsection (1) are-

> *(a)*   that the person assessed to provisional salaries tax has become entitled during the year of assessment to an allowance under Part V, which allowance was not taken into account in the ascertainment of his net chargeable income for the year preceding the year of assessment or in estimating the sum in respect of which such person is liable to pay provisional salaries tax;

> *(b)*   that the net chargeable income during the year of assessment of the person assessed to provisional salaries tax is, or is likely to be, less than 90% of the net chargeable income for the year preceding the year of assessment or of the estimated sum in respect of which such person is liable to pay provisional salaries tax;

> *(c)* that the person assessed to provisional salaries tax has ceased, or will before the end of the year of assessment cease, to derive income chargeable to salaries tax; or
>
> *(d)* that the person assessed to provisional salaries tax has objected under section 64 to his assessment to salaries tax for the year preceding the year of assessment.

(3) On receipt of an application under subsection (1), the Commissioner shall consider the same and may hold over the payment of the whole or part of the provisional salaries tax.

(4) The Commissioner shall, by notice in writing, inform the person applying under subsection (1) of his decision.

(5) *(Repealed)*

Provisional salaries tax to be applied against salaries tax

63F.(1) When any person had paid provisional salaries tax in respect of any year of assessment, the Commissioner shall, not later than when he gives notice of assessment of salaries tax, apply the amount of provisional salaries tax so paid in payment first of-

> *(a)* the salaries tax payable by that person for that year of assessment; then
>
> *(b)* the provisional salaries tax payable in respect of the year of assessment succeeding that year of assessment,

and shall refund to the person paying the provisional salaries tax the amount of the provisional salaries tax not so applied.

(2) *Repealed)*

PART XB - Provisional Profits Tax

Liability for provisional profits tax

63G. Every person who is chargeable to profits tax under Part IV in respect of the year of assessment commencing on 1 April 1975 or any succeeding year of assessment shall be liable to pay provisional profits tax in respect of that year of assessment in accordance with this Part.

Amount of provisional profits tax

63H.(1) Subject to subsections (1A), (2), (3) and (4), provisional profits tax in respect of any year of assessment shall be payable at the standard rate by reference to the amount of assessable profits for the year preceding the year of assessment, but after the set off of any loss available for set off in the year of assessment under section 19 or 19C.

(1A) In the case of-

    (a)   a corporation; and

    (b)   a corporation ("relevant corporation") to which a share of the assessable profits of a partnership is apportioned under section 22A and is charged in the partnership name under section 22,

provisional profits tax shall be charged on the assessable profits of that corporation, or on that share of the assessable profits of that relevant corporation, as the case may be, at the rate specified in Schedule 8.

(2) In calculating any assessable profits for a year preceding a year of assessment for the purposes of computing provisional profits tax under subsection (1), there shall be disregarded any loss available for set off in that year.

(3) Where the amount of assessable profits of a person for the year preceding the year of assessment was calculated on a basis period of more or less than 1 year, an assessor may estimate the sum in respect of which such person is liable to pay provisional profits tax in that year of assessment.

(4) If a person commences to carry on a trade, profession or business in Hong Kong on a day within a year of assessment commencing on or after 1 April 1974, an assessor may estimate the sum in respect of which such person is liable to pay provisional profits tax in that year and the succeeding year of assessment.

(5) If a person is liable to pay provisional profits tax, an assessor shall, as soon as may be after the expiration of the time limited by the notice requiring that person to furnish a return under section 51(1), assess or estimate the amount of provisional profits tax which he is liable to pay.

(6) Notwithstanding subsection (5), an assessor may assess or estimate the amount of provisional profits tax which any person is liable to pay if he is of the opinion that the person is about to leave Hong Kong or that for any other reason it is expedient to do so.

(7) When an assessor has assessed or estimated the amount of provisional profits tax which a person is liable to pay, the Commissioner shall give a notice to that person stating the amount of provisional profits tax to be paid, and such due date for payment thereof as may be fixed by the Commissioner.

(7A) Where in any year of assessment a notice for payment of provisional profits tax has been given under subsection (7) and thereafter the rate of provisional tax for that year of assessment is amended, the amount of provisional profits tax stated in the notice shall nevertheless be payable.

(8) For the purposes of Part XII, provisional profits tax shall be deemed to be a tax charged under this Ordinance and a notice under subsection (7) shall be deemed to be a notice of assessment.

Demands for provisional profits tax

63I.   In any year of assessment, a notice for payment of provisional profits tax may be-

> *(a)*   given separately to the person liable to pay that provisional profits tax; or

> *(b)*   included in a notice of assessment to profits tax.

Holding over of payment of provisional profits tax

63J.(1) Where in relation to any year of assessment a person is liable to pay provisional profits tax, he may, by notice in writing lodged with the Commissioner not later than-

> *(a)*   28 days before the day by which the provisional profits tax is to be paid; or

> *(b)*   14 days after the date of the notice for payment of provisional profits tax under section 63H(7),

whichever is the later, apply to the Commissioner on any of the grounds specified in subsection (2) to have the payment of the whole or part of such tax held over until he is required to pay profits tax for that year of assessment or, in the case of an application on the ground set out in subsection (2)(e), until-

> **(i)**   the determination of the objection or settlement thereof under section 64(3); or

> **(ii)**   he is required to pay profits tax for that year of assessment,

whichever is the sooner.

(2) The grounds referred to in subsection (1) are-

> *(a)*   that the assessable profits for the year of assessment of the person assessed to provisional profits tax are, or are likely to be, less than 90% of the assessable profits for the year preceding the year of assessment or of the estimated sum in respect of which the person is liable to pay provisional profits tax;

> *(b)*   that the amount of any loss brought forward for set off to that year of assessment under section 19 or 19C has been omitted or is incorrect;

> *(c)*   that the person assessed to provisional profits tax has ceased, or will before the end of the year of assessment cease, to carry on his trade, profession or

business and that the assessable profits to be assessed under section 18D for that year of assessment are, or are likely to be, less than the assessable profits for the year preceding the year of assessment or of the estimated sum in respect of which the person is liable to pay provisional profits tax;

(d) that the person assessed to provisional profits tax has elected or is deemed to have elected to be personally assessed under Part VII for that year of assessment and that such personal assessment is likely to reduce his liability to tax; or

(e) that the person assessed to provisional profits tax has objected under section 64 to his assessment to profits tax for the year preceding the year of assessment.

(3) On receipt of an application under subsection (1), the Commissioner shall consider the same and may hold over the payment of the whole or part of the provisional profits tax.

(4) The Commissioner shall, by notice in writing, inform the person applying under subsection (1) of his decision.

Provisional profits tax to be applied against profits tax

63K. When any person has paid provisional profits tax in respect of any year of assessment, the Commissioner shall, not later than when he gives notice of assessment of profits tax, apply the amount of provisional profits tax so paid in payment first of-

(a) the profits tax payable by that person for that year of assessment; then

(b) the provisional profits tax payable in respect of the year of assessment succeeding that year of assessment,

and shall refund to the person paying the provisional profits tax the amount thereof not so applied.

PART XC - Provisional Property Tax

Liability for provisional property tax

63L.   Every person who is chargeable to property tax under Part II in respect of any year of assessment commencing on or after 1 April 1983 shall be liable to pay provisional property tax in respect of that year of assessment in accordance with this Part.

Amount of provisional property tax

63M.(1) Provisional property tax in respect of any year of assessment shall be payable at the standard rate on the net assessable value of land or buildings or land and buildings for the year preceding the year of assessment.

(2) Where the amount of assessable value of land or buildings or land and buildings for the year preceding the year of assessment was calculated in respect of a period of less than one year, an assessor may estimate the assessable value in respect of which provisional property tax is payable.

(3) Where a person becomes chargeable to property tax during a year of assessment, an assessor may estimate the assessable value in respect of which provisional property tax is payable in that year and the succeeding year of assessment.

(4) Where a person is liable to pay provisional property tax, an assessor shall, as soon as may be after expiration of the time limited by the notice requiring that person to furnish a return under section 51(1), assess or estimate the amount of provisional property tax which he is liable to pay.

(5) Notwithstanding subsection (4), an assessor may assess or estimate the amount of provisional property tax which any person is liable to pay if he is of the opinion that the person is about to leave Hong Kong or that for any other reason it is expedient to do so.

(6) When an assessor has assessed or estimated the amount of provisional property tax which a person is liable to pay, the Commissioner shall give a notice to that person stating the amount of provisional property tax to be paid, and such due date for payment thereof as may be fixed by the Commissioner.

(7) Where in any year of assessment a notice for payment of provisional property tax has been given under subsection (6) and thereafter the allowance mentioned in section 5(1A) or the rate of provisional property tax for that year of assessment is amended, the amount of provisional property tax stated in the notice shall nevertheless be payable.

(8) For the purposes of Part XII, provisional property tax shall be deemed to be a tax charged under this Ordinance and a notice under subsection (7) shall be deemed to be a notice of assessment.

Demands for provisional property tax

63N.   In any year of assessment, a notice for payment of provisional property tax may be-

> *(a)*   given separately to the person liable to pay that provisional property tax; or

> *(b)*   included in a notice of assessment to property tax.

Holding over of payment of provisional property tax

63O.(1) Where in relation to any year of assessment a person is liable to pay provisional property tax, he may, by notice in writing lodged with the Commissioner not later than-

> *(a)*   28 days before the day by which the provisional property tax is to be paid; or

> *(b)*   14 days after the date of the notice for payment of provisional property tax under section 63M(6),

whichever is the later, apply to the Commissioner on any of the grounds specified in subsection (2) to have the payment of the whole or part of such tax held over until he is required to pay property tax for that year of assessment or, in the case of an application on the ground set out in subsection (2)(d), until-

> **(i)**   the determination of the objection or settlement thereof under section 64(3); or

> **(ii)**   he is required to pay property tax for that year of assessment,

whichever is the sooner.

(2) The grounds referred to in subsection (1) are-

> *(a)*   that the assessable value for the year of assessment is, or is likely to be, less than 90% of the assessable value for the year preceding the year of assessment or of the estimated assessable value in respect of which the person is liable to pay provisional property tax;

> *(b)*   that the person assessed to provisional property tax has ceased, or will before the end of the year of assessment cease, to be an owner of land or buildings or land and buildings and that the assessable value for the year of assessment is, or is likely to be, less than the assessable value for the year preceding the year of assessment or the estimated sum in respect of which the person is liable to pay provisional property tax;

> *(c)*   that the person assessed to provisional property tax has elected or is deemed to have elected to be personally assessed under Part VII for that year of

assessment and that such personal assessment is likely to reduce his liability to tax; or

(d)   that the person assessed to provisional property tax has objected under section 64 to his assessment to property tax for the year preceding the year of assessment.

(3) On receipt of an application under subsection (1), the Commissioner shall consider the same and may hold over the payment of the whole or part of the provisional property tax.

(4) The Commissioner shall, by notice in writing, inform the person applying under subsection (1) of his decision.

Provisional property tax to be applied against property tax

63P.   When any person has paid provisional property tax in respect of any year of assessment, the Commissioner shall, not later than when he gives notice of assessment of property tax, apply the amount of provisional property tax so paid in payment first of-

(a)   the property tax payable by that person for that year of assessment; then

(b)   the provisional property tax payable in respect of the year of assessment succeeding that year of assessment,

and shall refund to the person paying the provisional property tax the amount thereof not so applied.

PART XI - Objections And Appeals

Objections

64.(1) Any person aggrieved by an assessment made under this Ordinance may, by notice in writing to the Commissioner, object to the assessment; but no such notice shall be valid unless it states precisely the grounds of objection to the assessment and, in the case of an assessment other than a provisional assessment, is received by the Commissioner within 1 month after the date of the notice of assessment:

Provided that-

(a)   if the Commissioner is satisfied that owing to absence from Hong Kong, sickness or other reasonable cause, the person objecting to the assessment was prevented from giving such notice within such period, the Commissioner shall extend the period as may be reasonable in the circumstances;

(b)   where any assessment objected to has been made under section 59(3) in the absence of any return required under section 51, no notice of objection against such assessment shall be valid unless, in addition to such notice being valid in accordance with the foregoing provisions of this subsection, the return required as aforesaid has been made within the period provided by this subsection for objecting to the assessment or within such further period as the Commissioner may approve for the making of such return;

(c)   where the assessment is a reassessment of the tax due from a person having the effect of either increasing or reducing that person's liability to tax, the person so reassessed shall have no further right of objection than he would have had if the reassessment had not been made except to the extent to which, by reason of the reassessment, a fresh liability in respect of any particular is imposed on him or an existing liability in respect of any particular is increased or reduced.

(1A)   For the purposes of subsection (1), where a person chargeable to tax is assessed under section 59(2)(b) or 60(1) in circumstances that, if the person had no other income, property or profits chargeable to tax under this Ordinance, the assessment would have been made under section 59(3)-

(a)   the provisions of proviso (b) to subsection (1) shall apply to any objection made against that assessment to the extent to which that person has failed to comply with section 51; and

(b)   no notice of objection against such assessment shall be valid unless and until that person has complied with section 51.

(2) On receipt of a valid notice of objection under subsection (1) the Commissioner shall consider

the same and within a reasonable time may confirm, reduce, increase or annul the assessment objected to, and for the purpose of discharging his functions under this subsection may, by notice in writing, require the person giving the notice of objection to furnish such particulars as the Commissioner may deem necessary with respect to the matters which are the subject of the assessment and to produce all books or other documents in his custody or under his control relating to such matters, and may summon any person who in his opinion is able to give evidence respecting the assessment to attend before him and may examine such person on oath or otherwise. Where the Commissioner proposes to examine any person on oath under this subsection, he shall, by prior notice in writing, afford a reasonable opportunity to the person giving the notice of objection or his authorized representative to be present at such examination.

(3) In the event of the Commissioner agreeing with any person assessed, who has validly objected to an assessment made upon him, as to the amount at which such person is liable to be assessed, any necessary adjustment of the assessment shall be made.

(4) In the event of the Commissioner failing to agree with any person assessed, who has validly objected to an assessment made upon him, as to the amount at which such person is liable to be assessed, the Commissioner shall, within 1 month after his determination of the objection, transmit in writing to the person objecting to the assessment his determination together with the reasons therefor and a statement of the facts upon which the determination was arrived at, and such person may appeal therefrom to the Board of Review as provided in section 66.

(5) The Commissioner shall for the purpose of this section have the powers granted under section 4(1)(d), (e), (f) and (g) of the Commissions of Inquiry Ordinance (Cap. 86), subject to the provisions of section 80 of this Ordinance.

(6) Any person, other than the person giving the notice of objection or his authorized representative, may be allowed by the Commissioner any reasonable expenses necessarily incurred by him in attending before the Commissioner under subsection (2).

(7) No objection by a person to a personal assessment on his total income under Part VII shall-

> *(a)* extend the time for making any objection under any other provision of this Ordinance;

> *(b)* make valid any objection which is otherwise invalid; or

> *(c)* authorize the revision of any amount which has been included in the total income of an individual pursuant to the provisions of section 42(1), where such amount has been the subject of, or formed a part of, any assessment made under Part II, III or IV which has become final and conclusive under section 70:

> Provided that nothing in this paragraph shall operate to prevent an objection by an individual on the grounds that an amount included in the calculation

under section 42 of his total income as a share of the assessable profits or losses of a partnership has not been ascertained in accordance with section 22A.

(8) Where an individual makes an objection in the circumstances described in the proviso to subsection (7)(c), such objection shall be deemed to be an objection by all the partners as to the share of assessable profits or losses ascertained under section 22A and any determination or agreement made under this section as to such Ascertainment shall be binding on all the partners.

(9) For the purposes of subsection (1) where a person is chargeable to salaries tax under section 10(3)(a), the spouse of that person shall have, subject to this subsection, the same right to object as has the person assessed, but any such objection shall be limited to the manner in which the assessable income or net assessable income of such spouse is to be determined, the entitlement of such spouse to any allowance under Part V or other matters to which that spouse could have objected had that spouse been the person so chargeable.

(10)   Where an objection to which subsection (9) applies is made-

> *(a)*   the powers of the Commissioner under subsection (2) shall include the power to annul such assessment and make an assessment against the person objecting;

> *(b)*   subsection (3) shall not apply but-

>> **(i)**   where the Commissioner agrees with both the spouse who has objected and his or her spouse as to the amount at which either of them is liable to be assessed, any necessary adjustment of the assessment shall be made; and

>> **(ii)**   where the Commissioner fails to come to any such agreement as is referred to in subparagraph (i), such agreement shall be deemed to be a failure to agree for the purposes of subsection (4), and the reference in that subsection to the person objecting shall be construed as a reference to the person objecting under paragraph (a) and his or her spouse, with the consequence that either or both of them may appeal to the Board of Review.

Constitution of the Board of Review

65.(1) For the purpose of hearing appeals in the manner hereinafter provided, there shall be a panel for a Board of Review consisting of a chairman and 10 deputy chairmen, who shall be persons with legal training and experience, and not more than 150 other members, all of whom shall be appointed from time to time by the Governor. The members of the panel shall hold office for a term of 3 years but shall be eligible for reappointment.

(2) There shall be a clerk to the Board of Review (hereinafter referred to as the Board) who shall be appointed by the Governor.

(3) (*Repealed*)

(4) 3 or more members of the panel, one of whom shall always be either the chairman or a deputy chairman, shall be nominated by the Chief Secretary and summoned by the clerk to attend meetings of the Board at which appeals are to be heard. At any such a meeting a quorum shall consist of 3 members. All matters coming before the Board shall be decided by a majority of votes and in the case of an equality of votes the chairman or deputy chairman shall have a second or casting vote.

(5) At the request of the Chief Secretary, the clerk to the Board shall summon a meeting of the Board consisting of all the members of the panel available in Hong Kong. At such a meeting a quorum shall consist of 5 members.

(6) The remuneration, if any, of the chairman, deputy chairmen and other members of the Board and the clerk to the Board shall be determined by the Governor.

(7) Where a person ceases to be chairman, a deputy chairman or a member of the panel and, at the time of that event, the person is involved in the hearing of an appeal by the Board, that person may continue to hear and determine that appeal.

Right of appeal to the Board of Review

66.(1) Any person (hereinafter referred to as the appellant) who has validly objected to an assessment but with whom the Commissioner in considering the objection has failed to agree may within-

> *(a)*   1 month after the transmission to him under section 64(4) of the Commissioner's written determination together with the reasons therefor and the statement of facts; or

> *(b)*   such further period as the Board may allow under subsection (1A),

either himself or by his authorized representative give notice of appeal to the Board; but no such notice shall be entertained unless it is given in writing to the clerk to the Board and is accompanied by a copy of the commissioner's written determination together with a copy of the reasons therefor and of the statement of facts and a statement of the grounds of appeal.

(1A)   If the Board is satisfied that an appellant was prevented by illness or absence from Hong Kong or other reasonable cause from giving notice of appeal in accordance with subsection (1)(a), the Board may extend for such period as it thinks fit the time within which notice of appeal may be given under subsection (1). This subsection shall apply to an appeal relating to any assessment in respect of which notice of assessment is given on or after 1 April 1971.

(2) The appellant shall at the same time as he gives notice of appeal to the Board serve on the Commissioner a copy of such notice and of the statement of the grounds of appeal.

(3) Save with the consent of the Board and on such terms as the Board may determine, an appellant may not at the hearing of his appeal rely on any grounds of appeal other than the grounds contained in his statement of grounds of appeal given in accordance with subsection (1).

Transfer of appeals under section 66 for hearing and determination by High Court instead of Board of Review

67.(1) Where notice of appeal is given to the Board under section 66, the appellant or the Commissioner may give notice in writing in accordance with this section that he desires the appeal to be transferred to the High Court:

Provided that if both the appellant and the Commissioner give such notice, the notice given by the Commissioner shall have no effect and shall be deemed not to have been given.

(2) A notice under subsection (1) shall, if given by the appellant, be given to the Commissioner, or, if given by the Commissioner, be given to the appellant, not later than 21 days after the date on which the notice of appeal is received by the clerk to the Board, and the person giving such notice shall at the same time send a copy thereof to the Board.

(3) If the person to whom notice is given under subsection (1) consents thereto, he shall, not later than 21 days after the date on which the notice is given, notify his consent in writing to the Board and serve a copy of such notification on the person giving the notice, and on receipt of such notification by the Board the clerk to the Board shall transmit the notice of appeal to the High Court together with the documents delivered to the Board under this section and section 66(1) in connection with the appeal.

(4) An appeal in respect of which notice of appeal is transmitted to the High Court under subsection (3) shall be heard and determined by the High Court as in all respects an appeal to the High Court against the determination to which the notice of appeal relates.

(5) The following provisions shall apply in relation to the hearing of an appeal under this section-

> *(a)*   the High Court shall give 14 clear days' notice to the appellant and the Commissioner of the date fixed for the hearing of the appeal, and may adjourn the hearing to any other date as the High Court may deem fit;

> *(b)*   the Commissioner shall be entitled to appear and be heard at the hearing of the appeal;

> *(c)*   save with the leave of the High Court and on such terms as to costs or otherwise as the High Court may order, the appellant shall not at the hearing of the appeal rely on any grounds of appeal other than the grounds contained in his statement of grounds of appeal given with the notice of appeal under section 66(1);

> *(d)* the onus of proving that the assessment appealed against is excessive or incorrect shall be on the appellant;
>
> *(e)* the High Court may summon any person appearing to the High Court to be able to give evidence respecting the appeal to attend at the hearing of the appeal and may examine any such person as a witness on oath or otherwise.

(6) An appeal in respect of which notice of appeal is transmitted to the High Court under subsection (3) shall not be withdrawn without the leave of the High Court and except on such terms as to costs or otherwise as the High Court may order.

(7) In determining an appeal under this section, the High Court may-

> *(a)* confirm, reduce, increase or annul the assessment determined by the Commissioner;
>
> *(b)* make any assessment which the Commissioner was empowered to make at the time he determined the assessment, or direct the Commissioner to make such an assessment, in which case an assessment shall be made by the Commissioner so as to conform to that direction;
>
> *(c)* make such order as to costs as the High Court may deem fit.

Hearing and disposal of appeals to the Board of Review

68.(1) Except where a notification of consent in respect of the transfer of any appeal under section 67 is received by the Board within the time allowed in that behalf by that section, every appeal under section 66 shall be heard by the Board in accordance with this section and the clerk to the Board shall, as soon as may be after the receipt of the notice of appeal, fix a time and place for the hearing of the appeal, and shall give 14 clear days' notice thereof to the appellant and the Commissioner:

Provided that the time so fixed for the hearing of the appeal shall not be earlier than-

> *(a)* in the case of an appeal in respect of which neither party to the appeal gives notice under section 67(1), the expiration of the time allowed by that section for giving such notice; or
>
> *(b)* in the case of an appeal in respect of which notice under section 67(1) is given-
>
> > **(i)** by the appellant; or
> >
> > **(ii)** by the Commissioner but not by the appellant,

the expiration of a period of 21 days after the date on which such notice is given.

(2) Subject to subsection (2B), an appellant shall attend at the meeting of the Board at which the appeal is heard in person or by an authorized representative.

(2A) At any time before the hearing of an appeal, the appellant may withdraw the appeal by notice in writing addressed to the clerk to the Board.

(2B) If, on the date fixed for the hearing of an appeal, the appellant fails to attend at the meeting of the Board either in person or by his authorized representative the Board may-

> *(a)*   if satisfied that the appellant's failure to attend was due to sickness or other reasonable cause, postpone or adjourn the hearing for such period as it thinks fit;

> *(b)*   proceed to hear the appeal under subsection (2D); or

> *(c)*   dismiss the appeal.

(2C) If an appeal has been dismissed by the Board under subsection (2B)(c) the appellant may, within 30 days after the making of the order for dismissal by notice in writing addressed to the clerk to the Board, apply to the Board to review its order and the Board may, if satisfied that the appellant's failure to attend at the meeting of the Board for the hearing of the appeal was due to sickness or any other reasonable cause, set aside the order for dismissal and proceed to hear the appeal.

(2D) The Board may, if satisfied that an appellant will be or is outside Hong Kong on the date fixed for the hearing of the appeal and is unlikely to be in Hong Kong within such period thereafter as the Board considers reasonable on the application of the appellant made by notice in writing addressed to the clerk to the Board and received by him at least 7 days prior to the date fixed for the hearing of the appeal, proceed to hear the appeal in the absence of the appellant or his authorized representative.

(2E) The Board may, if it hears an appeal in the absence of an appellant or his authorized representative under subsection (2D), consider such written submissions as the appellant may submit to the Board.

(3) The assessor who made the assessment appealed against or some other person authorized by the Commissioner shall attend such meeting of the Board in support of the assessment.

(4) The onus of proving that the assessment appealed against is excessive or incorrect shall be on the appellant.

(5) All appeals shall be heard in camera, but any appeal may be reported in such publications as may be approved by the Attorney General in such a manner that the identity of the appellant is not disclosed.

(6) The Board shall have power to summon to attend at the hearing any person whom it may consider able to give evidence respecting the appeal and may examine him as a witness either on oath or otherwise. Any person so attending may be allowed by the Board any reasonable expenses necessarily incurred by him in so attending.

(7) At the hearing of the appeal the Board may, subject to the provisions of section 66(3), admit or reject any evidence adduced, whether oral or documentary, and the provisions of the Evidence Ordinance (Cap. 8), relating to the admissibility of evidence shall not apply.

(8)   *(a)*   After hearing the appeal, the Board shall confirm, reduce, increase or annul the assessment appealed against or may remit the case to the Commissioner with the opinion of the Board thereon.

       (b)   Where a case is so remitted by the Board, the Commissioner shall revise the assessment as the opinion of the Board may require and in accordance with such directions (if any) as the Board, at the request at any time of the Commissioner, may give concerning the revision required in order to give effect to such opinion.

(9)   Where under subsection (8), the Board does not reduce or annul such assessment, the Board may order the appellant to pay as costs of the Board a sum not exceeding $5,000, which shall be added to the tax charged and recovered therewith.

(10)   The Board shall for the purpose of this section have the powers granted under section 4(1)(d), (e), (f) and (g) of the Commissions of Inquiry Ordinance (Cap. 86), subject to the provisions of section 80 of this Ordinance.

Appeals to the High Court

69.(1)   The decision of the Board shall be final:

Provided that either the appellant or the Commissioner may make an application requiring the Board to state a case on a question of law for the opinion of the High Court. Such application shall not be entertained unless it is made in writing and delivered to the clerk to the Board, together with a fee of $640, within 1 month of the date of the Board's decision. If the decision of the Board shall be notified to the Commissioner or to the appellant in writing, the date of the decision, for the purposes of determining the period within which either of such persons may require a case to be stated, shall be the date of the communication by which the decision is notified to him.

(2) The stated case shall set forth the facts and the decision of the Board, and the party requiring it shall transmit the case, when stated and signed, to the High Court within 14 days after receiving the same.

(3) At or before the time when he transmits the stated case to the High Court, the party requiring it shall send to the other party notice in writing of the fact that the case has been stated on his application and shall supply him with a copy of the stated case.

(4) Any judge of the High Court may cause a stated case to be sent back for amendment and thereupon the case shall be amended accordingly.

(5) Any judge of the High Court shall hear and determine any question of law arising on the stated case and may in accordance with the decision of the court upon such question confirm, reduce, increase or annul the assessment determined by the Board, or may remit the case to the Board with the opinion of the court thereon. Where a case is so remitted by the court, the Board shall revise the assessment as the opinion of the court may require.

(6) In any proceedings before the High Court under this section, the court may make such order in regard to costs in the High Court and in regard to the sum paid under subsection (1) as to the court may seem fit.

(7) Appeals from decisions of the High Court under this section shall be governed by the provisions of the Supreme Court Ordinance (Cap. 4), the Rules of the Supreme Court (Cap. 4 sub. leg.), and the Orders and Rules governing appeals to the Privy Council.

Right to appeal directly to Court of Appeal against decision of Board of Review

69A.(1) Notwithstanding section 69, the appellant or the Commissioner may, with the leave of the Court of Appeal granted on the application of the appellant or the Commissioner, as the case may be, appeal directly to the Court of Appeal against the decision of the Board.

(2) Leave to appeal under this section may be granted on the ground that in the opinion of the Court of Appeal it is desirable that, by reason of the amount of tax in dispute or of the general or public importance of the matter or its extraordinary difficulty or for any other reason, the appeal be heard and determined by the Court of Appeal instead of the High Court.

(3) Section 69 shall apply in relation to appeals under this section as it applies in relation to appeals under that section except that for references in that section to the High Court or a judge of the High Court there shall be substituted references to the Court of Appeal.

Assessments or amended assessments to be final

70.　　Where no valid objection or appeal has been lodged within the time limited by this Part against an assessment as regards the amount of the assessable income or profits or net assessable value assessed thereby, or where an appeal against an assessment has been withdrawn under section 68(2A) or dismissed under subsection (2B) of that section, or where the amount of the assessable income or profits or net assessable value has been agreed to under section 64(3), or where the amount of such assessable income or profits or net assessable value has been determined on objection or appeal, the assessment as made or agreed to or determined on objection or appeal, as the case may be, shall be final and conclusive for all purposes of this Ordinance as regards the amount of such assessable income or profits or net assessable value:

Provided that nothing in this Part shall prevent an assessor from making an assessment or additional assessment for any year of assessment which does not involve re-opening any matter which has been determined on objection or appeal for the year.

Powers of assessor to correct errors

70A.(1) Notwithstanding the provisions of section 70, if, upon application made within 6 years after the end of a year of assessment or within 6 months after the date on which the relative notice of assessment was served, whichever is the later, it is established to the satisfaction of an assessor that the tax charged for that year of assessment is excessive by reason of an error or omission in any return or statement submitted in respect thereof, or by reason of any arithmetical error or omission in the calculation of the amount of the net assessable value (within the meaning of section 5(1A)), assessable income or profits assessed or in the amount of the tax charged, the assessor shall correct such assessment:

Provided that under this section no correction shall be made to any assessment in respect of an error or omission in any return or statement submitted in respect thereof as to the basis on which the liability to tax ought to have been computed where the return or statement was in fact made on the basis of or in accordance with the practice generally prevailing at the time when the return or statement was made.

(2) Where an assessor refuses to correct an assessment in accordance with an application under this section he shall give notice thereof in writing to the person who made such application and such person shall thereupon have the same rights of objection and appeal under this Part as if such notice of refusal were a notice of assessment.

Husband and wife

70B. Where, following an election under section 41(1A) for personal assessment by a husband and wife, either spouse makes an objection, appeal or application under this Part in respect of any assessment made in consequence of the election-

> *(a)*   the other spouse shall be deemed to be joined in the objection, appeal or application;

> *(b)*   nothing in section 70 shall prevent a re-assessment being made in respect of either spouse; and

> *(c)*   amended assessments may be issued to both spouses.

PART XII - Payment And Recovery Of Tax

Provisions regarding payment of tax

71.(1) Tax charged under the provisions of this Ordinance shall be paid in the manner directed in the notice of assessment on or before a date specified in such notice. Any tax not so paid shall be deemed to be in default, and the person by whom such tax is payable, or where any tax is payable by more than one person or by a partnership then each of such persons or each partner in the partnership, shall be deemed to be a defaulter for the purposes of this Ordinance.

(2) Tax shall be paid notwithstanding any notice of objection or appeal, unless the Commissioner orders that payment of tax or any part thereof be held over pending the result of such objection or appeal:

Provided that where the Commissioner so orders he may do so conditionally upon the person who or on whose behalf the objection or appeal is made providing security for the payment of the amount of tax or any part thereof the payment of which is held over either-

> *(a)* by purchasing a certificate issued under the Tax Reserve Certificates Ordinance (Cap. 289); or

> *(b)* by furnishing a banker's undertaking,

as the Commissioner may require.

(3) Where the Commissioner is of opinion either that the tax or any part thereof held over under subsection (2) is likely to become irrecoverable, or that the person objecting or appealing is unreasonably delaying the prosecution of his objection or appeal, he may cancel any order made under that subsection and make such fresh order as the case may appear to him to require.

(4) Where, upon the final determination of an objection or appeal under Part XI, or upon any order made by the Commissioner, any tax which has been held over under subsection (2) becomes payable or the tax charged is increased, the Commissioner shall give to the person objecting or appealing a notice in writing fixing a date on or before which any tax or balance of tax shall be paid. Any tax not so paid shall be deemed to be in default.

(5) Where any tax is in default, the Commissioner may in his discretion order that a sum or sums not exceeding 5% in all of the amount in default shall be added to the tax and recovered therewith.

(5A) Where on the expiry of a period of 6 months from the date when any tax is deemed to be in default, whether such date was before or after I August 1984, there remains unpaid any amount of the aggregate of-

> *(a)* the tax deemed to be in default; and

> *(b)* any sum added thereto under subsection (5),

the Commissioner may order that a sum or sums not exceeding 10% in all of the unpaid amount shall be added to the unpaid amount and recovered therewith.

(5B) Any amount charged by the Commissioner prior to 1 August 1984 in the purported exercise of his powers under subsection (5A) by way of surcharge upon the unpaid amount of any sum added to tax under subsection (5) shall, notwithstanding that the tax was not in default at the time of making such charge, be deemed to have been validly charged and to be recoverable as if the tax had been in default at the time of making such charge.

(6) Notwithstanding anything contained in the previous subsections of this section the Commissioner may agree to accept payment of tax by instalments.

(7) Where the Commissioner exercises his powers under the proviso to subsection (2) and a person is required to purchase a certificate under paragraph (a) of that proviso-

> *(a)*   a certificate in an amount equal to the tax or any part thereof the payment of which is held over shall be purchased within a period of 14 days from the date of the order of the Commissioner, or on or before the date for the payment of tax specified in the notice of the assessment, whichever is the later, failing which the provisions of subsection (2) shall apply as they would if there had been no order;

> *(b)*   the Commissioner shall, when he issues a certificate so purchased, note on it particulars sufficient to identify the objection or appeal to which it relates;

> *(c)*   upon the withdrawal or final determination of the objection or appeal a certificate or part of a certificate so purchased shall be accepted by the Commissioner in payment of so much of the tax held over as becomes or is found to become payable, and no interest shall be payable upon any certificate or part of a certificate so accepted;

> *(d)*   where, upon the final determination of the objection or appeal, and after all tax held over which becomes, or is found to be, payable has been paid in the manner specified in paragraph (c), any certificate or part of a certificate so purchased has not been accepted as payment by the Commissioner under paragraph (c), the holder thereof may surrender that certificate or part to the Commissioner and-

>> **(i)**   if 36 months or less since the date of purchase of the certificate has elapsed, at his option require the Commissioner to-

>>> **(A)**   issue a new certificate in the place of the old certificate or part of the old certificate bearing the same date of issue and rate of interest as that old certificate; or
>>> **(B)**   repay the principal value represented by the certificate or part

together with the interest thereon at the rate prescribed by the rules from the date of issue of the certificate to the date of the final determination of the objection or appeal; or

(ii) if more than 36 months since the date of purchase of the certificate has elapsed, the Commissioner shall repay to the holder the principal value represented by the certificate or part together with interest thereon, at the rate prescribed by the rules, from the date of issue of the certificate to the date of the final determination of the objection or appeal; and

(e) no certificate so purchased shall be valid for any purpose except as specified in the preceding paragraphs.

(8) The provisions of subsection (7) shall apply notwithstanding anything to the contrary in the rules relating to such certificates made under the Tax Reserve Certificates Ordinance (Cap. 289) and any reference to the rules relating to such in that subsection shall refer to the rules so made.

(9) Where the Commissioner exercises his powers under the proviso to subsection (2) and a person is required to furnish a banker's undertaking under paragraph (b) of that proviso, the undertaking shall-

(a) be in a form acceptable to the Commissioner;

(b) be furnished to the Commissioner within a period of 14 days from the date of the order of the Commissioner, or on or before the date for the payment of the tax specified in the notice of assessment, whichever is the later;

(c) be given by a bank (as defined in the Banking Ordinance (Cap. 155));

(d) not be revocable without the consent of the Commissioner;

(e) be expressed to be an undertaking to pay-

(i) an amount equal to the tax or any part thereof the payment of which is held over; and

(ii) interest on that amount, from the date for the payment of the tax specified in the notice of assessment to the date of withdrawal or final determination of the objection or appeal, at the rate specified in subsection (11); and

(f) provide for payment to the Commissioner upon written notification to the bank by the Commissioner that the objection or appeal has been withdrawn or finally determined and that the amount, and interest, stated by him is now due,

and if such person fails to supply such an undertaking in such manner the provisions of subsection (2) shall apply as they would if there had been no order.

(10) Where the Commissioner makes an order under subsection (2) but does not exercise his powers under the proviso thereto, interest shall be payable on so much of the amount of the tax or any part thereof the payment of which is held over as becomes payable or is found to become payable upon the withdrawal or final determination of the objection or appeal, from the date for the payment of the tax specified in the notice of assessment or the date of the order, whichever is the later, to the date of withdrawal or final determination of the objection or appeal, at the rate specified in subsection (11).

(11) The rate of interest specified for the purposes of subsections (9)(e)(ii) and (10) shall be the rate fixed by the Chief Justice by notice in the Gazette under section 50 of the District Court Ordinance (Cap. 336).

Tax to include fines, etc.

72. In the succeeding sections of this Part, "tax" includes any sum or sums added under section 71(5) or (5A) by reason of default, together with any fines, penalties, fees, or costs incurred, and any interest payable under section 71(9)(e)(ii) or (10).

73-74. (*Repealed*)

Tax recoverable as a civil debt through the District Court

75.(1) Tax due and payable under this Ordinance shall be recoverable as a civil debt due to the Crown.

(2) Whenever any person makes default in payment of tax the Commissioner may recover the same by action in the District Court notwithstanding that the amount is in excess of the sum mentioned in section 33 of the District Court Ordinance (Cap.336).

(3) In proceedings under this section for the recovery of tax the production of a certificate signed by the Commissioner stating the name and last known postal address of the defaulter and particulars of the tax due by him shall be sufficient evidence of the amount so due and sufficient authority for a District Court to give judgment for the said amount.

(4) In proceedings under this section for the recovery of tax the court shall not entertain any plea that the tax is excessive, incorrect, subject to objection or under appeal, but nothing in this subsection shall be construed so as to derogate from the powers conferred by the proviso to section 51(4B)(a) to give judgment for a less sum in the case of proceedings for the penalty specified therein.

(5) In any proceedings in the District Court under this section, the Commissioner may appear in person or may be represented either by a legal officer within the meaning of the Legal Officers Ordinance (Cap. 87) or by any other person authorized by him in writing.

75A. (*Repealed*)

Recovery of tax from a debtor of the taxpayer

76.(1) Where tax payable by a person is in default, or a person charged to tax has quieted Hong Kong or in the opinion of the Commissioner is likely to quit Hong Kong without paying all the tax charged to him, and it appears to the Commissioner to be probable that any other person (hereinafter in this subsection referred to as "the third party")

> (*a*)   owes or is about to pay money to such person (hereinafter in this subsection referred to as "the taxpayer"); or

> (*b*)   holds money for or on account of the taxpayer; or

> (*c*)   holds money on account of some other person for payment to the taxpayer; or

> (*d*)   has authority from some other person to pay money to the taxpayer,

the Commissioner may give the third party notice in writing (a copy of which shall be sent by post to the taxpayer) requiring him to pay such moneys not exceeding the amount of tax in default or charged, as the case may be, to the officer named in the notice. The notice shall apply to all such moneys which are in the third party's hands or due from him or about to be paid by him at the date of receipt of such notice or which come into his hands or become due from him or about to be paid by him at any time within a period of 30 days thereafter.

(2) Any person who has made any payment in pursuance of this section shall be deemed to have acted under the authority of the person by whom the tax was payable or on whom it was charged and of all other persons concerned, and is hereby indemnified in respect of such payment against all proceedings civil or criminal notwithstanding the provisions of any written law, contract or agreement.

(3) Any person to whom notice has been given under subsection (1) who is unable to comply therewith shall within 14 days of the expiration of the period of 30 days from the date of receipt of such notice give notice in writing to the Commissioner acquainting him with the facts.

(4) Any person to whom a notice has been given under subsection (1) who could have complied therewith but failed to do so within 14 days after the expiration of the period referred to in subsection (1), shall be personally liable for the whole of the tax which he was required to pay, and such tax may be recovered from him by all means provided in this Ordinance for the recovery of tax from a person who has made default in payment.

Recovery of tax from persons leaving Hong Kong

77.(1) If the Commissioner, or an officer of the Inland Revenue Department not below the rank of chief assessor authorized in writing by the Commissioner for the purpose ("authorized officer"), satisfies a District Judge, by statement made on oath-

> *(a)*   that a person has not paid all tax assessed upon him; and

> *(b)*   that there are reasonable grounds for believing that the person intends to depart, or has departed, from Hong Kong to reside elsewhere,

and if the District Judge is satisfied that it is in the public interest to ensure that the person does not depart from Hong Kong or, if he returns, does not depart again, without first paying the tax or furnishing security to the satisfaction of the Commissioner for payment of that tax, he shall issue a direction ("departure prevention direction") to the Director of Immigration and the Commissioner of Police directing them to prevent the person from departing from Hong Kong without paying such tax or furnishing such security.

(2) The District Judge shall, as soon as practicable after he makes a departure prevention direction under subsection (1), cause a copy of it to be served upon the person who is the subject of the direction, if he can be found, but, whether or not a copy is so served, the direction comes into force immediately upon being issued and continues in force until-

> *(a)*   the tax is paid;

> *(b)*   security is furnished to the satisfaction of the Commissioner for payment of the tax; or

> *(c)*   the departure prevention direction is set aside by the High Court under subsection (9).

(3) Where-

> *(a)*   an immigration officer or immigration assistant (within the meaning of section 2(1) of the Immigration Ordinance (Cap. 115)); or

> *(b)*   a police officer,

believes on reasonable grounds that-

> **(i)**   a person the subject of a departure prevention direction made under subsection (1) is about to depart from Hong Kong; and

> **(ii)**   the Commissioner has not authorized the person to depart from Hong Kong nor has the High Court suspended or otherwise varied the departure prevention direction so as to permit the person to depart from Hong Kong,

172

he may take such measures including the use of such force as may be necessary to prevent the departure of that person from Hong Kong.

(4) Where-

    (a) a copy of a departure prevention direction has been served on the person the subject of it or the person has been verbally advised of its existence by a person referred to in subsection (3)(a) or (b); and

    (b) the Commissioner has not authorized the person to depart from Hong Kong nor has the High Court suspended or otherwise varied the departure prevention direction so as to permit the person to depart from Hong Kong,

the person commits an offence if he departs or attempts to depart from Hong Kong, and an immigration officer, immigration assistant or police officer may arrest him without a warrant.

(5) Any person who commits an offence under subsection (4) is liable to a fine of $20,000 and to imprisonment for 6 months.

(6) Where a departure prevention direction made under this section is in force, the Commissioner may, if he thinks fit, on the written application of the person the subject of the direction or, in the absence of any such application, of his own initiative, authorize, in writing, the person to depart from Hong Kong on one or more occasions as specified in the authorization.

(7) Where-

    (a) the tax owing has been paid or security has been furnished to the satisfaction of the Commissioner for payment thereof;

    (b) a departure prevention direction is set aside or temporarily suspended under this section; or

    (c) the Commissioner authorizes a person to depart from Hong Kong on one or more occasions,

the Commissioner shall, as soon as practicable, notify-

    (i) the Director of Immigration; and

    (ii) the Commissioner of Police,

that the person is permitted to depart from Hong Kong.

(8) Where a person the subject of a departure prevention direction applies under subsection (6) and the Commissioner does not see fit to authorize his departure, the Commissioner shall, as soon as practicable, serve a notice ("notice of decision") upon the person.

(9) A person aggrieved by a departure prevention direction under subsection (1) or a notice of decision under subsection (8), as the case may be, may appeal to the High Court which may-

    (a)   make an order setting aside the departure prevention direction subject to such conditions as the Court may consider necessary, including the supplying of security to the Commissioner as specified by the Court;

    (b)   make an order temporarily suspending or otherwise varying the departure prevention direction, and the Court may attach such conditions to the suspension or variation as it considers necessary; or

    (c)   dismiss the appeal.

(10)   Service of-

    (a)   a copy of a departure prevention direction under subsection (2) shall be effected personally on the person who is the subject of it;

    (b)   a notice of decision under subsection (8) may be effected personally on the person who is the subject of it or by post addressed to that person at his last known place of abode, business or employment.

(11) Where a direction was issued by a District Judge under section 77 as repealed by the Inland Revenue (Amendment) (No. 3) Ordinance 1993, that direction shall be deemed to be a departure prevention direction issued under this section and the provisions of this section shall apply to it accordingly.

(12) In this section, "High Court" has the same meaning as in section 2 of the Supreme Court Ordinance (Cap. 4) and includes the Registrar and a Master as defined in that Ordinance.

(13) In proceedings under this section, the production of a certificate signed by the Commissioner or an authorized officer stating the name and last known postal address of the person referred to in subsection (1) and particulars of the unpaid tax assessed upon him shall be sufficient evidence of the amount and a court shall not entertain any plea that the tax is excessive, incorrect, subject to objection or under appeal.

(14) The Commissioner or an authorized officer may apply ex parte to the District Court for a departure prevention direction.

(15) In any proceedings in the District Court under this section, the Commissioner or an authorized officer, as the case may be, may appear in person or may be represented either by a legal officer within the meaning of the Legal Officers Ordinance (Cap. 87) or by any other person authorized in writing by the Commissioner.

Refusal of clearance to ships and aircraft where tax is in default

77A.(1) In addition to any other powers of collection and recovery provided by this Ordinance, where a person has been charged to tax in respect of his profits from the business of shipowner or charterer or aircraft owner or charterer and such tax is in default and whether such person has been assessed directly or in the name of some other person, the Commissioner, with the prior approval of the Chief Secretary, may issue to the Director of Marine, the Director of Civil Aviation or other authority by whom clearance may be granted, a certificate containing the name or names of the said person and the particulars of the tax in default.

(2) On receipt of such certificate the Director of Marine, the Director of Civil Aviation, or other authority, shall be empowered and is hereby required to refuse clearance from any port, aerodrome or airport or place within Hong Kong to any ship or aircraft owned wholly or partly or chartered by such person until the said tax has been paid or until security for payment has been given to the satisfaction of the Commissioner.

(3) No civil or criminal proceedings shall be instituted or maintained against the Crown, the Chief Secretary, the Commissioner, the Director of Marine, the Director of Civil Aviation or other authority, in respect of a refusal of clearance under this section, nor shall the fact that a ship or aircraft is detained under this section affect the liability of the owner, charterer or agent to harbour, airport or other dues and charges for the period of detention.

78. *(Repealed)*

PART XIII - Repayment

Tax paid in excess to be refunded

79.(1) If it is proved to the satisfaction of the Commissioner by claim duly made in writing within 6 years of the end of a year of assessment or within 6 months after the date on which the relevant notice of assessment was served, whichever is the later, that any person has paid tax in excess of the amount with which he was properly chargeable for the year, such person shall be entitled to have refunded the amount so paid in excess:

Provided that nothing in this section shall operate to extend or reduce any time limit for objection, appeal or repayment specified in any other section or to validate any objection or appeal which is otherwise invalid, or to authorize the revision of any assessment or other matter which has become final and conclusive.

(2) An executor, trustee or receiver shall have the same right to make a claim under the provisions of subsection (1) as the person whom he represents would have had if such person had not been prevented from making such claim by his death, incapacity, bankruptcy or liquidation and shall be entitled to have refunded to him for the benefit of such person or such person's estate any tax paid in excess within the meaning of subsection (1).

(3) Where a non-resident person has been assessed in the name of another person under section 20A or 20B and the tax so assessed has been paid by the other person, the other person or the non-resident person, but not both, may make a claim under subsection (1) for a refund of tax overpaid. In the event of a refund being made to the other person his receipt shall be a valid discharge in respect of the amount of overpaid tax so refunded.

PART XIV - Penalties And Offences

Penalties for failure to make returns, making incorrect returns, etc.

80.(1) Any person who without reasonable excuse-

> *(a)*   fails to comply with the requirements of a notice given to him under section 51(3), 51A(1), 52(1) or (2), or 64(2); or

> *(b)*   fails to attend in answer to a summons issued under section 64(2) or 68(6), or having attended fails to answer any questions put to him, being questions which, under section 64(2) or 68(6), as the case may be, may be put to him; or

> *(c)*   fails to comply with the requirements of section 5(2)(c), 51(6), (7) or (8), 51C(1), 51D(1), 52(4), (5), (6) or (7), or 76(3),

shall be guilty of an offence: Penalty a fine of $5,000, and the court may order the person convicted within a time specified in the order to do the act which he has failed to do.

(1A)   *(Repealed)*

(2)   Any person who without reasonable excuse-

> *(a)*   makes an incorrect return by omitting or understating anything in respect of which he is required by this Ordinance to make a return, either on his behalf or on behalf of another person or a partnership;

> *(b)*   makes an incorrect statement in connection with a claim for any deduction or allowance under this Ordinance;

> *(c)*   gives any incorrect information in relation to any matter or thing affecting his own liability to tax or the liability of any other person or of a partnership;

> *(d)*   fails to comply with the requirements of a notice given to him under section 51(1) or (2A); or

> *(e)*   fails to comply with section 51(2),

shall be guilty of an offence: Penalty a fine of $5,000 and a further fine of treble the amount of tax which has been undercharged in consequence of such incorrect return, statement or information, or would have been so undercharged if the return, statement or information had been accepted as correct, or which has been undercharged in consequence of the failure to comply with a notice under section 51(1) or (2A) or a failure to comply with section 51(2), or which would have been undercharged if such failure had not been detected.

(2A)   In the case of an offence under subsection (2)(d), the court may order the person convicted to comply with the requirements of the notice given to him under section 51(1) or (2A) within such time as may be specified in the order.

(2B)   Any person who does not comply with an order of the court under subsection (1) or (2A) or under section 51(4B)(b) shall be guilty of an offence: Penalty a fine of $5,000.

(3) No person shall be liable to any penalty under this section unless the complaint concerning such offence was made in the year of assessment in respect of or during which the offence was committed or within 6 years after the expiration thereof.

(4) Any person who aids, abets or incites another person to commit an offence under this section shall be deemed to have committed the same offence and to be liable to the same penalty.

(5) The Commissioner may compound any offence under this section and may before judgment stay or compound any proceedings thereunder.

80A.   *(Repealed)*

Breach of secrecy and other matters to be offences

81.   Any person who-

> *(a)*   acts under this Ordinance without taking an oath of secrecy as required by section 4(2); or

> *(b)*   acts contrary to the provisions of section 4(1) or to an oath taken under section 4(2); or

> *(c)*   aids, abets, or incites any other person to act contrary to the provisions of section 4,

shall be guilty of an offence: Penalty a fine of $50,000.

Penal provisions relating to fraud, etc.

82.(1) Any person who willfully with intent to evade or to assist any other person to evade tax-

> *(a)*   omits from a return made under this Ordinance any sum which should be included; or

> *(b)*   makes any false statement or entry in any return made under this Ordinance; or

(c)   makes any false statement in connection with a claim for any deduction or allowance under this Ordinance; or

(d)   signs any statement or return furnished under this Ordinance without reasonable grounds for believing the same to be true; or

(e)   gives any false answer whether verbally or in writing to any question or request for information asked or made in accordance with the provisions of this Ordinance; or

(f)   prepares or maintains or authorizes the preparation or maintenance of any false books of account or other records or falsifies or authorizes the falsification of any books of account or records; or

(g)   makes use of any fraud, art, or contrivance, whatsoever or authorizes the use of any such fraud, art, or contrivance,

shall be guilty of an offence: Penalty on summary conviction a fine of $5,000 and a further fine of treble the amount of tax which has been undercharged in consequence of the offence or which would have been undercharged if the offence has not been detected, and to imprisonment for 6 months, and on indictment a fine of $20,000 and a further fine of treble the amount of tax so undercharged or which would have been so undercharged and to imprisonment for 3 years.

(2) The Commissioner may compound any offence under this section and may before judgment stay or compound any proceedings thereunder.

Additional tax in certain cases

82A.(1) Any person who without reasonable excuse-

(a)   makes an incorrect return by omitting or understating anything in respect of which he is required by this Ordinance to make a return, either on his behalf or on behalf of another person or a partnership; or

(b)   makes an incorrect statement in connection with a claim for any deduction or allowance under this Ordinance; or

(c)   gives any incorrect information in relation to any matter or thing affecting his own liability to tax or the liability of any other person or of a partnership; or

(d)   fails to comply with the requirements of a notice given to him under section 51(1) or (2A); or

(e)   fails to comply with section 51(2),

shall, if no prosecution under section 80(2) or 82(1) has been instituted in respect of the same facts, be liable to be assessed under this section to additional tax of an amount not exceeding treble the amount of tax which-

    (i)   has been undercharged in consequence of such incorrect return, statement or information, or would have been so undercharged if the return, statement or information had been accepted as correct; or

    (ii)   has been undercharged in consequence of the failure to comply with a notice under section 51(1) or (2A) or a failure to comply with section 51(2), or which would have been undercharged if such failure had not been detected.

(2) Additional tax shall be payable in addition to any amount of tax payable under an assessment, or an additional assessment under section 60.

(3) An assessment of additional tax may be made only by the Commissioner personally or the deputy commissioner personally.

(4) Before making an assessment of additional tax the Commissioner or the deputy commissioner, as the case may be, shall-

    (a)   cause notice to be given to the person he proposes so to assess which shall-

        (i)   inform such person of the alleged incorrect return, incorrect statement or incorrect information or alleged failure to comply with the requirements of the notice given to him under section 51(1) or (2A) or the alleged failure to comply with section 51(2) in respect of which the Commissioner or deputy commissioner intends to assess additional tax under subsection (1);

        (ii)   include a statement that such person has the right to submit written representations to him with regard to the proposed assessment on him of additional tax;

        (iii)   specify the date, which shall not be earlier than 21 days from the date of service of the notice, by which representations which such person may wish to make under subparagraph (ii) must be received;

    (b)   consider and take into account any representations which he may receive under paragraph (a) from or on behalf of a person proposed to be assessed for additional tax.

(4A)   Notwithstanding subsection (4), if the Commissioner or deputy commissioner is of the opinion that the person he proposes to assess to additional tax under subsection (1) is about to leave Hong Kong, he need not serve a notice under subsection (4)(a), but may assess that person to additional tax under subsection (1).

(5) Notice of intention to assess additional tax and notice of an assessment to additional tax shall be given in the same manner as is provided in section 58(2) in respect of a notice of assessment under section 62.

(6) Where a person who is liable to be assessed to additional tax has died, an assessment to additional tax may be made on his executor, and the additional tax shall be recovered as a debt due from and payable out of the deceased person's estate.

(7) A person who has been assessed to additional tax under subsection (1) shall not be liable to be charged on the same facts with an offence under section 80(2) or 82(1).

Appeals against assessment to additional tax to Board of Review

82B.(1) Any person who has been assessed to additional tax under section 82A may, within 1 month after notice of assessment is given to him, give notice of appeal to the Board; but no such notice shall be entertained unless it is given in writing to the clerk to the Board and is accompanied by-

> *(a)*   a copy of the notice of assessment;

> *(b)*   a statement of the grounds of appeal from the assessment;

> *(c)*   a copy of the notice of intention to assess additional tax given under section 82A(4), if any such notice was given; and

> *(d)*   a copy of any written representations made under section 82A(4).

(2)   On an appeal against assessment to additional tax, it shall be open to the appellant to argue that-

> *(a)*   he is not liable to additional tax;

> *(b)*   the amount of additional tax assessed on him exceeds the amount for which he is liable under section 82A;

> *(c)*   the amount of additional tax, although not in excess of that for which he is liable under section 82A, is excessive having regard to the circumstances.

(3)   Sections 66(2) and (3), 68, 69 and 70 shall, so far as they are applicable, have effect with respect to appeals against additional tax as if such appeals were against assessments to tax other than additional tax.

Tax payable notwithstanding proceedings

83. The institution of proceedings for, or the imposition of, a penalty, fine, or term of imprisonment under this Part shall not relieve any person from liability to assessment or payment of any tax for which he is or may be liable.

Prosecutions, sanction of Commissioner

84.(1) No prosecution in respect of an offence under section 80 or 82 may be commenced except at the instance of or with the sanction of the Commissioner.

(2) Nothing in this section shall derogate from the powers of the Attorney General in respect of the prosecution of criminal offences.

PART XV - General

Power to make rules

85.(1) The Board of Inland Revenue may from time to time make rules generally for carrying out the provisions of this Ordinance and for the ascertainment and determination of any class of income or profits.

(2) Without prejudice to the generality of the foregoing power such rules may-

(a) prescribe the procedure to be followed on application for refunds and relief;

(b) provide for any matter which by this Ordinance is to be or may be prescribed;

(c) for the purpose of any of the provisions of this Ordinance, prescribe what is or is deemed to be included in, or excluded from, the expression "machinery or plant" and the expression "implement, utensil or article"

(3) Such rules may prescribe fines recoverable on summary conviction for any contravention thereof or failure to comply therewith not exceeding in each case a sum of $200.

(4) All such rules made by the Board of Inland Revenue shall be submitted to the Governor, and shall be subject to the approval of the Legislative Council.

Board of Inland Revenue to specify forms

86.(1) The Board of Inland Revenue may specify any forms which may be necessary for carrying this Ordinance into effect.

(2) Where a specimen of any form bears an endorsement, purporting to be signed by the secretary to the Board of Inland Revenue, to the effect that the form is specified by the Board of Inland Revenue, it shall be presumed, until the contrary is proved, that the form is a form specified by the Board of Inland Revenue under subsection (1).

General power of Governor in Council to exempt

87. The Governor in Council may by order exempt any person, office or institution from payment of the whole or any portion of any tax chargeable under this Ordinance.

87A. *(Repealed)*

Exemption of charitable bodies

88. Notwithstanding anything to the contrary in this Ordinance contained there shall be exempt and there shall be deemed always to have been exempt from tax any charitable institution or trust of a public character:

Provided that where a trade or business is carried on by any such institution or trust the profits derived from such trade or business shall be exempt and shall be deemed to have been exempt from tax only if such profits are applied solely for charitable purposes and are not expended substantially outside Hong Kong and either-

> *(a)*   the trade or business is exercised in the course of the actual carrying out of the expressed objects of such institution or trust; or

> *(b)*   the work in connection with the trade or business is mainly carried on by persons for whose benefit such institution or trust is established.

Transitional provisions

89.(1) The transitional provisions of Schedule 5 shall have effect in relation to the amendments made by the Inland Revenue (Amendment) (No. 3) Ordinance 1989.

(2) In relation to amendments made by the Inland Revenue (Amendment) (No. 2) Ordinance 1993 -

> *(a)*   it is declared that the amendments shall be without prejudice to the provisions of Part XIV; and

> *(b)*   the transitional provisions of Schedule 7 shall have effect.

(3) The transitional provisions of Schedule 9 shall have effect in relation to recognized occupational retirement schemes approved under section 87A prior to the repeal of that section by the Inland Revenue (Amendment) (No. 5) Ordinance 1993.

SCHEDULE I

[ss. 2 & 5]

STANDARD RATE

For the years of assessment 1947/48 to 1949/50 inclusive   -   10%.

For the years of assessment 1950/51 to 1965/66 inclusive   -   12 ½%.

For the years of assessment 1966/67 to 1983/84 inclusive   -   15%.

For the years of assessment 1984/85 to 1986/87 inclusive   -   17%.

For the year of assessment 1987/88   -   16½%.

For the year of assessment 1988/89   -   15½%.

For the year of assessment 1989/90 and until superseded   -   15%.

SCHEDULE 2

[ss. 13 & 43 (1)]

RATES

For the years of assessment 1947/48 to 1949/50 inclusive

Second Column   Third Column

(a)	Upon the first $5,000	¼ standard rate
(b)	Upon the next $5,000	¼ standard rate
(c)	- do -	¾ standard rate
(d)	- do -	The full standard rate
(e)	- do -	1¼ standard rate
(f)	- do -	1½ standard rate
(g)	- do -	1¾ standard rate
(h)	Upon the remainder	Twice the standard rate

Note: Where a person is liable to the appropriate tax for a part only of any year of assessment the amounts in the second column against items (a) to (g) will be reduced in the proportion which the number of days he is so liable bears to the number of days in that year of assessment.

For the years of assessment 1950/51 to 1965/66 inclusive

Second Column   Third Column

(a)	Upon the first $5,000	$^{1}/_{5}$ standard rate
(b)	Upon the next $5,000	$^{2}/_{5}$ standard rate
(c)	- do -	$^{3}/_{5}$ standard rate
(d)	- do -	$^{4}/_{5}$ standard rate
(e)	- do -	The full standard rate
(f)	- do -	$1^{1}/_{5}$ standard rate
(g)	- do -	$1^{2}/_{5}$ standard rate
(h)	- do -	$1^{3}/_{5}$ standard rate
(i)	- do -	$1^{4}/_{5}$ standard rate
(j)	Upon the remainder	Twice the standard rate

For the years of assessment 1966/67 to 1971/72 inclusive

Second Column		Third Column
(a)	Upon the first $5,000	2¾%
(b)	Upon the next $5,000	5½%
(c)	- do -	8¼%
(d)	- do -	11%
(e)	- do -	14%
(f)	- do -	17%
(g)	- do -	20%
(h)	- do -	23%
(i)	- do -	26%
(j)	Upon the remainder	30%

For the year of assessment 1972/73

Second Column		Third Column
(a)	Upon the first $5,000	2½%
(b)	Upon the next $5,000	5%
(c)	- do -	7½%
(d)	- do -	10%
(e)	- do -	12½%
(f)	- do -	15%
(g)	- do -	17½%
(h)	- do -	20%
(i)	- do -	22½%
(i)	- do -	25%
(k)	- do -	27½%
(l)	Upon the remainder	30%

For the years of assessment 1973/74 to 1977/78 inclusive

Second Column		Third Column
(a)	Upon the first $10,000	5%
(b)	Upon the next $10,000	10%
(c)	- do -	15%
(d)	- do -	20%
(e)	- do -	25%
(f)	Upon the remainder	30%

For the years of assessment 1978/79 to 1984/85 inclusive

Second Column		Third Column
(a)	Upon the first $10,000	5%
(b)	Upon the next $10,000	10%
(c)	- do -	15%
(d)	- do -	20%
(e)	Upon the remainder	25%

For the years of assessment 1985/86 to 1986/87 inclusive

Second Column		Third Column
(a)	Upon the first $10,000	5%
(b)	Upon the next $10,000	10%
(c)	- do -	15%
(d)	Upon the next $20,000	20%
(c)	Upon the remainder	25%

For the year of assessment 1987/88

Second Column		Third Column
(a)	Upon the first $10,000	5%
(b)	Upon the next $10,000	10%
(c)	Upon the next $20,000	15%

(d) Upon the next $20,000 20%
(e) Upon the remainder 25%

For the years of assessment 1988/89 and 1989/90

Second Column   Third Column

(a) Upon the first $10,000 3%
(b) Upon the next $10,000 6%
(c) - do - 9%
(d) - do - 12%
(e) - do - 15%
(f) - do - 18%
(g) - do - 21%
(h) Upon the remainder 25%

For the year of assessment 1990/91

Second Column   Third Column

(a) Upon the first $10,000 2 per cent
(b) Upon the next $10,000 4 per cent
(c) - do - 9 per cent
(d) - do - 12 per cent
(e) - do - 15 per cent
(f) - do - 18 per cent
(g) - do - 21 per cent
(h) Upon the remainder 25 per cent

For the years of assessment 1991/92 and 1992/93

Second Column   Third Column

(a)	Upon the first $20,000	2%
(b)	Upon the next $20,000	9%
(c)	Upon the next $20,000	17%
(d)	Upon the remainder	25%

For the year of assessment 1993/94

Second Column		Third Column
(a)	Upon the first $20,000	2%
(b)	Upon the next $30,000	9%
(c)	Upon the next $30,000	17%
(d)	Upon the remainder	25%

For the year of assessment 1994/95 and each year after that year

Second Column		Third Column
(a)	Upon the first $20,000	2%
(b)	Upon the next $30,000	9%
(c)	Upon the next $30,000	17%
(d)	Upon the remainder	20%

SCHEDULE 3

[s. 16(2)(b) & (6)]

PUBLIC UTILITY COMPANIES

The Hong Kong Electric Company, Limited.
China Light and Power Company, Limited.
The Hong Kong and China Gas Company, Limited.

FOURTH SCHEDULE

[s. 27(3)]

ALLOWANCES

For the year of assessment 1989/90

First Column (section)	Second Column (the prescribed amount or percentage)

1.   Section 28 (basic allowance)-

(a)	subsection (1)(a)	$32,000
(b)	subsection (1)(b), being the first reference to the prescribed amount	$ 7,000
(c)	subsection (1)(b), being the references to the prescribed amount in subparagraphs (i) and (ii)	$39,000
(d)	subsection (1)(b), being the prescribed percentage	10%

2.   Section 29 (married person's allowance)-

(a)	subsection (3)(a)	$66,000
(b)	subsection (3)(b), being the first reference to the prescribed amount	$14,000
(c)	subsection (3)(b), being the references to the prescribed amount in subparagraphs (i), (ii) and (iii)	$80,000
(d)	subsection (3)(b), being the prescribed percentage	10%

3.   Section 30 (dependent parent allowance)-

(a)	subsection (3)(a)	$11,000
(b)	subsection (3)(b)	$ 3,000
(c)	subsection (4)(a)	$ 1,200

4.   Section 31 (child allowance)-

(a)   subsection (1)

(i)	$13,000 for the first child
(ii)	$9,000 for the second child
(iii)	$3,000 for the third child
(iv)	$2,000 each for the fourth, fifth and sixth child

| | | (v) | $1,000 for each subsequent child |
| (b) | subsection (5) | | $34,000 |

5. Section 32(1) (single parent allowance) $20,000

For the year of assessment 1990/91

First Column (section)		Second Column (the prescribed amount or percentage)

1. Section 28 (basic allowance)-
   (a) subsection (1)(a) $32,000
   (b) subsection (1)(b), being the first
        reference to the prescribed amount $ 7,000
   (c) subsection (1)(b), being the references
        to the prescribed amount in subparagraphs
        (i) and (ii) $39,000
   (d) subsection (1)(b), being the prescribed
        percentage 0%

2. Section 29 (married person's allowances)
   (a) subsection (3)(a) $66,000
   (b) subsection (3)(b), being the first
        reference to the prescribed amount $14,000
   (c) subsection (3)(b), being the references
        to the prescribed amount in subparagraphs
        (i), (ii) and (iii) $80,000
   (d) subsection (3)(b), being the prescribed
        percentage 0%

3. Section 30 (dependent parent allowance)-
   (a) subsection (3)(a) $12,000
   (b) subsection (3)(b) $ 3,000
   (c) subsection (4)(a) $ 1,200

4. Section 31 (child allowance)-
   (a) subsection (1)
        (i) $14,000 for the first child
        (ii) $10,000 for the second child
        (iii) $3,000 for the third child
        (iv) $2,000 each for the fourth, fifth and sixth child
        (v) $1,000 for each subsequent child
   (b) subsection (5) $36,000

5. Section 32(1) (single parent allowance) $20,000

For the year of assessment 1991/92

First Column   Second Column
(section)   (the prescribed amount or percentage)

1.   Section 28 (basic allowance)-
        (a)   subsection (1)(a) $34,000
        (b)   subsection (1)(b), being the first
                reference to the prescribed amount $ 7,000
        (c)   subsection (1)(b), being the references
                to the prescribed amount in subparagraphs
                (i) and (ii) $41,000
        (d)   subsection (1)(b), being the prescribed
                percentage   0%

2.   Section 29 (married person's allowance)-
        (a)   subsection (3)(a) $68,000
        (b)   subsection (3)(b), being the first
                reference to the prescribed amount $14,000
        (c)   subsection (3)(b), being the references
                to the prescribed amount in subparagraphs
                (i), (ii) and (iii) $82,000
        (d)   subsection (3)(b), being the prescribed
                percentage   0%

3.   Section 30 (dependent parent allowances)
        (a)   subsection (3)(a) $12,000
        (b)   subsection (3)(b) $ 3,000
        (c)   subsection (4)(a) $ 1,200

4.   Section 31 (child allowance)-
                (a)   subsection (1)
                                (i) $14,000 for the first child
                                (ii) $10,000 for the second child
                                (iii) $3,000 for the third child
                                (iv) $2,000 each for the fourth, fifth and sixth child
                                (v) $1,000 for each subsequent child
        (b)   subsection (5) $36,000

5.   Section 32(1) (single parent allowance) $20,000

For the year of assessment 1992/93

First Column	Second Column
(section)	(the prescribed amount or percentage)

1.   Section 28 (basic allowance)-

    (a)   subsection (1)(a) $39,000

    (b)   subsection (1)(b), being the first reference to the prescribed amount $ 7,000

    (c)   subsection (1)(b), being the references to the prescribed amount in subparagraphs (i) and (ii) $46,000

    (d)   subsection (1)(b), being the prescribed percentage   0%

2.   Section 29 (married person's allowances)

    (a)   subsection (3)(a) $78,000

    (b)   subsection (3)(b), being the first reference to the prescribed amount $14,000

    (c)   subsection (3)(b), being the references to the prescribed amount in subparagraphs (i), (ii) and (iii) $92,000

    (d)   subsection (3)(b), being the prescribed percentage   0%

3.   Section 30 (dependent parent allowance)-

    (a)   subsection (3)(a) $13,500

    (b)   subsection (3)(b) $ 3,000

    (c)   subsection (4)(a) $ 1,200

4.   Section 31 (child allowance)-

    (a)   subsection (1)

        (i) $15,500 for the first child

        (ii) $11,500 for the second child

        (iii) $3,000 for the third child

        (iv) $2,000 each for the fourth, fifth and sixth child

        (v) $1,000 for each subsequent child

    (b)   subsection (5) $39,000

5.   Section 32(1) (single parent allowance) $23,000

For the year of assessment 1993/94

First Column (section)	Second Column (the prescribed amount or percentage)

1.   Section 28 (basic allowance)-

(a)	subsection (1)(a)		$ 49,000
(b)	subsection (1)(b), being the first reference to the prescribed amount		$ 7,000
(c)	subsection (1)(b), being the references to the prescribed amount in subparagraphs (i) and (ii)		$ 56,000
(d)	subsection (1)(b), being the prescribed percentage		0%

2.   Section 29 (married person's allowance)

(a)	subsection (3)(a)		$ 98,000
(b)	subsection (3)(b), being the first reference to the prescribed amount		$ 14,000
(c)	subsection (3)(b), being the references to the prescribed amount in subparagraphs (i), (ii) and (iii)		$112,000
(d)	subsection (3)(b), being the prescribed percentage		0%

3.   Section 30 (dependent parent allowance)

(a)	subsection (3)(a)	$ 17,000
(b)	subsection (3)(b)	$ 3,000
(c)	subsection (4)(a)	$ 1,200

4.   Section 31 (child allowance)-

(a)   subsection (1)

(i)	$17,000 for the first child
(ii)	$17,000 for the second child
(iii)	$3,000 for the third child
(iv)	$2,000 each for the fourth, fifth and sixth child
(v)	$1,000 for each subsequent child

(b)   subsection (5) $ 46,000

5.   Section 32(1) (single parent allowance) $ 27,000

For the year of assessment 1994/95 and each year after that year

First Column (section)	Second Column (the prescribed amount or percentage)

1.   Section 28 (basic allowance)-

    (a)   subsection (1)(a) $ 65,000

    (b)   subsection (1)(b), being the first
            reference to the prescribed amount $ 7,000

    (c)   subsection (1)(b), being the references
            to the prescribed amount in subparagraphs
            (i) and (ii) $ 72,000

    (d)   subsection (1)(b), being the prescribed
            percentage   0%

2.   Section 29 (married person's allowance)

    (a)   subsection (3)(a) $130,000

    (b)   subsection (3)(b), being the first
            reference to the prescribed amount $ 14,000

    (c)   subsection (3)(b), being the references
            to the prescribed amount in subparagraphs
            (i), (ii) and (iii) $144,000

    (d)   subsection (3)(b), being the prescribed
            percentage   0%

3.   Section 30 (dependent parent allowance)

    (a)   subsection (3)(a) $ 20,000

    (b)   subsection (3)(b) $ 3,000

    (c)   subsection (4)(a) $ 1,200

4.   Section 30A (dependent grandparent allowance)-

    (a)   subsection (3)(a) $ 20,000

    (b)   subsection (3)(b) $ 3,000

    (c)   subsection (4)(a) $ 1,200

5.   Section 31 (child allowance)-

    (a)   subsection (1)

                      (i) $20,000 for the first child

                      (ii) $20,000 for the second child

                      (iii) $3,000 for the third child

                      (iv) $2,000 each for the fourth, fifth and sixth child

                      (v) $1,000 for each subsequent child

    (b)   subsection (5) $ 52,000

6.   Section 32(1) (single parent allowance) $ 32,000

FIFTH SCHEDULE

[s. 89]

Transitional Provisions Relating To The Inland Revenue (Amendment) (No. 3) Ordinance 1989

1.　　In this Schedule

"amending Ordinance" means the Inland Revenue (Amendment) (No. 3) Ordinance 1989;

"tax" means salaries tax and tax under a personal assessment under Part VII;

"1989 tax year" means the year of assessment commencing 1 April 1989; and reference to other tax years shall be construed in an analogous manner.

2.　No assessment to tax in respect of the 1989 tax year made prior to 1 April 1990 shall be variable after 1 April 1990 by the Commissioner by reason of the amendment to the Ordinance by the amending Ordinance save under and in accordance with this Schedule and, until and unless such variation takes place, the correctness or otherwise of such assessment or anything done by the Commissioner in relation thereto shall be determined by the provisions of this Ordinance as they were at the time that the assessment was made notwithstanding the application of the amending Ordinance to the 1989 tax year.

3.　Where the person charged by an assessment to which paragraph 2 relates or his wife (not being a wife living apart from her husband) derives assessable income in respect of the 1989 tax year subsequent to the date of the assessment then, if such income if taken into account prior to the commencement of the amending Ordinance would have increased the amount payable under such assessment, nothing in Part XI shall prevent an assessor from making an assessment or additional assessment for the 1989 tax year which gives effect to the provisions of this Ordinance as amended by the amending Ordinance.

4.　Where a person has been assessed to tax by such an assessment as is described in paragraph 2 and either he or his wife (not being a wife living apart from her husband) derives assessable income in respect of the 1989 tax year prior to the date of the assessment which was not included in that assessment, then the amending Ordinance shall not apply to that income which shall be assessable to tax as if that Ordinance had not been enacted except that such income may be taken into account in the event of an assessment or additional assessment under paragraph 3.

5.　Notwithstanding the repeal of sections 13(2), 58A and 63C(1A) (the repealed provisions), where any lump sum payment to which proviso (i) to section 11D(b) relates is received on or after 1 April 1989 but before 1 April 1992 and is related back under that proviso to the 1988 tax year or any previous year of assessment on the application of the person entitled to claim, then that person and his or her spouse shall be deemed to have elected to be separately assessed in relation to any tax chargeable on such sum in accordance with section 58A as it applied prior to such repeal and the repeated provisions shall apply accordingly with the effect that, subject to those provisions, the person making the application under that provision shall be solely chargeable to tax upon that sum.

6. Where a person, not being a person to whom section 63C(1A), prior to its repeal by the amending Ordinance then applied, has been assessed to provisional salaries tax for the 1989 tax year in respect of income derived by him and his wife, then the provisional salaries tax paid in pursuance of such assessment shall be applied

> *(a)*   firstly in payment of the salaries tax payable by that person for the 1989 tax year;

> *(b)*   secondly, in payment of the provisional salaries tax payable by that person for the 1990 tax year;

> *(c)*   thirdly, in payment of the salaries tax payable by his wife for the 1989 tax year;

> *(d)*   fourthly, in payment of the provisional salaries tax payable by his wife for the 1990 tax year,

and any tax paid which cannot be so applied shall be refunded to the person paying it.

SCHEDULE 6

[s. 26A(2) & (3)]

PART I - Instruments

1. A bill of exchange within the meaning of section 3 of the Bills of Exchange Ordinance (Cap. 19).

2. A promissory note within the meaning of section 89 of the Bills of Exchange Ordinance (Cap. 19).

3. Any other instrument which evidences an obligation to pay a stated or determinable amount to bearer or to order, on or before a fixed time, with or without interest, being an instrument by the delivery of which, with or without endorsement, the right to receive that stated or determinable amount, with or without interest, is transferable.

PART II - Bodies

1.   The Asian Development Bank.

2.   The International Bank for Reconstruction and Development.

3.   The International Finance Corporation.

4.   The European Investment Bank.

5.   The European Bank for Reconstruction and Development.

6.   The Inter-American Development Bank.

7.   The Nordic Investment Bank.

8.   The European Company for the Financing of Railroad Rolling Stock.

SCHEDULE 7

[s. 89(2)]

Transitional Provisions Relating To The Inland Revenue (Amendment) (No. 2) Ordinance 1993

1. In this Schedule "amending Ordinance" means the Inland Revenue (Amendment)(No. 2) Ordinance 1993.

2. No assessment to tax in respect of the year of assessment commencing on 1 April 1993 issued prior to 1 April 1994 shall be variable by the Commissioner by reason of the amendment to the Ordinance by the amending Ordinance.

3. In respect of the year of assessment commencing on 1 April 1993, in the case where a person charged by an assessment in respect of that year owns more than one property, any provisional property tax paid for that year of assessment by reason of separate assessments for each of those properties shall be aggregated into a single sum prior to being applied in accordance with section 63P.

SCHEDULE 8

[ss. 14(2) & 63H(1A)]

Rate Of Profits Tax In Respect Of A Corporation

For the years of assessment 1992/93 and 1993/94   17½%

For the year of assessment 1994/95 and until superseded   16½%

SCHEDULE 9

[s. 89]

Transitional Provisions Relating To The Inland Revenue (Amendment) (No. 5) Ordinance 1993

1.   In this Schedule

"amending Ordinance" means the Inland Revenue (Amendment) (No. 5) Ordinance 1993;

"retirement scheme" means a retirement scheme as defined in section 2(1) prior to the commencement of section 2 of the amending Ordinance.

2.   Notwithstanding the repeal of section 87A by the amending Ordinance, where an application for approval of a retirement scheme under that section was received by the Commissioner before such repeal, the Commissioner may approve the scheme as if that section has not been repealed, and where such approval has been given the scheme shall be deemed to have been approved by the Commissioner under that section immediately prior to its repeal by the amending Ordinance.

3.   The approval given by the Commissioner to any retirement scheme under section 87A prior to its repeal by the amending Ordinance shall-

>   *(a)*   continue to be effective unless and until it is-
>
>>   **(i)**   deemed to have been withdrawn under subparagraph (b); or
>>
>>   **(ii)**   withdrawn under paragraph 4;
>
>   *(b)*   be deemed to have been withdrawn-
>
>>   **(i)**   upon the scheme becoming a recognized occupational retirement scheme other than by virtue of paragraph (a) of the definition of "recognized occupational retirement scheme" in section 2(1);
>>
>>   **(ii)**   where an application is made under section 7 or 15 of the Occupational Retirement Schemes Ordinance (Cap. 426) in respect of the scheme before the commencement of section 3 of that Ordinance but the application has not been disposed of prior to the commencement of that section, on the date on which the application is finally disposed of;
>>
>>   **(iii)**   where an application made under section 7 or 15 of the Occupational Retirement Schemes Ordinance (Cap. 426) in respect of the scheme is rejected and an appeal (if any) against such rejection is dismissed before the commencement of section 3 of that Ordinance, on that date of commencement; or

(iv) where no application for registration or exemption under the Occupational Retirement Schemes Ordinance (Cap. 426) has been made prior to the date of commencement of section 3 of that Ordinance, on that date of commencement.

4. The Commissioner may withdraw the approval given to any retirement scheme under section 87A prior to its repeal by the amending Ordinance if any term or condition of the scheme is altered unless-

(a) the alteration is made solely to secure the issue of an exemption certificate in respect of the scheme or registration of the scheme under section 7 or 18 of the Occupational Retirement Schemes Ordinance (Cap. 426); or

(b) in the case of any other alteration, the Commissioner is notified in writing of such alteration within 1 month after it is made and the scheme, as altered, complies substantially with the requirements set out in paragraph 7.

5. Where an application is made under section 7(1) or 15 of the Occupational Retirement Schemes Ordinance (Cap. 426) in respect of a retirement scheme which was approved for the time being by the Commissioner under section 87A before its repeal by the amending Ordinance, the employer who operates the scheme shall as soon as reasonably practicable after the determination of the application or appeal (if any) give a notice in writing to the Commissioner of the result of the application and, where an appeal has been made against the refusal of such application under section 19 of the Occupational Retirement Schemes Ordinance (Cap. 426), the result of such appeal.

6. Section 17(1)(j) applies to a retirement scheme as defined in section 2(1) prior to the commencement of section 2 of the amending Ordinance.

7. The requirements referred to in paragraph 4(b) are-

(a) the retirement scheme shall be exclusively for the benefit of the employee or employees and of the spouse, children, surviving dependents, or legal personal representatives of an employee;

(b) each employee concerned shall be entitled to defined benefits and the terms and conditions of the retirement scheme shall have been made known to all the employees concerned;

(c) the benefits afforded by the retirement scheme shall accrue only-

(i) on retirement from the service of the employer at some specified age of not less than 45 years; or

(ii) on retirement after some specified period of service with the employer of not less than 10 years; or

(iii)   on attaining the age of 60 years or some specified age for retirement whichever is the later; or

(iv)   on earlier incapacity or death:

Provided where, however, the retirement scheme provides for proportionate or reduced benefits in the event of an employee leaving the employer's service prior to attaining the specified age or completing the specified period of service, the provision for such benefits shall not in itself disqualify the scheme from retaining the approved status;

(d)   the nature of the benefits afforded by the retirement scheme shall be the same in relation to all the persons to whom the scheme relates but a scheme relating to more than one class of employee may be regarded as so many separate schemes for this purpose;

(e)   where the retirement scheme is conducted by a third party to whom the employer makes periodical contributions, the diversion of such contributions to any purposes (Other than those of the scheme) and the refund of such contributions to the employer shall, except with the consent of the Commissioner and subject to subparagraph (f), be prohibited;

(f)   the employer shall have no lien on any sum or other benefit to which the employee would be entitled under the retirement scheme except-

(i)   to the extent that the employer has suffered a loss due to a dishonest act committed by the employee; or

(ii)   to the extent of a debt acknowledged in writing by the employee as owing to the employer.

ARRANGEMENT BETWEEN THE MAINLAND OF CHINA AND THE HONG KONG SPECIAL ADMINISTRATIVE REGION FOR THE AVOIDANCE OF DOUBLE TAXATION ON INCOME

Article 1

Permanent establishment and its business profits

1. The profits of an enterprise of One Side shall be taxable only on that Side unless the enterprise carries on business on the Other Side through a permanent establishment situated therein. If the enterprise carries on business as aforesaid, the profits of the enterprise may be taxed on the Other Side but only so much of them as is attributable to that permanent establishment.

2. The term "permanent establishment" means a fixed place of business through which the business of an enterprise is wholly or partly carried on.

3. The term "permanent establishment" includes in particular:

> *(1)* a place of management;
>
> *(2)* a branch;
>
> *(3)* an office;
>
> *(4)* a factory;
>
> *(5)* a workshop;
>
> *(6)* a mine, an oil or gas well, a quarry or any other place of extraction of natural resources.

4. The term "permanent establishment" also includes:

(1) a building site, a construction, assembly or installation project or supervisory activities in connection therewith, but only where such site, project or activities continue for a period of more than 6 months;

(2) services, including consultancy services, furnished by an enterprise of One Side, through employees or other personnel on the Other Side, provided that such services have been furnished for the same project or a connected project for a period or periods exceeding in the aggregate 6 months in any 12-month period.

5. Notwithstanding the provisions of paragraphs 2 to 4 of this Article, the term "permanent establishment" shall be regarded as not including:

(**1**) the use of facilities solely for the purpose of storage, display or delivery of goods or merchandise belonging to the enterprise;

(**2**) the maintenance of a stock of goods or merchandise belonging to the enterprise solely for the purpose of storage, display or delivery;

(**3**) the maintenance of a stock of goods or merchandise belonging to the enterprise solely for the purpose of processing by another enterprise;

(**4**) the maintenance of a fixed place of business solely for the purpose of purchasing goods or merchandise, or of advertising, or of collecting information, for the enterprise;

(**5**) the maintenance of a fixed place of business solely for the purpose of carrying on, for the enterprise, any other activity of a preparatory or auxiliary character;

(**6**) the maintenance of a fixed place of business solely for any combination of the activities mentioned in sub-paragraphs (1) to (5) of this paragraph, provided that the overall activity of the fixed place of business resulting from this combination is of a preparatory or auxiliary character.

6.   Notwithstanding the provisions of paragraphs 2 and 3 of this Article, where a person, other than an agent of an independent status to whom the provisions of paragraph 7 of this Article apply, is acting on One Side on behalf of an enterprise of the Other Side and has, and habitually exercises, an authority to conclude contracts in the name of the enterprise, that enterprise shall be regarded as having a permanent establishment on the first-mentioned Side in respect of any activities which that person undertakes for the enterprise, unless his activities are limited to those mentioned in paragraph 5 of this Article which, if exercised through a fixed place of business, would not make this fixed place of business a permanent establishment under the provisions of that paragraph.

7.   An enterprise of One Side shall not be regarded as having a permanent establishment on the Other Side merely because it carries on business on that Other Side through a broker, general commission agent or any other agent of an independent status, provided that such persons are acting in the ordinary course of their business. However, when the activities of such an agent are devoted wholly or almost wholly on behalf of that enterprise, he will not be regarded as an agent of an independent status within the meaning of this paragraph.

8.   The fact that a company which is a resident of One Side controls or is controlled by a company which is a resident of the Other Side or which carries on business on that Other Side (whether through a permanent establishment or otherwise), shall not of itself constitute either company a permanent establishment of the other.

Article 2

Shipping, air and land transport

1. Revenue and profits from the operation of ships, aircraft or land transport vehicles carried on by an enterprise of One Side on the Other Side shall be exempt from tax (which, in the case of the Mainland of China, includes Business Tax) on the Other Side.

2. The provisions of paragraph 1 of this Article shall also apply to revenue and profits derived from the participation in a pool, a joint business or an international operating agency.

Article 3

Personal services

1. Independent personal services:

(1) Income derived by a resident of One Side in respect of professional services or other activities of an independent character shall be taxable only on that Side except in any one of the following circumstances, where such income may also be taxed on the Other Side:

> *(i)*　　if he has a fixed base regularly available to him on the Other Side for the purpose of performing his activities; in such case, only so much of the income as is attributable to that fixed base may be taxed on that Other Side;

> *(ii)*　　if he stays on the Other Side for a period or periods exceeding in the aggregate 183 days in the calendar year concerned; in such case, only so much of the income as is derived from his activities performed on that Other Side may be taxed on that Other Side.

(2) The term "professional services", in particular, includes independent scientific, literary, artistic, educational or teaching activities as well as the independent activities of physicians, lawyers, engineers, architects, dentists and accountants.

2. Dependent personal services:

(1) Subject to the provisions of paragraph 3 of this Article, salaries, wages and other similar remuneration derived by a resident of One Side in respect of an employment shall be taxable only on that Side unless the employment is exercised on the Other Side. If the employment is so exercised, such remuneration as is derived therefrom may be taxed on the Other Side.

(2) Notwithstanding the provisions of sub-paragraph (1) of this paragraph, remuneration derived by a resident of One Side in respect of an employment exercised on the Other Side shall be taxable only on the first-mentioned Side if:

(i)   the recipient stays on that Other Side for a period or periods not exceeding in the aggregate 183 days in the calendar year concerned; and

(ii)   the remuneration is paid by, or on behalf of, an employer who is not a resident of that Other Side; and

(iii)   the remuneration is not borne by a permanent establishment or a fixed base which the employer has on that Other Side.

(3) Notwithstanding the provisions of sub-paragraphs (1) and (2) of this paragraph remuneration derived in respect of an employment exercised aboard a ship, an aircraft or a land transport vehicle operated in international traffic by an enterprise of One Side shall be taxable only on the Side in which the enterprise is situated.

3. Directors' fees:

Notwithstanding the provisions of paragraphs 1 and 2 of this Article, directors' fees and other similar payments derived by a resident of One Side in his capacity as a member of the board of directors of a company which is a resident of the Other Side may be taxed on that Other Side.

4. Artistes and athletes:

Notwithstanding the provisions of paragraphs 1 and 2 of this Article:

(1) income derived by a resident of One Side as an entertainer, such as a theatre, motion picture, radio or television artiste, or a musician, or as an athlete, from his personal activities as such exercised on the Other Side may be taxed on that Other Side.

(2) where income in respect of personal activities exercised by an entertainer or an athlete in his capacity as such accrues not to the entertainer or athlete himself but to another person, that income may be taxed on the Side on which the activities of the entertainer or athlete are exercised.

Article 4

Methods of elimination of double taxation

1. In the Mainland of China, double taxation shall be eliminated as follows:

Where a resident of the Mainland of China derives income from the Hong Kong Special Administrative Region, the amount of tax paid in the Hong Kong Special Administrative Region in respect of that income in accordance with the provisions of this Arrangement shall be allowed as a credit against the Mainland tax imposed on that resident. The amount of credit, however, shall not exceed the amount of the Mainland tax computed in respect of that income in accordance with the taxation laws and regulations of the Mainland of China.

2. In the Hong Kong Special Administrative Region, double taxation shall be eliminated as follows:

Subject to the provisions of the taxation laws and regulations of the Hong Kong Special Administrative Region regarding the allowance of deduction or credit against the Hong Kong Special Administrative Region tax of tax paid in any place other than the Hong Kong Special Administrative Region, where a resident of the Hong Kong Special Administrative Region derives income from the Mainland of China, the amount of tax paid in the Mainland of China in respect of that income in accordance with the provisions of this Arrangement shall be allowed as a credit against the Hong Kong Special Administrative Region tax imposed on that resident. The amount of credit, however, shall not exceed the amount of the Hong Kong Special Administrative Region tax computed in respect of that income in accordance with the taxation laws and regulations of the Hong Kong Special Administrative Region.

Article 5

Consultation

The competent authorities of the two Sides shall endeavour to resolve by consultation any difficulties or doubts arising as to the interpretation or application of this Arrangement. They may also consult together for the elimination of double taxation in cases not provided for in this Arrangement. In order to facilitate reaching consensus, representatives of the competent authorities of the two Sides may proceed with consultation by an oral exchange of opinions.

Article 6

Personal Scope and Taxes Covered

1. Personal scope

(1) This Arrangement shall apply to a person who is a resident of One Side or a resident of both Sides. The term "resident" means any person who is liable to tax of One Side by reason of his residence, domicile, place of effective management, place of head office or any other criterion of a similar nature in accordance with the laws of the respective Sides.

(2) Where by reason of the provisions of sub-paragraph (1) of this paragraph an individual is a resident of both Sides, his status shall be determined as follows:

> *(i)*   he shall be regarded as a resident of the Side on which he has a permanent home available to him; if he has a permanent home available to him on both Sides, he shall be regarded as a resident of the Side with which his personal and economic relations are closer ("centre of vital interests");

> *(ii)*   if the Side on which he has his centre of vital interests cannot be determined, or if he has not a permanent home available to him on either Side, he shall be regarded as a resident of the Side on which he has an habitual abode;

> *(iii)*   if he has an habitual abode on both Sides or on neither of them, the competent

authorities of the two Sides shall settle the question by consultation.

(3) Where by reason of the provisions of sub-paragraph (1) of this paragraph a person other than an individual is a resident of both Sides, the competent authorities of the two Sides shall determine its residential status by consultation.

2. Taxes covered

Subject to any other provisions, the existing taxes to which this Arrangement shall apply are:

(1) In the Mainland of China:

>   *(i)*   Individual Income Tax;
>
>   *(ii)*   Foreign Investment Enterprises Income Tax and Foreign Enterprises Income Tax

(herein referred to as "Mainland tax")

(2) In the Hong Kong Special Administrative Region:

>   *(i)*   Profits Tax;
>
>   *(ii)*   Salaries Tax;
>
>   *(iii)*   Tax charged under Personal Assessment

(herein referred to as "Hong Kong Special Administrative Region tax").

(3) This Arrangement shall also apply to any identical or substantially similar taxes which are imposed after the date when this Arrangement comes into effect in addition to, or in place of, the existing taxes referred to above. The competent authorities of the two Sides shall notify each other of any substantial changes which have been made in their respective taxation laws within a reasonable period of time after such changes.

Article 7

General definitions

1. For the purposes of this Arrangement, unless the context otherwise requires:

(1) the terms "One Side" and "the Other Side" mean the Mainland of China or the Hong Kong Special Administrative Region as the context requires;

(2) the term "person" includes an individual, a company and any other body of persons;

(3) the term "company" means any body corporate or any entity which is treated as a body corporate for tax purposes;

(4) the terms "enterprise of One Side" and "enterprise of the Other Side" respectively mean an enterprise carried on by a resident of One Side and an enterprise carried on by a resident of the Other Side;

(5) the term "shipping, air and land transport" means any transport by ships, aircraft or land transport vehicles operated by an enterprise of One Side, except when the ships, aircraft or land transport vehicles are operated solely between places on the Other Side;

(6) the term "competent authority" means, in the case of the Mainland of China, the State Administration of Taxation or its authorized representatives and, in the case of the Hong Kong Special Administrative Region, the Commissioner of Inland Revenue of the Hong Kong Special Administrative Region Government or his authorized representatives.

2. As regards the application of this Arrangement by One Side, any term not defined herein shall, unless the context otherwise requires, have the meaning which it has under the laws of that Side concerning the taxes to which this Arrangement applies.

Hong Kong as a Tax Haven for International Business

by

Adam Starchild

Tax havens are very much in the news, and stories about small- and medium-sized companies mushrooming overnight and multi-national giants amassing fabulous fortunes via tax haven operations are growing. They may sound like Alice in Wonderland fairy tales to most people, but to the sophisticated entrepreneur, use of foreign tax havens for such advantages is an everyday business opportunity.

The use of a foreign corporation domiciled in any one of the famous company tax havens such as Hong Kong, Panama, the Bahamas, or Bermuda (among others, can enhance the profitability of any international business.

Many European and American companies are expanding and diversifying overseas as a means of growth and as a hedge against economic ups and downs in their country of origin. By incorporating a tax haven operation to accumulate tax-free income, accomplishment of multi-national objectives is accelerated. An international trading or freight operation can be established in a tax haven to be used as a conduit for international sales activity and financing. Such operations can accumulate trade discounts, commissions, advertising allowances, etc., completely tax-free while the parent or associated company can assume tax deductions by absorbing administrative and selling costs.

Before getting into the ways in which tax haven operations are used by various types of businesses, it is of eminent importance that the distinct difference is understood between two seemingly similar terms: "tax avoidance" and "tax evasion." Tax evasion has dubious and illegal overtones: for example, a company might falsify its financial statements so as to conceal its full liability to the tax authorities — that would be tax evasion — an infraction of the law and a very serious one.

Tax avoidance, on the other hand, is a legitimate method of minimizing or negating the tax factor. In simple terms, it is utilizing "loopholes" in tax laws and exploiting them within legal perimeters. This is the cornerstone of the tax haven concept.

Certain offshore companies can defer any tax until the profits are repatriated to the investor's home country. These are generally companies actively engaged in the conduct of a local business. In most import-export or other international trade activities, such a definition is especially easy to meet. A retailer, or group of retailers, could set up their own wholesale buying opertion in a convenient tax haven, such as Hong Kong, and put all of their Asian business through it. The profits of the Hong Kong firm would accumulate tax-free, and could be invested in other foreign operations.

In addition, a great many countries offer tax holidays of 5 to 20 years for new export manufacturers or assembly operations, often including smaller companies down to as few as ten employees. A company or group of companies could easily invest some of their foreign profits in such a venture, continuing to build for tax-free profits. Such concessions often include an exemption from customs duties on raw materials and equipment.

Most developed countries do tax the current income of certain types of corporations controlled by their residents, such as leasing companies, and other financial enterprises dealing the parent company. But this concept of a controlled foreign corporation applies usually to passive or tax-haven type corporations, not to active businesses. But even for a passive business, a joint venture with foreign partners on a 50-50 basis will allow the income to accumulate tax-free since the company is not controlled by national of either country. If you are leasing equipment, consider a joint venture with your foreign partner whereby you set up a jointly owned company to receive some of the income. You will both profit by it, and have a tax-free pool of funds to invest together in other ventures. Such profits will not be taxed in the country of either partner until they are repatriated, since they are not controlled by either country's citizen.

Countries which have no income tax include Bermuda, the Bahamas, the Cayman Islands, Nevis, and the Turks & Caicos Islands. A number of countries do not tax foreign source income, including Panama and Hong Kong.

Many businessmen looking for tax haven opportunities would envy the daily opportunities open to international traders, and yet most international traders rarely use these opportunities — or even understand them. 100% tax-free dollars will grow a whole lot faster than 50% after-tax dollars.

Setting Up Your Tax Haven-Based Trading Operation

A firm I can personally give my highest recommendation to is ICS Trust (Asia) Limited, based in Hong Kong.

The handover of the former British Crown Colony of Hong Kong to China is complete, and it is now called the Hong Kong Special Administrative Region, generally abbreviated to Hong Kong S.A.R., even on official documents.

As more than one local businessman has put it, "now that the politicians and journalists are gone (from covering the handover), we can get down to *business*." This attitude is typical of Hong Kong, still a true capitalist center. In fact, many of the wealthy who left to obtain second citizenships in Canada, Australia, and elsewhere, have now returned home to continue building their fortunes.

The major advantage of Hong Kong is simply that it is a real business center, not just a tax haven. One of the consequences of that is the ability to add value to services that are provided in only skeleton form in other tax havens. The reinvoicing business is a prime example. Most tax haven jurisdictions host a number of trading companies that do nothing more than reinvoicing. But one Hong Kong firm has now developed this traditional service into a "real" business mode, with an ability to arrange local trade financing. This is a healthy step away from traditional tax havenry into a true offshore **business** center.

ICS Trust Company Limited is part of the ICS International group of companies headquartered in Hong Kong. This highly successful entrepreneurial group was started by Elizabeth L. Thomson. Elizabeth describes herself as "a lawyer by profession" (2 law degrees, a member of 4 Law Societies internationally), "an entrepreneur by choice"! She has helped innumerable people start new enterprises in many parts of the globe and is well known in Hong Kong for her work with women entrepreneurs.

With a staff of 40 at ICS, every aspect of your business is covered — from deciding to incorporate, to obtaining financing from the bank, to managing your paper work including Letters of Credit, to investing your hard earned profits! ICS is truly a "one stop shop" for entrepreneurs.

Their clients range from multinational companies for whom they run Direct Import Programs worth millions of dollars to individuals who seek tax sheltering and estate planning on an international scale. As an entrepreneurial group, they attract many entrepreneurs as clients — business people who have grown their business to a level of maturity and profits that requires expansion into Asia for many diverse reasons.

Instead of just a paper thin traditional tax haven reinvoicing company, with ICS you can develop a real business in Hong Kong. With their extensive banking contacts, ICS professionals will "shop" for the best letter of credit facilities that Hong Kong's competitive banking scene can offer, likely better facilities than you can find at home. Depending upon the client, ICS can often arrange letter of credit banking facilities for clients with either a low or zero margin deposit, usually required by the opening bank. By freeing up your collateral and capital, they provide you with more purchasing power to increase sales and gain higher profits.

Most of these reinvoicing transactions are usually effected such that they are tax free in Hong Kong. There is no withholding tax on dividends so it is often possible to engage in international trade through a HK company and obtain dividends from that company tax free.

ICS will also work with international banks and factors in Hong Kong and overseas to arrange financing, secured primarily on the strength of purchase orders from your clients. Working with banks, factories, shipping companies and freight forwarders, ICS will structure a transaction to increase the likelihood of obtaining flexible, low cost facilities.

The goods do not need to go through HK for us to use a HK vehicle to pass title. Most of their clients ship from a third country direct to their own country.

Although the traditional Hong Kong focus is on firms who trade in goods, it is also possible to use these structures in cases where services are to be provided from overseas. For example, a firm could contract out a study to a company in Hong Kong. This Hong Kong company could then sub-contract out the work to a third party firm and the profit kept in Hong Kong, tax free.

If you import goods from Asia for sale to large chains, ICS can help you expand your credit facilities and increase your domestic sales by establishing and running a Direct Import Program for you. Combined with their international trade finance capabilities, the Direct Import Program is a powerful tool for generating more profits.

The primary goal of the Direct Import Program is to maximize your profits by making your customers perceive that they are buying "direct." This is achieved by:

- setting up a subsidiary company in Hong Kong

- getting your buyers to open their L/C or orders to this subsidiary

- liaising with suppliers to ensure goods are to specification.

The Direct Import Program works because of two powerful reasons:

- The trend in the retail industry is for buyers to "buy direct" from the Orient. Having a subsidiary in Hong Kong which receives orders or L/Cs greatly enhances this perception.
- Large retail chains often can obtain freight and insurance at significant savings because of their economies of scale. Selling FOB Asia can often result in a lower selling price for the importer but with the same profit.

ICS will set up and manage the subsidiary company for you, and prepare financing proposals for presentation to local banks. When everything is complete, goods are shipped directly from the Asian factory to the customer. The fact that you are now seen as an Asian supplier (and not the middleman) is often an important factor that clinches the deal. The added prestige of a Hong Kong office makes the customer think he or she is buying "direct" and therefore receiving the lowest price.

To get started, you should contact ICS with as much detail as possible about your business and its trading activities.

For further information, contact:

Mr. Kishore K. Sakhrani, Director
ICS Trust (Asia) Limited
8th Floor, Henley Building
Five Queen's Road, Central
Hong Kong
Telephone: +852 2854 4544
Fax: +852 2543 5555

You will be well-advised and well-serviced in the hands of this fine company.

Sources of Help for Offshore Investing

Britannia Corporate Management Limited

Another business specializing in the formation of offshore corporations and trusts is Britannia Corporate Management Limited, located in the Cayman Islands. Its president, Gary F. Oakley, is a Canadian with over 18 years of Cayman Islands residency. Britannia is licensed to manage investment holding and trading companies, real estate holding companies, patent holding companies, and insurance holding companies. It is licensed to incorporate and manage corporations registered in the Cayman Islands. As such, the firm can service as the registered office of a corporation, provide its secretary, officers and directors, or undertake any day-to-day functions that may be required. More information can be obtained by writing the following:

Britannia Corporate Management Limited
Attn: New Clients Information
P. O. Box 1968
Whitewall Estates, Grand Cayman
Cayman Islands

Britannia can be reached by fax at +1 345 949 0716, marking your fax "Attention New Clients Information.

Skye Fiduciary Services Limited

Skye Fiduciary Services Limited are among the foremost experts in offshore planning. Under the direction of its chairman Charles Cain, formerly managing director of the second merchant bank to open in the Isle of Man, Skye Fiduciary is the most experienced offshore corporate and trust management business in the jurisdiction. Although Skye offers a full range of company and trust management services, their expertise in designing novel company structures to meet the needs of foreign clients is unique.

For further information, write the following:

Skye Fiduciary Services Limited
Attn: New Clients Department
2 Water Street
Ramsey, Isle of Man 1M8 1JP
United Kingdom

Their telephone number is +44 1624 816117. Fax service is available at +44 1624 816645; marking your fax "Attention: New Clients Information".

JML Swiss Investment Counsellors

One of the leaders in Swiss financial management is JML Swiss Investment Counsellors, a firm which offers a unique style of financial management. Clients can customize and control their own portfolios and still receive comprehensive management advice from some of the world's best experts on financial matters.

Recognizing that investors have differing goals, time frames, and tolerance for risk, JML's managers work with their individual clients to help them target their unique objectives. This naturally requires continued surveillance and analysis of worldwide economic trends, political events, financial markets, currencies, and other factors which could make some investments particularly attractive and others most unfavorable. Few individuals have the time or expertise to undertake this kind of evaluation themselves.

Further information about JML can be obtained by writing the following:

JML Jurg M. Lattmann AG
Swiss Investment Counsellors
Germaniastrasse 55, Dept. 212
CH-8033 Zurich, Switzerland

Their telephone number is (41) 1 368-8233 and their fax number is (41) 1 368-8299, marking your fax "Attention Department 212".

Weber Hartmann Vrijhof & Partners

While there are many excellent Swiss investment financial managers, another one of particular note is the management firm of Weber Hartmann Vrijhof & Partners. Offering management services for the portfolios of both individuals and companies, the firm excels at providing personal attention to its clients. Weber Hartmann Vrijhof & Partners was established in 1992 by Hans Weber, Robert Vrijhof, and Adrian Hartmann. The three men have substantial experience in finance and investment. Weber managed Foreign

Commerce Bank (FOCOBANK) in Switzerland for nearly 30 years as its president and CEO, Vrijhof was a former vice-president and head of FOCOBANK'S portfolio management group, and Hartmann was head of FOCOBANK'S North American subsidiary in Vancouver. Weber Hartmann Vrijhof & Partners offers specialized investment services designed to meet the individual needs of their clients.

The minimum opening portfolio to be managed by this firm is $250,000 or equivalent. The management team here normally recommends that a portion of the portfolio be invested in hard currencies other than the U.S. dollar including the Swiss franc, French franc, German mark, and Dutch guilder. Respected for their conservative approach to portfolio management, the partners assist clients with opening a custodial account at one of the major private Swiss banks, so that all client securities are held by the bank, not the investment manager.

A large percentage of their clients are based in the United States. One of their main goals has always been to get a certain portion of their clients' wealth out of the U.S. dollar and into European hard currencies such as Swiss francs, Deutschmarks, and Dutch guilders, and then build a portfolio with a mix of bonds and shares.

For more information, you can write to the following:

Weber Hartmann Vrijhof & Partners Ltd.
Attn: New Clients Department
Zurichshstrasse 110B
CH-8134 Adilswil, Switzerland

Their telephone number is (41-1) 709-11-15 and their fax number (41-1) 709-11-13, marking your fax "Attention New Clients Department".

Dunn & Hargitt International Group

Recently, many international investors have become dissatisfied with the small annual return on Euro-dollar deposits.

This is why private and institutional investors throughout the world are looking at other areas where returns can be in the area of 20-25% a year, to help offset the high annual rates of inflation on luxury goods.

The Dunn & Hargitt International Group, founded in 1961, has specialized in doing research for developing Portfolio Management Programs that have the potential of providing investors with a high return on their capital by investing in a diversified portfolio trading in the commodity, currency, precious metals, and financial futures markets in the United States and throughout the world.

The Dunn & Hargitt group offers investors the possibilitiy of participating in several of the different pools that are managed by them by investing through the investment programs that are offered by their affiliate, Winchester Life in Gibraltar, but which are actually managed by The Dunn & Hargitt International Group.

At the time of publication they are offering three possible investment alternatives, including The Winchester Life Umbrella Account (which allows 100% of a client's money to be invested in a diversified futures portfolio), The Winchester Life 100% Guaranteed Investment Account (in which Lloyds Bank acts as custodian trustee and US Government Zero Coupon Treasury Bonds are set aside to guarantee the client's capital), and The Winchester Life 150% Guaranteed Investment Account (which is a similar program, but guaranteeing that the client will receive at least 150% of the value deposited with a maturity date at least ten years in the future).

The average net return for the 150% Guaranteed Investment Account over the last six years would have been 22% a year. The average net return on the 100% Guaranteed Investment Account over the last six years would have been 27% a year. The average annual net return for The Winchester Life Umbrella Account over the last twelve years would have been 35% a year.

The minimum accounts accepted are $20,000 for The Winchester Life Umbrella Account, $20,000 for The Winchester Life 100% Guaranteed Account, and $50,000 for The Winchester Life 150% Guaranteed Account.

Although commodities are a speculative form of investment, investors everywhere are diversifying part of their portfolios to take part in the considerable potential profit opportunities that are available in the commodity, currency, precious metals and financial futures markets. The programs devised by the Dunn & Hargitt International Group will make profits if significant trends develop in either direction; i.e. up or down. This does not mean that short term results are always profitable, however the Dunn & Hargitt proven trading systems can provide above average returns over the longer term. Their objective is to make a profit for their clients of between 20% and 40% per annum and their computer trading systems are geared to this level of performance.

For more information, contact:

The Dunn & Hargitt International Group
c/o Dunn & Hargitt Research S.A.
Department S-697
P.O. Box 3186
Road Town, Tortola
British Virgin Islands

The structure of the Dunn & Hargitt Group has been established so that no taxes are withheld from the client's investment on the international commodity, currency, precious metals and financial futures markets. Because of this they can only manage money for investors who are neither citizens nor residents of the United States.

The Dunn & Hargitt International Group offers complete confidentiality to all of its clients, and will not reveal any information on a client or on its accounts to any third parties.

About the Author

This special afterword was prepared by Adam Starchild who over the past 25 years has been the author of over two dozen books, and hundreds of magazine articles, primarily on business and finance. His articles have appeared in a wide range of publications around the world — including *Business Credit, Euromoney, Finance, The Financial Planner, International Living, Offshore Financial Review, Reason, Tax Planning International, The Bull & Bear, Trust & Estates*, and many more.

Now semi-retired, he was the president of an international consulting group specializing in banking, finance and the development of new businesses, and director of a trust company.

Although this formidable testimony to expertise in his field, plus his current preoccupation with other books-in-progress, would not seem to leave time for a well-rounded existence, Starchild has won two Presidential Sports Awards and written several cookbooks, and is currently involved in a number of personal charitable projects.

His personal website is at http://www.adamstarchild.com

www.ingramcontent.com/pod-product-compliance
Lightning Source LLC
Chambersburg PA
CBHW080443030726
47592CB00011B/2958